Invisible Mothers

Invisible Mothers

Unseen Yet Hypervisible
after Incarceration

Janet Garcia-Hallett

UNIVERSITY OF CALIFORNIA PRESS

University of California Press
Oakland, California

© 2022 by Janet Garcia-Hallett

Library of Congress Cataloging-in-Publication Data

Names: Garcia-Hallett, Janet, 1989– author.
Title: Invisible mothers : unseen yet hypervisible after incarceration /
    Janet Garcia-Hallett.
Description: Oakland, California : University of California Press,
    [2022] | Includes bibliographical references and index.
Identifiers: LCCN 2022020917 (print) | LCCN 2022020918 (ebook) |
    ISBN 9780520315044 (cloth) | ISBN 9780520315051 (paperback) |
    ISBN 9780520974029 (epub)
Subjects: LCSH: Women ex-convicts—New York (State)—New
    York—Social conditions—21st century. | Minority women—New
    York (State)—New York—Social conditions—21st century. |
    Prisoners—Deinstitutionalization—New York (State)—New
    York—21st century. | Mothers—New York (State)—New
    York—21st century.
Classification: LCC HV9306.N6 G37 2022 (print) | LCC HV9306.N6
    (ebook) | DDC 364.808209747—dc23/eng/20220716
LC record available at https://lccn.loc.gov/2022020917
LC ebook record available at https://lccn.loc.gov/2022020918

31 30 29 28 27 26 25 24 23 22
10 9 8 7 6 5 4 3 2 1

In loving memory of my godson,
Nolan Rafael Fuentes-Cousain.

Blessed and Highly Favored

Contents

Introduction   *1*

1. Motherwork: "It's Always Been a Very Demanding Job"   *28*

2. Custody and Housing: "I Just Want My Baby Back"   *62*

3. Employment and Finances: "I Just Want to Be Able to Provide"   *93*

4. Life in Recovery: "There's No Turning Back"   *130*

Conclusion   *172*

Appendix A: Research Design   *191*

Appendix B: Summary of the Mothers   *199*

Notes   *205*

References   *217*

Index   *233*

Introduction

That visibility which makes us most vulnerable is that which
also is the source of our greatest strength.

—Audre Lorde, *Sister Outsider*

I am a product of a historical Black mecca: Harlem. In the early 1900s,
Harlem was a major landing ground during the Black Migration, in
which Black individuals left the South to relocate to the North. It became the heart of a Black cultural movement, the Harlem Renaissance,
that inspired and nurtured Black artists. Harlem still houses the world-
famous Apollo Theater and the Cotton Club, where legendary artists
like Duke Ellington, Josephine Baker, and Billie Holiday made appear-
ances. Over time, Black activists like Malcolm X, Martin Luther King
Jr., Marcus Garvey, Angela Davis, and many others have drawn large
crowds to Harlem to listen to their speeches against racial oppression
and to internalize their words uplifting the Black Power movement. In
the late twentieth century, however, Harlem was hard hit by the war on
crime and war on drugs, which politicians used to justify political reliance on punitive sentencing policies and imprisonment. The public narrative of Harlem as a magnet for Black culture and civil rights activism
shifted to dialogues that imagined and constructed Harlem as a place
filled with crime, drugs, and turmoil.

This was the context of my youth, occasionally visiting historical
landmarks in my community, yet constantly witnessing the growing
takeover of penal control. While walking with my mother to C-Town,
the nearest supermarket on 116th Street, I made sure to keep my eyes
focused on the ground to avoid stepping on dirty needles and crack
vials. Occasionally we would grab our shopping cart and walk to the

Pathmark supermarket on 125th Street for cheaper deals on groceries. Along the way, it was common—and somewhat expected—to see people actively using drugs or under the influence, including parents of peers from my school. Interventions from child welfare services meant that some of my school friends lived with extended family members or were placed in the foster care system, where they were sometimes exposed to worse conditions and emotional treatment. Eventually I began to notice the missing faces of people whom I had been accustomed to seeing under the influence of drugs or alcohol as I walked home from school or walked to the nearby bodega. Although their absence originally brought me hope that they were receiving help, I eventually learned that an absent face meant another person had been incarcerated and taken by the penal transformation in my community. People were being stigmatized for resorting to drug use as a coping mechanism to racialized poverty and oppression, and they were being incarcerated for merely surviving their circumstances. Witnessing these events at an early age allowed me to realize that the takeover of penal institutions was just another way for the government to avoid providing the much-needed resources that marginalized groups needed to survive. I realized that the purpose of state systems is not to help people in Black and brown communities like Harlem, but to keep us under state control and confine us. Instead of providing us with adequate social services, we as a people are criminalized, pulled from the community, and incarcerated behind bars.

My upbringing in Harlem sparked my growing interest in the disproportionate treatment of people of color in the criminal legal system. The return to the community post-incarceration—what criminologists call the "prisoner reentry" process—is full of systemic problems in finding housing and obtaining work with a criminal record. Jeremy Travis argues that these punishments are invisible in that they are additional punishments mostly out of the public's eyesight, they are implemented beyond the defined punishments stated during sentencing, and they are typically excluded in national debates and decisions concerning sentencing policies.[1] Discussions about invisible punishments, however, have largely focused on men in the criminal legal system, since men outnumber women across various components of the system: men make up 93% of prison populations (those with longer sentences, charged with more serious offenses), 84% of those in jails (awaiting trial and arrested for minor offenses), and the majority of people on community-based supervision (75% of those on probation and 87% of those on parole are men).[2] Nevertheless, the focus on men obscures the disproportionate impact of the penal takeover on women, particularly the drastic increase in incarceration rates that women experienced during the war on drugs compared to men.[3] Growing up in Harlem during the war on drugs, I witnessed this growing removal of women firsthand. By being ignored and disregarded as victims of punitive carceral systems, women remain relatively invisible as potential recipients of reentry support.

Though feminist scholars have helped bring academic attention to women in the criminal legal system, the focus is often negative, centered around the negative effects of maternal incarceration on the children left behind. Of the women incarcerated in US state prisons, 62% are mothers of underage children.[4] Only a few advocates and criminologists like Bahiyyah Muhammad explore the resiliency and success of these children as they overcome parental incarceration. Media, researchers, social service providers, and politicians predominantly emphasize the negative effects of incarceration on mothers' children, both during and after imprisonment. These public discourses highlight the negative effects maternal incarceration has on children's perceived academic performance and preparedness, residential instability, and behavioral problems.[5] This focus on children is guided by notions of them as innocent bystanders or silent victims of their mothers' decisions, perpetuating mother blaming. Blaming mothers for exposing their children to maternal incarceration disregards the patriarchy, misogyny, and systemic racism that marginalize and criminalize mothers of color, pushing them into the auspices of penal control. This book, *Invisible Mothers*, diverges from the focus on the negative effects of maternal incarceration on mothers' children because it does not adequately problematize the oppression that influences maternal incarceration or explore the social-structural effects of maternal incarceration on the mothers themselves. Instead, *Invisible Mothers* shares the voices, challenges, and needs of traditionally silenced mothers in the criminal legal system.

Women's (in)visibility to the general public as respectable human beings worthy of acknowledgment and inclusion is a function of their role as mothers and their enactment of motherhood. On the one hand, women are rendered invisible in a patriarchal society in which men are viewed as the more dominant group and are given positions of power and control. To complicate matters further, gendered expectations of women to become mothers and sexist ideologies that mothers should be responsible for childcare responsibilities place mothers in charge of parental labor. Women's mothering labor, however, is largely private and invisible to others who are oblivious to mothers' daily financial, emotional, and practical struggles of caring for children. These gendered and undervalued caregiving expectations of women leave mothers generally unrecognized and undervalued as invisible mothers. On the other hand, mothering labor often only becomes visible through "othering," in which the public critiques women and treats them as being different or "other than" mainstream ideals of how mothers should behave. When incarcerated, mothers are stigmatized for supposedly challenging dominant ideologies of motherhood that dictate good mothers are docile, fragile, innocent, and harmless. Incarceration therefore leaves mothers in a double bind as they remain invisible as mothers and unrecognized for their mothering, yet at the same time they are visible as "others" when it concerns their criminality and involvement in carceral systems.[6] To demonstrate how mothers in the criminal legal system can be invisible as *mothers* yet simultaneously visible as *others*, I use "(m)others" throughout this book when referring to the stigmatized treatment or public perceptions of these mothers as supposedly mothering in ways "other than" what is normatively expected or accepted of women with children.

Invisible Mothers highlights the voices of the most traditionally silenced mothers: mothers of color. They experience oppression and inequities not only as women but also as women of underrepresented racial-ethnic groups. Their social position as women of color leaves them cumulatively marginalized across gender, race, and ethnicity; then they are expected to navigate motherhood with such restricted access to opportunities. As an Afro-Latina mother who grew up in a marginalized community, I empathize with mothers of color and understand their plights pre- and post-incarceration. Therefore, I have made it my mission to share their personal narratives in this book, which draws on Black feminist thought as a critical social theory devoted to empowering women of color by resisting oppressive practices toward them and strengthening efforts that address their needs.[7] *Invisible Mothers* examines the paradox of visibility and invisibility in how social institutions treat mothers of color as invisible mothers who are restricted from equal opportunities but also are simultaneously treated as visible (m)others who are criminalized and penalized for surviving their marginalization.[8] This book argues that the process of navigating motherhood as visible (m)others complicates the post-incarceration reentry process, and inversely that the reentry process for mothers of color makes navigating motherhood more difficult. The book treats mothering and reentry as two journeys that must be examined in tandem to fully understand post-incarceration life for mothers of color. All things considered, *Invisible Mothers* is devoted to enhancing the visibility of mothers of color and to exposing and contesting their marginalization as they navigate motherhood and reentry after incarceration.

SOCIAL CONSTRUCTIONS OF MOTHERHOOD

Matricentric feminism is a mother-centered feminism that recognizes the unique social position and experiences of mothers and that specifically places mothers' interests and needs at the forefront of theoretical, empirical, and policy work.[9] Adrienne Rich highlights motherhood as an invisible institution—unseen and untouched—that functions under our patriarchal society, in which male control disempowers mothers and limits mothers' decision-making power in everyday life. In this way, the patriarchal institution of *motherhood* shapes mothers' oppression; the concept of *mothering*, however, concerns the experiences of mother work. Feminists argue that *motherhood* as an institution should not be confused with experiences of *mothering*, noting that the former is a controlling state of male-defined oppression and disempowerment while the latter is woman defined and can be viewed as empowering.[10] As Andrea O'Reilly explains, "matricentric feminism understands motherhood to be socially and historically constructed, and positions mothering more as a practice than an identity."[11]

The concept of *motherwork* captures the unpaid and invisible labor of caring for children in which caregiving remains centered around mothers, despite shifts in gender expectations over time. Although mothering is work, women's motherwork is not equally visible to the general public, and not all women's motherwork is respected or validated. For instance, there is a cultural ambivalence in how society believes women should mother their children. Yet amid cultural images and ideals of motherhood, mothers "can never fully do it right."[12] Public interpretations of motherhood center around ideologies of intensive mothering, which is "child-centered, expert-guided, emotionally absorbing, labor-intensive, and financially expensive."[13] Such high standards for motherhood, however, are embedded in a hegemony of racialized, gendered, and middle-class beliefs of what mothering should look like. Gender and race are social constructs that are coupled with one another and shape the mothering experience; "race is 'gendered' and gender is 'racialized,' so that race and gender fuse to create unique experiences and opportunities for all groups."[14] Fused together, racialized and gendered treatment creates unique and diverging experiences between Black mothers and white mothers. Given the historical racial oppression of Black individuals as less than white normative standards, I intentionally capitalize *Black* throughout this book while avoiding such racial capitalization for *whites* as a means to counteract the white privilege and white supremacy that are ingrained in our society.

White mothers have historically been afforded racial privileges that provide them the generational wealth and financial stability to enact financially expensive mothering. Racial privileges generally give white mothers the flexibility of labor-intensive mothering when they are protected from systemic racism in health care, housing, employment, and educational systems, to name a few areas. White mothers benefit from white privilege, in which their lives or the lives of their children literally do not depend on surviving racial oppression, as those of Black families do. Still, white (upper) middle-class standards remain the most visible model of mothering.

Society expects all mothers to uphold primary caregiving responsibilities for underage children by specifically living up to white middle-class ideologies of motherhood. Yet white middle-class motherhood, as a normative cultural construct, essentially thrives on Black mothers being framed as "other than" their white counterparts, as well as on their motherwork being regarded as relatively deviant compared to that of white mothers. The term *intersectionality* underscores that individuals can experience multiple social inequalities that overlap with one another and affect the overall lived experience.[15] Black mothers, in particular, experience discrimination at the intersection of multiple interlocking oppressions associated with gender, class, race, ethnicity, and more. For instance, "U.S. Black women encounter societal practices that restrict us to inferior housing, neighborhoods, schools, jobs, and public treatment[,] and [these societal practices] hide this differential consideration behind an array of common beliefs about Black women's intelligence, work habits, and sexuality."[16] Black mothers are rendered invisible when government structures do not allocate resources to their communities or to specific policies and practices that cater to their interests or needs. They run into a maternal wall that blocks Black mothers (and Black women perceived as mothers) from job opportunities, while reaching a sexist and racist glass ceiling that hinders Black women from progressing and moving up in the workplace.[17] Black mothers routinely face brutality from law enforcers and public servants who verbally express a disregard for their pregnancies and who treat these mothers and their children as fair game for physical harm and violence.[18] Black mothers confront such public hatred directed against them and are forced to survive a patriarchal and racist society as perceived (m)others.

Black mothers are systematically restricted from available resources and stripped of equal opportunities given to white mothers to *do* mothering. Such racialized oppression makes motherwork particularly taxing on Black mothers. Society then blames Black mothers for their unfortunate circumstances by disregarding the presence of the racial-ethnic discrimination and prejudice that create and maintain social inequalities. In fact, white normative discussions often dismiss, belittle, and undervalue Black mothering experiences compared to those of white mothers. This Black/white racial dichotomy and binary way of thinking reinforces racialized constructions of intensive mothering that instigate othering, in which Black mothers are demeaned as (m)others who are less than or "other than" perceived norms of the white mother. *Invisible Mothers* does not replicate or support white normative discussions of Black motherwork that vilify Black and brown bodies. Instead, this book intentionally uses an intersectional framework to highlight the role of interlocking social positions in navigating the institution of motherhood and also integrates Black feminist thought, which is designed to empower Black women and mothers and to resist their multifaceted oppression.[19]

Dichotomizing Race and Homogenizing Ethnicities

The shared struggle *Invisible Mothers* aims to highlight is that the visibility of mothers of color is contingent upon their perceived adherence to or divergence from white normative meanings of motherhood. More specifically, if they adhere to ideologies of intensive mothering, mothers of color remain invisible under broad discussions of normative mothering; when they somehow diverge from these ideologies of mothering, however, they become visible through a blurred lens that focuses on them as "others" or, in this case, "(m)others." In this way, visibility is not a zero-sum matter in which mothers of color either have it as a whole or do not; rather, they are in a double bind of being simultaneously invisible mothers and visible (m)others.

In addition, this book recognizes that there may also be intraracial nuances in mothers' visibility that can shape their treatment and experiences in navigating motherhood. Despite the knowledge gained from research on mothering while Black, the use of a Black/white racial dichotomy may treat underrepresented ethnicities (like African Americans and West Indians) as a homogenous group. Overlooking ethnicity suggests that society treats all Black ethnic groups the same, and a Black/white racial dichotomy likely misses some nuances in their treatment and experiences.[20] Discourse about racial-ethnic experiences of womanhood and motherhood, however, are examined in great length in sociology, gender studies, and ethnic studies. This work shows that employers, politicians, and social service providers, among others, may interact with people beyond large racial umbrellas and treat them according to stereotypes and prejudices that are more specifically tied to ethnic background such as for African American, Latina, and West Indian women.[21]

Due to the empirical limitations and social implications of Black/white racial dichotomies, from this point forward *Invisible Mothers* diverts from this racial dichotomy unless referring to research on Black mothers and their racialized experiences. Otherwise, *Invisible Mothers* specifically identifies the ethnicities of women and mothers as either African American, West Indian, or Latina and uses "women of color" and "mothers of color" as inclusive phrases for their shared experiences across ethnicity. The use of women of color and mothers of color in this book is more appropriate to capture both the similarities and nuances of navigating motherhood among underrepresented racial-ethnic groups. This approach is in line with Andrea Ritchie's work on Black women and women of color: "When using 'women of color,' I do so in the hopes of gesturing toward common ground and sites of shared struggle, while simultaneously honoring [ethnic] difference."[22] The mothers are described as "mothers of color" when highlighting their common ground, and their ethnic identities are identified occasionally throughout the book when the mothers' narratives are specifically associated with their ethnic background. For convenience, appendix B includes the ethnic background(s) for each mother.

Honoring ethnic nuances and recognizing that stereotypes may differ for ethnic groups, the following sections review various controlling images of African American, West Indian, and Latina women. Controlling images are essentially socially constructed depictions that are upheld by the general public and embedded within social systems like the child welfare system. Unfortunately, the "controlling" aspect of these images is that they may manipulate public perceptions of underrepresented women as (m)others and can be used to justify the social inequalities they face.[23] Thus, it is important to understand the controlling images of

African American, West Indian, and Latina women to adequately grasp the unique obstacles they face in combatting gendered and racial-ethnic subordination and in navigating the institution of motherhood.

African American Women. As slaves, African American women "were classified as 'breeders' as opposed to 'mothers.'"[24] They were dehumanized as animals whose worth was based on their ability to reproduce more slaves and, in turn, provide slave owners with more product. This dehumanization and exploitation of African American women remains prevalent today, though it is more covertly reinforced within controlling images.

Controlling images of African American women include the Sapphires, Jezebels, and Mammies. Historical caricatures of Sapphires are portrayals of "angry Black women" who are loud, outspoken, and bitter and thus disregarded as undeserving of public time or attention. The sexualized Jezebels (or modern-day "hoochie mamas") are represented as sexually promiscuous and thus treated as deserving of sexual abuse or assault. The asexual and maternal Mammies are depictions of selfless house slaves (or modern-day domestic servants) devoted to providing childcare for white children. Compared to the Jezebel and the Sapphire, the Mammy is the only controlling image that suggests some maternal role, albeit to the extent that her maternal care is performed as an exploited service to white children while society disregards her personal maternal interests. In essence, Black women were visible as mammies to white children during their enslavement, while their invisibility as mothers justified forcibly removing them from their own children.

These representations of African American women portray them as violating social norms of "true womanhood" (as pure and passive) and of "true motherhood" (as the intensive mothering of biological children). These images not only reinforce patriarchal notions of gender roles, but they are intertwined with racial-ethnic biases and hierarchical undertones, intentionally degrading African American women and mothers to purposefully justify and maintain their oppression. Though these controlling images of African American women emerged from slavery as a means to justify labor exploitation, racial violence, and white supremacy, modernized depictions continue today as a way to maintain inequality (in labor, sexual exploitation, and racism).

West Indian Women. Scholars suggest that compared to the US context, racism is less institutionalized in West Indian countries given that these countries are mostly inhabited by people of color.[25] They argue that in this region, conflicts are not predominantly "whites against Blacks. It is now mainly Blacks against Blacks; Blacks against browns; high browns against low browns; Africans against Indians."[26] As a result, we observe ample Afro-Indo conflict in West Indian countries like Trinidad and Tobago with large Indian populations. For instance, Caribbean feminist studies highlight how West Indian women of Indian descent are more likely depicted as sexually pure, innocent, and submissive women and mothers, while those of African descent are hypersexualized and stereotyped as being loud and independent.[27] In her work conceptualizing "difference" in this global region, professor Rhoda Reddock argues that because Afro and Indo ethnic groups are "defined in opposition to each other," these socially constructed differences promote more division across cultural spaces and further restrict opportunities for these women in a patriarchal society.[28]

Research shows that West Indian mothers, like many mothers across the world, may migrate to the United States for financial opportunities and as a means to feed their children who remain in their home countries.[29] Although this is not the reality for all West Indian immigrant mothers, when they are of African descent their visibility as workers has become a function of what they can do for affluent white families and how much they can mother white children as nannies. More specifically, West Indian women of African descent are often offensively depicted as inferior domestic servants with the natural skills to be of service to those more dominant over them: affluent white families.[30] Such controlling images of these West Indian women as domestic servants illustrate the paradox of their visibility as "the help" that is regarded for the services they can provide to affluent white families and their children, while simultaneously being invisible as mothers to their own children. The ethnoracial and classist "othering" embedded in these images works to justify their labor exploitation for low pay, their exposure to verbal and sexual abuse from employers, and their being (dis)regarded as disposable objects.[31]

Latina Women. We see considerable overlap between controlling images of African American, West Indian, and Latina women, particularly historical depictions of the Mammy and modern-day depictions of West Indian and Latina domestic servants to be exploited for their services.[32] A controlling image of both African American and Latina women is that of the Welfare Queen, which wrongfully and condescendingly represents them as leeches on state services. These images emerged through political rhetoric during the mid- to late 1900s. Politicians like Ronald Reagan tried to minimize welfare assistance by misrepresenting African American and Latina mothers as blameworthy for their circumstances for supposedly having "too many" children and as being undeserving of cash assistance due to their poor decisions and perceived abuse of the system.[33] These controlling images of Welfare Queens attribute social inequalities to individual downfalls, reinforcing notions of African American and Latina mothers as bad (m)others who are subordinate to white mothers. These depictions also fueled an anti-immigrant narrative about Latina mothers "taking over" the country and draining state resources, supposedly justifying social and political action to restrict their citizenship and limit their access to state resources.[34]

Some controlling images of Latinas can also be found within historical and cultural archetypes of La Virgen de Guadalupe as well as legends regarding and disapproving of La Llorona and La Chingada (La Malinche). These images depict the good, pure woman that others should aspire to, while illustrating the deviant women that others should avoid becoming. For instance, La Virgen de Guadalupe is idealized as a sexually pure, spiritual figure who is docile. Though there are some similarities with the Mammy in that both are pure and docile, La Virgen de Guadalupe is viewed as a model, religious figure (while the Mammy is not) and also serves as a protector to all (not just as childcare for white children). La Llorona is another controlling image of Latinas, which translates to "the weeping woman." The legend of La Llorona is that she is a mother who drowned her two children in a river (whether through neglect or with her own hands) and is left crying in everlasting turmoil as she searches the river for her deceased children. Another controlling image is La Chingada (La Malinche), which translates to "the fucked one (the raped one)" and is a negative portrayal of a prostitute who has betrayed her community and the institution of motherhood. She is depicted as a hypersexualized woman—like the Jezebel—and she is scapegoated as a societal failure for not behaving like a nun (like La Virgen de Guadalupe). She can also be tied to modern-day notions and stereotypes of Latina women as being "hot-blooded" and *caliente mamacitas* (which translates to hot little mamas).

Sociologists Pierrette Hondagneu-Sotelo and Ernestine Avila note that all things considered, "cultural symbols that model maternal femininity, such as the *Virgen de Guadalupe*, and the negative femininity, such as *La Llorona* and *La Malinche*, serve to control [Latina] women's conduct by prescribing idealized visions of motherhood."[35] Put simply, controlling images of La Virgen de Guadalupe are used to try to control Latina women's conduct to fit preconceived notions of womanhood and motherhood as a sexually pure and religious protector. Mothers seemingly contradicting this normative standard are condemned as visible (m)others, exposing them to derogatory labels and condescending treatment.

Women of Color. These gendered, classed, and ethnoracial depictions of African American, West Indian, and Latina women reflect "the dominant group's interest in maintaining Black women's subordination," as noted by Patricia Hill Collins in *Black Feminist Thought.*[36] Controlling images of these women's perceived deviance from white middle-class motherhood thrive within structures of inequality by affecting access to resources, such as welfare assistance. They influence how social institutions respond to women's motherwork and reinforce differential treatment toward women of color. All in all, biased constructs of womanhood and motherhood present a distorted vision of African American, West Indian, and Latina mothers, with prejudiced assessments that seemingly justify their oppression in state systems.

PENAL CONTROL OF (M)OTHERS OF COLOR

Across various social institutions, mothers of color are criminalized for their motherwork; that is, they are turned into "criminals" by some socially constructed definition of crime tied to their mothering or that disproportionately affects mothers of color. As *Criminalized Mothers, Criminalizing Mothering* argues, "Extra-legal processes—social work, health care and medicine, child welfare—also function to criminalize certain kinds of mothering through a discourse and set of practices that blame, shame, and punish mothers."[37] For instance, in support of the patriarchal interests of society, state structures regulate women's mothering from the moment a child is conceived, with state laws regulating what mothers are allowed to do with their bodies during pregnancy. Additionally, mothers of color are generally forced to mother through inadequate or unequal resources that complicate motherwork. Despite these structural inequalities, a maternal focus on having food on the table and putting clothes on their children's backs is no longer sufficient in a society that emphasizes intensive mothering. Social workers in all fifty states are also considered mandated reporters who must report (though subjectively) any suspected incidents of child neglect, but the heightened interaction that mothers of color have with social service providers generally increases the chances that their motherwork will be under state scrutiny and deemed as intentional child neglect.[38] Mothers of color thus often find themselves losing the battle against normative white middle-class standards, then being penalized by the child welfare system that can remove children from their care. Research demonstrates that removing children from their mothers' care is publicly defended by a focus within the child welfare system on "saving children" and providing them with "care," yet this children-focused priority simultaneously reinforces the image and treatment of their mothers as visible Others who are to face "justice" and be punished in a state of penal control.[39]

Mothers of color not only fight against patriarchal and class-based power structures in social services, they do so while also battling institutional racism. Known for her work on critical race theory and feminist jurisprudence, law professor Angela P. Harris argues that "racism constantly changes in form but not in effect."[40] A long-standing form of institutional racism entails carceral systems, which are essentially the legal oppression of women of color and, more specifically, mothers of color. Andrea Ritchie's work demonstrates that oppressive policing results from state agents and state institutions policing motherwork with a blatant disregard for women of color as mothers: "Police officers commit violence against mothers of color with impunity, while simultaneously criminalizing them for the slightest actual or perceived harm to their fetus or child."[41] In this way, women of color are criminalized by discriminatory policies and policing practices, then pulled into correctional facilities.

In fact, African American women are overrepresented in correctional facilities. In 2017, African American women accounted for approximately 19% of women sentenced to imprisonment even though they are only 13% of the female population in the United States.[42] The percentage of Latina women sentenced to imprisonment, however, is more representative of the Latina population in the United States: approximately 18% for both.[43] In addition to their representation in carceral systems compared to their representation in the country, women of color are disproportionately incarcerated compared to white women. Before going to trial, prosecutors may use the threat of long sentences to encourage women to plead guilty for a reduced sentence, waiving their right to a jury trial even if they do not agree to the charges.[44] Yet white women have a better chance of receiving no jail time with their plea deals, reinforcing racial and ethnic disparities in plea bargain outcomes, rates of incarceration, and parental separation for nonviolent offenses.[45] In 2018, African American women were imprisoned at twice the rate of white women, while Latina women were incarcerated at a rate 1.3 times that of white women.[46] These incarceration rates do not result from committing more crime but rather from punitive carceral policies that affect women of color more under the guise of "public safety."

This public safety rhetoric is evident in US drug policies, which criminalize substance use by incarcerating individuals for merely possessing their drug of choice.[47] Even though whites are more likely to use drugs, the hypersurveillance of Black and brown communities overwhelmingly criminalizes women of color for their substance use, while politicians advocate for penal control of them instead of empowering community-based support and treatment.[48] Public concerns about substance abuse have been centered around pregnant women of color, who are already systematically oppressed at the intersection of race and gender, then reported by medical professionals and neglected by social workers who are required to act according to punitive policies. Punitive policies designed to police the mothering behaviors of women of color are about state making—defining the institution of motherhood around gendered, racial-ethnic, and classed norms. This book shares a different way of thinking about the impact of punitive policies on the lives of mothers of color.

Scholars argue that once she is within the grasp of the criminal legal system, "dominant ideologies about good motherhood and good womanhood influence how the police, courts, and corrections staff treat and interpret a woman and evaluate her behavior."[49] Women in the criminal legal system have long been plagued by this notion of their double deviance for engaging in crime and challenging socially constructed gender roles. Thus, it is no surprise that even though the number of incarcerated parents in both state and federal prisons increased by 79% between 1991 and 2007, the number of incarcerated mothers rose at a much faster rate than their male counterparts: 122% and 76%, respectively.[50] Society expects mothers to perform intensive mothering, with the belief that this should be done while they are living with children. Yet when judges have some discretion in bail and sentencing decisions, carceral systems are more punitive toward criminalized (m)others of color who do not live with their children.[51] More specifically, carceral systems are more likely to reprimand these mothers with incarceration for seemingly deviating from social constructions of motherhood. "Black women offenders," as sociologist Jeanne Flavin argues, "are subjected to a double-edged sword, rewarded if they are perceived as good parents but punished more severely if they are not."[52] These seemingly colorblind and gender-neutral policies aggravate social inequalities for mothers of color.

Even though most mothers provide for their children without engaging in crime, some who are less financially stable may commit crimes as a means of protecting and financially supporting their children.[53] Additionally, the state punishes the survival actions of poor mothers of color as crimes while largely ignoring the survival crimes of wealthier white mothers. A prime example of this discrepancy is rich white mothers being given a slap on the wrist in college admission scandals, while poor mothers of color have been more punitively punished for enrolling their children in school districts where they do not live. This illustrates the differential state response to wealthy white mothers, who used their wealth to circumvent a system and "buy" an education (that they could have worked for), and to the poor mothers of color, who are deemed to be "stealing" an education that was not afforded to them (because they lived in less prosperous areas). These mothers made sacrifices to provide for their children, as any mother would, doing so by any means necessary. Yet compared to their white counterparts, mothers of color are disproportionately confined in the criminal legal system as offenders, rather than being understood as survivors of their environment and systemic marginalization.

Research shows that in some instances, holding an identity as a "bad mother" was likely worse than being identified as a "criminal."[54] Society views incarcerated and formerly incarcerated mothers as *criminals* first and *mothers* second, if they are even recognized and respected as mothers at all. Despite their resilience in mothering through social-structural barriers, public discourse about mothers of color criminalizes them as the problem rather than recognizing them for their survival mechanisms. These public perceptions and punitive carceral policies strip the visibility of mothers of color as being people who matter and reinforce blemished images of them as (m)others who need to be under penal control. Without centering the motherwork of women of color, we are essentially doing ourselves a disservice when we attempt to understand mothers' experiences in carceral systems. Thus, *Invisible Mothers* is grounded on the belief that maternal experiences post-incarceration cannot be detached from mothers' treatment and experiences as criminalized people under penal control.

Mothering through Incarceration

Institutional barriers can undermine women's mothering while they are incarcerated. Research shows that 54% of mothers in state facilities communicate monthly with their children by phone.[55] Yet incarcerated mothers may be restricted by allotted time frames in which they can call their children or be discouraged from making prison calls by the expensive charges to family members. Approximately 66% of mothers in state facilities have monthly contact via mail, but children are often discouraged from writing back because they prefer direct contact with their mothers.[56] Despite this preference for in-person communication, most incarcerated mothers—about 76%—do not receive visits from their children.[57] Limited visitation from children is tied to barriers such as the long distances to correctional facilities, expensive travel costs, caregivers' willingness or ability to take children to visit their mothers, inconvenient time frames for visits, and displeasure with one's emotional state after a visit.[58] Some incarcerated mothers also note that they do not want their children to visit them, preferring instead to shield them from unpleasant security screenings and prison environments.[59] Such limited visitation, however, may interfere with women's ability to do mothering to their liking. In fact, 64% of incarcerated mothers worry that incarceration affects their maternal role, and 55% of incarcerated mothers believe their children do not receive the maternal attention they need.[60]

Carceral systems not only restrict women's resources to do mothering, they simultaneously reinforce white, middle-class social constructions of motherhood.[61] For instance, correctional facilities implement parenting programs to teach women how to "do" motherhood through communication skills, such as how to bond with children during reading time and playtime. This individual focus of carceral programs assumes that "success," which is subjectively defined, is a matter of "fixing" the mothers to fit into normative motherhood, as if their circumstances were devoid of structural oppression. In fact, Carolyn Sufrin found that within one carceral program that claimed to be evidence based, "there is no mention of institutionalized racism, poverty, lack of access to mental and medical health care, sentencing laws, or other sociopolitical factors that have contributed to the mass incarceration of parents over the last four decades."[62] This demonstrates a problematic paradox in restricting women's resources and disregarding the carceral role of these barriers that render them invisible mothers while simultaneously

encouraging and sometimes forcing mothers to aspire to social constructions of motherhood (in order to be seen as visible mothers).

Although research shows that motherhood is a vital source of motivation during incarceration, the invisible punishments of carceral systems
present several hurdles that persist well after mothers' incarceration.[63]
Mothers of color are exposed to structural injustices in society that not
only ensnare them into correctional facilities but also follow them back
into the community post-release. They face obstacles in gaining employment with a criminal record, in obtaining suitable housing after losing
it during confinement, and in securing custody of their children given
state-imposed requirements—all of which may overlap and complicate
the mothering experience. Everything considered, sociologists highlight
that "competing demands may seriously interfere with successful reintegration: The woman will need an apartment to regain custody of
their children, she will need a job to get an apartment, she will need to
get treatment for her addiction to be able to work, and initial contact
with her children may only be possible during business hours if they
are in custody of the state."[64] These competing demands on formerly
incarcerated mothers amount to interwoven needs, yet—as invisible
(m)others—social supports are severely limited due to state neglect to
provide them with adequate resources.

Invisible Mothers demonstrates these competing demands from state
structures, which intervene in women's mothering efforts after their release. As a result of such state interventions, mothers are hypervigilant
in protecting their children from racialized state violence, they purposefully support each other through "collective motherwork" in communities of color, and they try to minimize state disruptions by gathering all
available resources and managing the emotional impact on children.[65]
In these ways, formerly incarcerated mothers of color exercise a variety
of motherwork strategies to tackle competing demands during reentry
and to overcome oppressive carceral regimes.[66] To more effectively assist these mothers, *Invisible Mothers* highlights their motherwork efforts and the interwoven needs for motherwork during reentry. This
assistance, however, requires an understanding of mothers' experiences
and treatment within a web of conflicting hierarchies regarding ethnoracial and gendered images of "bad" (m)others.

Underrepresented racial-ethnic groups like African American, West
Indian, and Latina women are typically considered together as "minorities," with little attention to how social-structural nuances in their treatment and circumstances might impact their motherwork and its place in

the reentry process post-incarceration. All three groups of mothers share similar experiences in mothering as they raise their children through discrimination and oppression, yet *Invisible Mothers* explores how minor nuances in social prejudices, family support, and community networks may complicate or mitigate these barriers differently among mothers of color.[67]

RESEARCH APPROACH

Though social science research has examined social perceptions and treatment of mothers of color in punitive carceral systems, less is known about how they understand their own experiences amid histories of oppression and how social service providers can use this information in anti-oppressive approaches. *Invisible Mothers* addresses two central questions. First, how do mothers navigate motherhood through various aspects of their reentry into the community after imprisonment? Second, how is this reentry process shaped by mothers' treatment and experiences at the intersectionality of gender, motherhood, racial-ethnic background, and criminal status?

Researchers often quantify the experiences of incarcerated and formerly incarcerated women and mothers in quantitative research, which may reinforce notions of "unfit" or bad (m)others when presented without a clear understanding of their full and personal narratives. Qualitative interviews are an ideal approach to study the navigation of post-incarceration motherhood because they can capture complex phenomena from the perspective of those who are most knowledgeable about their own experiences. In 2014 I began interviewing formerly incarcerated mothers of color in New York City to gather the personal narratives that are often overlooked in other less-interactive data collection approaches. To preserve their anonymity, I present and highlight their narratives here using pseudonyms (i.e., fake names). *Invisible Mothers* explores how mothers understand their challenges and experiences navigating motherhood post-incarceration and examines how navigating motherhood shapes reentry into the community. Appendix A includes detailed information on how I recruited mothers for interviews, the interviewing process, and data analysis procedures.

Invisible Mothers aims to highlight intraracial experiences and nuances among mothers of color by focusing on formerly incarcerated mothers of African American, West Indian, and Latina background. Existing quantitative data sets may be limited in their ability to detect these nuances between ethnic groups when labeling them under the "Black" racial umbrella or classifying the racial group and its ethnic subgroups as "Black or African American alone."[68] If ethnicity is known, quantitative researchers may still exclude or overlook ethnic groups like West Indian and Latina mothers, deeming their presence relatively small and unimportant while reinforcing Black/white dichotomies. Qualitative data, on the other hand, is particularly useful to understand mothers' self-identification, provide an accurate representation of their experiences, and suggest resources and practices that tie in with their maternal realities post-incarceration.

In total, I interviewed 37 formerly incarcerated mothers of color. As many as 21 identified with an African American background, 15 identified with a Latin American background, 8 identified with a West Indian background, and 1 participant identified as Black but could not describe an ethnicity with which she identified. Given the high chances of inter-ethnic relations in a diverse city like New York City, I expected some mothers to identify with more than one ethnicity; some did, describing themselves as ethnically mixed and shaping the overlap in numbers for ethnic representation. This demonstrates the variety in ethnic background that can go unrecognized in criminal justice research exploring large racial dichotomies.[69] The represented Spanish-speaking countries and US territories include the Dominican Republic, Puerto Rico, Spain, Ecuador, Guatemala, and Cuba. The represented West Indian countries include Jamaica, Haiti, Barbados, St. Croix, and Trinidad and Tobago. Appendix B charts the ethnic background(s) of each participant. Throughout *Invisible Mothers*, I identify the ethnicities of the mothers as either African American, West Indian, or Latina when ethnicity is directly associated with their narratives, and I use *women of color* and *mothers of color* as inclusive terms for shared experiences across their ethnicities.

A summary of the mothers is available in appendix B, which provides demographic characteristics of the mothers such as their ages, the lengths of their last incarcerations, length of time since their release, ethnic backgrounds, degrees of contact with their children, and employment statuses. The mothers ranged from 24 to 63 years old, with an average age of 43. They had 2 to 3 biological children on average, with one mother having as many as 10 children. The 37 mothers had a total of 101 children among them. The youngest child was 3 months old, while the oldest was a 44-year-old son, but the average child's age when the mothers were interviewed was approximately 19 years old.[70] When relevant to the discussion, children's ages are identified; otherwise, the children's underage or adult status is available in appendix B.

Given that women's visibility as (m)others is a function of their criminal record, it is important to understand the mothers' involvement in the criminal legal system and what they were last incarcerated for. Of the 37 mothers, 21 (57%) had been incarcerated more than once, while the remaining 16 (43%) had pled guilty to or been convicted of only one offense each, excluding technical violations. Mothers were incarcerated on a variety of both misdemeanor and felony charges. Drug crimes (i.e., the possession or sale of controlled substances) were the most common causes of incarceration. Twenty-six of the thirty-seven mothers (70%) had histories of substance use; for the majority of them, this use had developed prior to motherhood, then later influenced their entry into the criminal legal system as mothers. In addition to drug crimes, the mothers were commonly charged with money crimes like identity theft, shoplifting, burglary, and grand larceny. While some had committed money crimes as teens and young adults for monetary survival and personal protection prior to motherhood, these crimes were typically ways to uphold familial responsibilities and to financially protect a collective unit.[71] Other crimes included prostitution, assault, weapons possession, and driving under the influence. On average, the mothers' most recent bout of incarceration ranged from a span of seven days to as long as five years, with an average of one year and three months.

Mothers had been in the community for an average of three years and four months when I interviewed them; this time ranged from as early as one and one-half weeks after release to as long as 16 years after their release. Over half of the mothers I interviewed were currently or had previously been on parole. It is possible that retrospective accounts several years after release might differ substantially from reentry narratives when recently released. As time passes, mothers may forget certain details, and their memories may over- or underestimate their emotional responses to things that happened a long time ago. For these reasons, criminologists generally focus on the first few years after incarceration to explore reentry obstacles. However, I did not impose limitations on who I interviewed based on how long mothers were in the community post-release. I interviewed 14 mothers within a year after their last incarceration, an additional 9 between one to three years post-incarceration, another 7 within three to five years post-incarceration, and only 7 mothers with more than five years in the community. Interviewing mothers with a range of time in the community can be beneficial because the impact of carceral systems extends well after mothers' incarceration. When I spoke with the mothers, 14 lived in transitional housing, 9 lived in shelters,

5 lived in families' homes, 4 lived in their own homes, and the remaining 5 were in a variety of living situations like homelessness, an in-patient drug treatment program, with a roommate, in a bedroom that a stranger was subletting, and one whose living situation was unknown. The 37 mothers lived in four of the five New York City boroughs, excluding Staten Island. Most of the women lived in the borough of Queens (N = 13), followed by Manhattan (N = 10), Brooklyn (N = 9), and the Bronx (N = 4); one woman (N = 1) was homeless and awaiting shelter placement at the time of her interview. Of the 37 mothers, 25 (68%) were unemployed and 28 (76%) had at least a high school diploma or had successfully passed the general equivalency diploma (GED) exam.

Two mothers had regained custody of children who were in the foster care system, two had children who were still in foster care, and seven had children who were adopted from foster care (three by family and four by nonfamily), including one mother with an additional child awaiting final adoption by her maternal grandmother. It is worth emphasizing, however, that custodial arrangements are not accurate representations of mother-child relationships or interaction. Mothers without custody of one or all of their underage children can still live and interact with them or remain the primary caregivers; similarly, mothers can legally have custody without living with or having contact with their children.[72] Mother-child interaction shapes motherwork beyond dichotomies of being residential versus nonresidential mothers or having custodial versus noncustodial arrangements. Thus, I did not limit my recruitment to mothers with normative classifications of motherhood such as having custody or living with their children.

Approximately one-third of the 37 mothers lived with at least one of their children: 6 lived with underage children, 3 lived with adult children, and 4 lived with both underage and adult children. However, the most common arrangement was for the mothers to have some form of contact with their children without physically living together (29 of 37 mothers, 78%; see appendix B). Residential expectations may differ according to children's ages, as society expects mothers to live with underage children more than with adult children. *Invisible Mothers* demonstrates that these nonresidential relationships are influenced by a variety of things such as barriers pre- and post-incarceration as well as social expectations that children will eventually transition into adulthood and move out of their parents' home.

As shown in appendix B, 9 mothers had no communication with a child. Of these 9 mothers, 6 had no communication with their adult children, while the remaining 3 had no communication with underage children. Additionally, no mothers with multiple children lacked communication with all of them; instead, the mothers often had differing degrees of communication with each of their children. For instance, of the 9 mothers without contact, 7 did not have communication with at least one of their multiple children but maintained contact with the rest; the remaining 2 mothers did not have contact with their only child.

Overall, *Invisible Mothers* presents reentry narratives from mothers living with their children, mothers not living with their children but remaining in contact, and mothers without communication with their children. Some individuals may question the extent of motherwork without having custody, living with, or communicating with their children, but it is important for reentry scholars to take an inclusive approach in thinking about motherwork. Doing so allows mothers to define their own maternal identities and acknowledges mothers' visibility across different circumstances. The mothers' narratives presented in this book demonstrate the importance of maternal inclusivity in understanding what motherwork entails, without imposing normative standards.

Given the various ways to incorporate and discuss interview data, it is important to highlight that *Invisible Mothers* uses a combination of two approaches. I present the mothers' narratives as transparent windows into their lived experiences and, in presenting their narratives, I also unpack the mothers' meaning making in how they understood their lived experiences. I treat our conversations as rich insight into the reality of mothers' experiences, eliciting information about their feelings, personal timelines, social circumstances, and the context of family relationships. To help readers understand the mothers' lived experiences, I contextualize their narratives by integrating information about larger social contexts like parole stipulations and state policies. When relevant, I also unpack their narratives for readers to understand how mothers made sense of their experiences and described their experiences to me as an outside person.

ORGANIZATION OF THE BOOK

This book is organized into four chapters exploring the invisible punishments women of color encounter while navigating motherhood post-incarceration. Although society and scholars often frame mothers of color in reentry as "criminals" or "offenders" first and mothers second, in this book I purposefully center how they perform post-incarceration motherwork as criminalized (m)others, without centering their criminality. I also shy away from a blanket understanding of mothering practices that stigmatizes formerly incarcerated mothers of color and devalues their motherwork. Instead, I present the women's reentry narratives as they reflect on various aspects of maternal life, illustrating their battles with normative standards of motherhood and highlighting their resiliency from controlling images of them as "criminals first, mothers second."

Combating the stigma and defamation of formerly incarcerated mothers of color as "bad" (m)others, chapter 1 demonstrates how they resist these labels and construct their actions as being motherly in nature and with a maternal purpose. Despite complicated circumstances and complex maternal relationships, their involvement in the criminal legal system does not prevent motherwork altogether. Chapter 1 explores how women of color engage in maternal labor and how they understand their motherwork within various living arrangements, custodial circumstances, and degrees of contact with their children. This chapter reviews common mothering efforts to gain positionality in their children's lives as their mothers, to make up for lost time with their children, to improve their children's circumstances, and to shift or expand attention to mothering their grandchildren as second chances to mend relationships. Mothers largely want to do right by their children and try to do so, yet this chapter highlights how penal control continues well after incarceration as mothers are released into the carceral state in Black and brown communities. Although their motherwork is typically overlooked or ignored as invisible mothers, they are simultaneously supervisible as they are hypersurveilled by law enforcement and judged by society based on social norms about "good" and "bad" behaviors.[73] Chapter 1 illustrates their efforts as criminalized (m)others of color to overcome state surveillance and interventions that threaten their mothering under the carceral state. This chapter also highlights their concerns and struggles to protect their children in a society that criminalizes people of color even when they are innocent. As law professor and social justice advocate Dorothy Roberts explains: "It is impossible to explain the depth of sorrow felt at the moment a mother realizes she birthed her precious brown baby into a society that regards her child as just another unwanted Black charge."[74] The mothers' narratives in chapter 1 suggest a unique maternal need to protect their children from racialized state oppression, from controlling images of ethnic groups, and from ethnic nuances in social treatment. This first chapter provides a broad context of post-incarceration motherwork and mothering as criminalized (m)others, followed by three additional chapters with in-depth discussions of focus areas within women's reentry into the community.

Chapter 2 explores mothers' experiences between the criminal legal system and the child welfare system as the state critiques their mothering, denounces their worthiness to mother, and then legally regulates their motherwork as visible (m)others through custody decisions. This chapter reviews how mothers of color are forced to demonstrate maternal fitness according to preconceived notions, defined by the state, of what it means to be suitable mothers. To regain custody of underage children, mothers are forced to meet a number of prerequisites, such as certifications from parenting programs; clean urine samples to demonstrate sobriety; and suitable housing for themselves and their children, which requires a form of income.[75] Although these mandates have been put in place to ensure mothers' preparation for custody, they represent obvious tensions between notions of care in the child welfare system (to protect children) and notions of justice in the criminal legal system (to control their mothers).[76] Chapter 2 demonstrates that African American, Latinx, and West Indian family members alongside community members generally supported the mothers through motherhood and in collectively fighting against state interventions that strip or suppress mothers' custodial rights. Yet the formerly incarcerated mothers expressed that these state interventions and custodial prerequisites were an extra load attached to the already heavy burdens of reentry. For instance, this chapter shows that the mothers experienced many difficulties trying to accommodate or negotiate with their children's caregivers as they underwent constant housing changes and strove to create a home environment post-incarceration. They discussed some of the racialized barriers to establishing a home as criminalized (m)others of color—whether or not this home environment was expected to include their children. Yet all in all, they attempted to establish a home with dependent children, they tried to please their children across different age groups, and they tried to maintain and enhance maternal relationships from within the shelter system and other forms of transitional or temporary housing arrangements.

Chapter 3 highlights mothers' efforts to enter and progress in the workforce after incarceration, situating their narratives within what we know about invisible punishments and marginalization across gender, race, ethnicity, and motherhood. Research shows that gender plays a significant role in the organization of the labor market and workplace as women face gender discrimination in hiring practices, lower pay compared to men, and systemic barriers to promotion, as well as gender harassment that pushes them out of male-dominated professions.[77] Such experiences with gender discrimination in the labor market and workplace are complicated by maternal expectations and obligations. Chapter 3 examines the role of motherhood in how women think about job opportunities as criminalized (m)others and highlights what they perceive as suitable employment for their maternal needs post-incarceration. Chapter 3 also explores how formerly incarcerated mothers are able to do motherwork despite low pay and unemployment. For instance, motherwork differed among the mothers based on their level of communication with children as well as their children's ages and dependency on them.

In addition to the mother-child aspects that shape motherwork and (un)employment experiences post-incarceration, chapter 3 also highlights differences in mothers' experiences tied to their social positions as African American, West Indian, and Latina mothers. Women of color, as a collective marginalized group, are hindered by common assumptions about their work ethic when they have a criminal record,[78] which often positions them as united against racial discrimination. Chapter 3 demonstrates, however, that African Americans and West Indians were also positioned as rival competitors to progress in the labor market and workplace because of public perceptions about each group's work ethic.[79] In addition to this conflict between the ethnic groups, chapter 3 also demonstrates the stigma and defamation from within their own ethnic communities and families. For instance, the mothers' narratives suggest nuances across ethnic communities in their willingness to support formerly incarcerated (m)others, pushing those of West Indian and Latin American background to take extra steps to avoid further stigma and dishonor to the family name. More specifically, even though family was generally essential in supporting mothers after incarceration, West Indian and Latina mothers were more likely to describe family's reluctance to offer financial help when (m)others had committed money crimes, since these contradicted cultural values about legitimate work and honorable income. Thus, in regard to racial-ethnic background, this chapter unpacks how cultural expectations about work and integrity intimately shaped mothers' reentry into the community after release.

Substance use has a vast presence among women in the criminal legal system and among the formerly incarcerated mothers I interviewed. Chapter 4 examines their goals, efforts, support networks, and challenges to recovery while navigating motherhood post-incarceration. Though motherhood often encouraged them to seek sobriety, it simultaneously introduced unique obstacles in mothers' recovery efforts. Chapter 4 highlights the problems they faced in coping with maternal and reentry stressors as they tried to avoid relapse. In doing so, it examines the role of positive social support networks in their recovery efforts, but it also highlights some of the complexities that exist within these support networks for visible (m)others. The mothers' narratives demonstrate that recovery is a function of their social interactions with people like family and intimate partners, but it is also shaped by their treatment resulting from societal perceptions of substance use, stigma of penal control, and carceral logics behind state surveillance. For instance, within ethnic communities, cultural beliefs about substance use exposed some of the mothers to more stigma and alienation, limiting the support they received and complicating their recovery efforts. Even in reentry programs for formerly incarcerated women, mothers are still vulnerable to judgment and hostility for stigmatized labels as "addicts" or bad (m)others, which are frequently uttered by other program participants without histories of substance use. Similarly, in treatment programs, the mothers found that treatment personnel and other women with longer sobriety questioned their recovery efforts and recovery progress. All in all, chapter 4 explores how, combined with common obstacles after their release, managing recovery is particularly unique and multifaceted for formerly incarcerated mothers of color.

The conclusion reviews the practical implications of the mothers' narratives for post-incarceration reentry and treatment programs servicing them, for program personnel and social service providers working with them, for community members supporting them, and for policy makers who have the power to curtail state violence toward them. It also includes suggestions for researchers studying the reentry process for mothers of color—specifically African American, West Indian, and Latina mothers—and conducting research that does not contribute to their stigmatization as (m)others. More specifically, it encourages researchers to explore intraracial and interethnic nuances in social interactions post-incarceration, to examine the role of cultural values and the impact of cultural transgressions on receiving family and community support, to expand on research about mothering infants and toddlers during reentry, and to explore mothers' intentions and actions during reentry compared to how these are viewed and received by their children. Overall, this book argues that formerly incarcerated mothers of color would benefit from more and adequate community-driven services that function outside of the punitive grasp of carceral systems. *Invisible*

Mothers concludes by advocating for and suggesting anti-carceral ways to support mothers of color through transformative efforts that do not contribute to their oppression within the criminal legal system.

In sharing mothers' narratives, I treat *Invisible Mothers* as a call to action to view and treat criminalized mothers of color as the visible mothers they are and fight to present themselves as. I encourage readers to acknowledge and reflect on the mothers' lived realities presented in this book and to avoid accepting public depictions of mothers of color as incarcerable subjects who need to be controlled and punished for their survival.

CHAPTER 1

Motherwork

"It's Always Been a Very Demanding Job"

"It's always been a very demanding job," said Vanessa about mother-work, the caring labor devoted toward children. She was a 25-year-old mother who lived in a shelter with her intimate partner and her only child. "I'm just 5!," interrupted her 5-year-old daughter, who was play-ing nearby. Though Vanessa believed motherhood in and of itself was a very demanding job, she cherished her maternal role. "I mean, some-times it's overwhelming. Sometimes it gets there . . . but it's nothing that I'd give up."

Approximately two years before we spoke, Vanessa had been released from incarceration for an assault charge. She had been found guilty of assault against someone who mistreated her daughter while babysitting. Vanessa believed her actions were justified since she was protecting her daughter, saying "it was all for her." She believed that mothers should care for their children, and that "good" mothers prioritize putting their children's interests before their own. This understanding of "good" mothers is similar to dominant social narratives about motherhood. In fact, while speaking with formerly incarcerated mothers like Vanessa, I found that despite their criminalized status and social assumptions about them as (m)others, their maternal ideals aligned with gendered notions of mothering. However, for Vanessa and many others like her, protecting her daughter had led to her incarceration.

Society places gendered expectations on women to serve as pri-mary caregivers, yet carceral systems hold women accountable to these expectations while simultaneously closing doors to opportunity and imposing barriers to progression. Vanessa found herself missing her daughter during her incarceration and not wanting to be away from her again. Despite the demanding nature of motherhood, the act of mothering and the desire to stay with her daughter motivated her actions post-incarceration. "I never let her out of my sight. Like, literally every day since [my release]. . . . I'm doing what I gotta do." Once released, however, mothers are not only tasked with trying to "get back in touch with what's going on on the outside," as Vanessa described, but they also must "get back on track with [their] children." This chapter illustrates common obstacles mothers encounter post-incarceration and also demonstrates how formerly incarcerated mothers implement many strategies to navigate the gendered consequences of penal control.

Though the institution of motherhood is often understood within the context of patriarchy and gendered expectations of women to be primary caregivers for children, motherhood must also be understood within the context of racial and ethnic oppression and inequalities. Vanessa's 5-year-old daughter continued to play nearby as we spoke. "Mommy," she said to catch her mother's attention. Both Vanessa and I turned our attention to the little girl. "Dark," she said, pointing to my bare arms. Then, pointing to her mother's arm, she said "Darker!" Her daughter was comparing the variations in our skin tone. Vanessa laughed, finding her daughter's observation funny. Shortly after that, her daughter redirected our attention back to our skin color. With one hand, she pointed to my arm. "Dark." With the other, she pointed to her mother. "Darker." At this point, Vanessa jokingly responded by pointing to her daughter's skin, "Yellow!" Even though Vanessa and I are both brown skinned, her daughter—who was lighter skinned—found it worthwhile to compare our skin tones. This may appear not that significant as children learn about the world, but it illustrates the visibility of skin color and demonstrates that young children are not oblivious to differences in skin color between and within racial groups.[1] Little did she know at such a young age that her visual appearance as a person of color would increasingly become the basis of assumptions about her as she grew older and the basis on which she would likely face marginalization in society.

Ultimately, how women experience and navigate motherhood is shaped by their social status as mothers of color, the resources that are available or unavailable to them, and their visibility and treatment as a marginalized group. In this chapter I illustrate how penal control extends well beyond the incarceration of mothers of color, affecting their mothering while under the carceral state in their communities and while navigating through parole. In what follows, I also highlight how formerly incarcerated mothers sometimes reframed social constructions of motherhood to best fit their circumstances as criminalized women of color. They often resisted such negative perceptions of them as "bad" or negligent (m)others and maintained identities as good mothers.

MOTHERING UNDER THE CARCERAL STATE AND THROUGH PAROLE

The carceral state, as described by Dr. Ruby Tapia, "encompasses the formal institutions and operations and economies of the criminal [legal] system proper, but it also encompasses logics, ideologies, practices, and structures that invest in tangible and sometimes intangible ways in punitive orientations to difference, to poverty, to struggles for social justice."[2] Embedded within the carceral state is the faulty logic that once individuals have supposedly "served their time" for any wrongdoing, restrictions on their freedoms should serve as a corrective tool. Though prisons and jails are formal institutions most frequently associated with the carceral state, penal control extends beyond prison bars or jail walls and continues through community-based parole supervision. Advocates of the criminal legal system claim that the purpose of parole is to serve as a transitional phase between confinement and freedom in the community, arguing that parole facilitates rehabilitation. In reality, however, parole is another form of incarceration without the physical barricades typically found in correctional facilities.

The emphasis of parole is on surveillance and the risk management of groups deemed as offenders, subjecting parolees to strict stipulations and stripping them of certain freedoms. Over half of the mothers I interviewed were or had been on parole. Even though physically situated in the community, the mothers faced various restrictions. Parole conditions include, but are not limited to, reporting frequently to parole officers, remaining in the designated city and state (unless permission is granted to leave), participating in a variety of programs (such as treatment programs), and notifying parole officers of any changes in residence or employment. Although parole may be pitched as a privilege because parolees are in the community, the mothers believed parole officers were allowed to "do whatever they want[ed] with [them]," putting mothers at risk of reincarceration. For instance, Marcia was reincarcerated on three occasions for parole violations of not reporting a change of address and absconding. Marcia shared that parole officers gave parolees ultimatums such as, "You either do this, or you go to jail!," illustrating the parole officers' hold on them and role as enforcers of penal control.

The women believed parole restrictions affected their lives in general but, more specifically, as mothers, arguing that "there's a difference for someone who has kids and someone who don't." According to Emma, formerly incarcerated mothers are particularly concerned about parole because it "is a surveillance state" that is unpredictable, time-consuming, and filled with stipulations that are more detrimental when women have children:

> A mother without children doesn't have to be concerned about the baggage of the system, like parole. Parole is a surveillance state: constantly have these stipulations, absorbs your time. Worry. Unpredictable when you gonna be released, when you have to make an appointment around holidays. It involves your radius—what you can't do. If your children are long distance, you can't travel because you need a pass.

Overall, mothers believed being on parole was "embarrassing" and "stressful" for them and their children, especially as they were susceptible to random visits from parole officers that increased their visibility as (m)others under the carceral state.

The stress of parole on their mothering was especially felt when mothers did not live with their children but maintained communication. Mothers on parole often have curfews that restrict them from being outside of their reported residence past a certain hour or from leaving before a given time, and they must account for travel time on public transportation as part of these restrictions. Marcia's curfew placed an inconvenient time constraint on visits to her two sons, who lived with their father. This hindered her ability to help watch them when their father was unavailable:

> I wanted to spend time with my kids. And [parole] avoided me from leaving my mom's house where I was paroled to, to spend two days with my kids. At times, my sons' father needed me to babysit or to go to a doctor's appointment and I couldn't. . . . So, yea, it did affect my sons' lives. It did affect my life as a mother in my sons' life.

Marcia would have liked to spend the weekends with her sons as a means of having quality time. Obtaining approval from parole to do so, however, was often an inconveniently long process that discouraged mothers from seeking this authorization. Thus, even when mothers tried to perform nonresidential motherwork after incarceration, their visibility and social position on parole hindered their ability to navigate motherhood with children they did not live with.

This chapter began with the story of Vanessa and her 5-year-old daughter to highlight Vanessa's motherwork after incarceration; I also interviewed Vanessa's mother, Vera, who had also been incarcerated and was on parole for six months when I met her. When asked to describe her experience on parole, Vera replied "not free." She elaborated on this lack of freedom:

> I'm out here, I don't have a cellblock to go in, I don't have someone to tell me: "Get up. Take a shower. It's lunchtime." But, you still don't feel like you're free out here either—you understand?—because there's so much stipulations.

Parole supervision, for instance, forbids parolees from fraternizing with others with criminal records unless permitted to do so by their parole officer. For Vera, this condition directly affected communication with her daughter Vanessa, with whom she shared a charge:

> There was a point where I couldn't even be around my daughter because she has a record, and on one of the cases we're joint. So, how does that feel to not be able to be around your child? That's my child!

Vera compared parole supervision to having a noose around her neck. In doing so, she associated being on parole with replicating the lynchings of Black people who were publicly shamed and punished for perceived wrongdoing. Sociologists, criminologists, and lawyers alike have published about modern-day lynchings arguing, "Today's lynching is incarceration. Today's lynch mobs are professionals. They have a badge; they have a law degree."[3] Not only is modern-day lynching widespread within carceral systems like prison and parole, but the latter continue to function as a form of racial control that disproportionately impacts Black and brown bodies.[4] Vera was three weeks shy of completing parole and saw this as an opportunity to remove the noose of penal control from her neck. In fact, she spoke as if it had already happened: "The noose is gone; the noose is above around from [my] neck." Even though Vera equaled the completion of parole to the removal of a noose, the following section demonstrates how mothers were still vulnerable to this hypothetical noose of penal control since their communities remained under siege by the carceral state.

Mothering under Siege in Communities of Color

As I walked through mothers' neighborhoods to meet them at or near their homes, the hypersurveillance of people of color was evident all around me. Mothers were essentially released from the confines of prison and jail cells and were living in a carceral state within their own communities, which not only surveilled them as formerly incarcerated (m)others but also surveilled their children, whom mothers wanted to protect. As a result, mothers faced the heavy burden of trying to keep their children safe in a society that criminalizes, penalizes, and kills people of color. As Bernadette explained, all women want "the same thing like: love, feelings, and [to] love they children. That much of the situation is like every mother: every mother wants to love they kids. But every mother of the races raise[s] they children entirely different." As in Bernadette's account, the mothers believed that as a result of their racial position and social treatment, they needed to be extremely protective of their children.

Lucy was one of the mothers who wanted to be interviewed at home. She lived in the Brownsville neighborhood, which is 76% Black and has the second-highest incarceration rate in New York City.[5] After exiting the train, I walked through the public housing development and saw various forms of police surveillance on that Thursday afternoon. Within a two-block radius, I saw at least two New York Police Department (NYPD) floodlight towers, which are essentially elevated floodlights located on wheels and parked by a sidewalk. These elevated floodlights were placed in areas that then mayor Bill de Blasio described as "obscure and problematic" to supposedly reduce crime, which in practice meant that these light towers were strategically and scornfully placed outside of predominantly Black and brown public housing developments. The use of such blinding light towers mimics the carceral power structure that philosopher Michel Foucault described: an elevated watchtower designed and operated to instill discipline and implement punishment.[6] As I continued to walk toward Lucy's home, I passed by a police car that was slowly circling the area. Unfamiliar with the neighborhood, I occasionally glanced at my phone to see the walking directions. Two police officers stood at a corner where I should have turned. Instead of walking past them, I found myself continuing to walk straight. As a brown-skinned Latina, a part of me did not want to walk past them since doing so would have caught their attention, increased my visibility to the officers, and potentially subjected me to an unwelcome interaction. I had convinced myself that I was supposed to walk in the direction away from the officers. I later wondered how residents felt about their visibility in this police presence.

As I spoke with Lucy, we sat next to each other on her living room couch. The apartment used to be her mother's, and Lucy had been living in it for about eighteen years. She described the area surrounding her apartment as "dangerous!" "In what way?" I asked. She clarified by saying, "You never know when they gonna start shooting. Oh God! It's a crisis." Lucy's description of crime in her area is consistent with New York City police data. Her local precinct is located in one of the most high-crime areas in Brooklyn and across the city. Such police data on high-crime areas, however, reproduce power structures and hypersurveillance in these racialized spaces, further criminalizing communities of color.[7]

Even though the role of police officers is arguably to protect children, police contributed to mothers' fears for their children's safety. While I was interviewing the mothers (2014–2015), significant media attention acknowledged the unarmed Black lives taken at the hands of police. When I asked Latoya what her biggest concern was regarding her two children, an 18-year-old son and a 14-year-old daughter, she responded:

> [T]hat my son will get shot down like a dog in the street by the police. . . . [Y]ou see it everywhere and it's like a real thing that's happening. And so, every time he goes outside, I'm not afraid of, like, so much someone in the street shooting him. I'm afraid of the police doing something to him, and that's my biggest fear.

Though Latoya focused on her son as a potential target of police maltreatment and murder, mothers shared these concerns for their daughters as well. Police violence is also prevalent against young Black women, and it also received increasing media attention during the time of my interviews. To name a few examples, media attention was directed to 14-year-old Dajerria Becton, who was thrown to the ground by an officer who then continued to kneel into the girl's back, as well as 16-year-old Shakara, who was still sitting at her desk when a school resource officer flipped the desk, dragged her and the desk a few feet away, then arrested her—all because she was using a cell phone. "You fear what might happen to your kid," said Bianca, a mother of 16- and 28-year-old daughters. She began to discuss police shootings of innocent children:

You hear about these kids getting shot by cops, and they're totally innocent. You just hear things that happen all over the United States. And it just
makes you want to hold on to your kid a little harder.

She continued:

It's hard too because you got to let them go live their life also. But, it's a hard
thing to do when you can't. . . . It's a catch [22]. You got to let them go out
into the world, but you just got to make sure that nobody is going to hurt
them when they walk out the door. So, wondering if you're going to see your
kid walk back to your door, that's a heavy feeling.

These accounts suggest the importance of understanding parenting within
the contexts of racial inequalities and discrimination intermingled within
the carceral state, which may surface in a variety of ways, such as police
use of force.

Consistent with sociological research, the mothers believed that, as
women of color, they needed to actively protect their children from the
carceral state and racialized state violence.[8] A consensus existed among
the mothers that a racialized need for protection led Black and brown
mothers to be more involved with their children compared to white
mothers. "Black women and Latina women are more loving and protective over their kids," explained Francesca, a mother who was Latina
and African American. "You gotta be on top of your kids," she said,
suggesting that Black and Latina mothers were protective of their children out of necessity, given the nature of their children's visibility in
society. When asked how important her racial-ethnic background was
in raising her children, Lucy, a Latina mother, noted that she wanted to
"raise them to be safe" and "try to keep them safe." As Susila Gurusami
has written in her work on formerly incarcerated Black women, "these
mothers locate the state as a primary danger in their children's lives."[9]
She argues that consequently, formerly incarcerated Black mothers engage in "hypervigilant motherwork" in which they anticipate state harm
and intervention and proactively work to protect their children from
the carceral state. Consistent with Gurusami's work, I found that the
women believed their mothering labor was essential to protect their
children from the potential troubles and racial discrimination they were
likely to tackle in society. Unfortunately, as long as society continues to
criminalize them as racial "minorities" and police officers continue to
harm and kill their children, mothers of color may continue to face circumstances that complicate their mothering and their efforts to protect
their children.

Ethnoracial Needs for Protection. Though the African American, Latina, and West Indian mothers believed there was a mutual maternal need to protect minoritized children, they also suggested that nuances existed in the treatment of ethnic groups within the Black racial umbrella. Specifically, a heightened need for protection was tied to societal perceptions of children's ethnic identity as being African American, compared to less relative need for protection if the mothers' children were perceived as Latinx or West Indian. This is consistent with research that shows African Americans are more inclined than Latinxs to discuss societal prejudices and prepare their children for biased treatment and suggests the same heightened preparation compared to West Indians.[10]

Marie considered herself Haitian American, while her son's father was African American. Even though Marie's son was of mixed ethnic background, she noted that official paperwork on people's racial-ethnic background "doesn't say West Indian." Instead, "there's only Black/African American," forcing members of society to "classify everyone who's Black as 'African American.'" This classification in official paperwork exemplifies the same way many people misconstrue race and ethnicity, assuming that those who are Black must be of African American background and overlooking the presence of other Black ethnic groups like Latinxs and West Indians. Similarly, Marie believed that children *perceived* as African American were destined to encounter hurdles in society and from the police. Even though her son was ethnically mixed, Marie believed he was vulnerable to negative treatment because of public views and assumptions about him specifically as African American and not necessarily due to his West Indian background. This is consistent with sociological research that finds "[w]ithout an accent or other clues to immediately telegraph their ethnic status to others, [West Indians] will be seen—and subjected to the same kind of racial exclusion— as black Americans [i.e., African Americans]."[11] Due to public views of African American males as perceived threats and her son's visibility with brown skin, Marie described having a greater need to protect him from "a lot of obstacles" that would inevitably surface from individual racism and racialized state violence. This is no surprise given the historical and systematic oppression of African American men and women in the United States.

As Marie's account suggests, social responses to perceived ethnic groups may influence ethnic nuances in women's motherwork. Specifically, mothers with children who have perceived visual markers of some African American background may perceive a greater social threat to their children and enact "hypervigilant motherwork," as described by Gurusami. This was evident with Marie; the thought of impending obstacles in her son's path contributed to another concern she had as a formerly incarcerated mother, believing her role as a parent was "*highly important*" to combat these ethnoracial barriers.

In all, women experience motherhood differently depending on their privilege, social status, and social perceptions.[12] Regardless of shared maternal interests among mothers, maternal demands can vary based on their social position within the carceral state and their need to prevent or overcome state violence toward them and their children.

MOTHERWORK AS THE "BAD" (M)OTHER

In conjunction with their surveillance under parole and within the carceral state more generally, the visibility of women of color has historically been grounded in gendered and racialized controlling narratives of them as "bad" (m)others. During enslavement, reproducing children was an aspect of their slave labor and exploitation as "breeders," and women of color were stripped of any rights to their own bodies, including personal decisions to become mothers or bear children. Currently, women of color continue to be viewed as breeders. They are portrayed as Welfare Queens who irresponsibly breed multiple children and abuse state resources, then are treated as women who demand state intervention because they are deemed "unfit" (m)others.[13] Incarceration further demonizes them as bad (m)others for seemingly doing something that landed them behind bars and away from their children. These narratives impose blame and demand personal responsibility for their actions, which society automatically assumes were not in the best interests of their children. Yet Vanessa's narrative at the beginning of this chapter shows that her incarceration was a direct result of protecting her daughter.

Women are judged as good or bad mothers based on social constructions of motherhood, but women do not experience motherhood in the same way. Mothers must find ways to overcome the racialized and gendered oppression imposed upon them as women of color, especially when criminalized and pushed into the criminal legal system. I found that the mothers did not believe good mothering required a constant physical presence; instead, the mothers' circumstances shaped their understanding of good mothering in which mothers may be physically, verbally, or emotionally available to children. Therefore, descriptions of "good" mothers must be understood *beyond* normative standards of intensive mothering and rather as they relate to common circumstances after incarceration, which often consist of nonresidential mothering, noncustodial mothering, and mothering without contact.

Nonresidential and Noncustodial Motherwork

Normative standards of intensive mothering imply that motherhood must be child-centered, financially committed, expensive, and a physical investment in nurturing children as primary caregivers.[14] Mothers without custody and mothers living apart from their children become visible to the general public for seemingly challenging these gendered and misogynistic expectations, subjecting them to criticism as bad (m)others. To complicate matters further, research shows that nonresidential and noncustodial arrangements are common realities for women in the criminal legal system because of disruptions to previous arrangements during prison time as well as interventions from the child welfare system before, during, and after incarceration.[15] This was the case for the women I interviewed. After their incarceration, half of the mothers with underage children did not have custody. In addition, the majority of the mothers did not live with at least one of their children (of all ages) but maintained some form of contact with them. The following discussion demonstrates how, despite these nonresidential and noncustodial arrangements, mothers emphasized *practical* meanings of motherhood that they were able to perform. In this way, formerly incarcerated mothers of color tried to alter the nature of their visibility as "bad" (m)others by reframing "good" mothering and doing motherwork that was realistic for them and their circumstances as criminalized women.

When I met Marcia, it was clear that she emphasized practical meanings of motherhood amid her complicated living circumstances and custodial arrangements. As I was exiting the bus in Brooklyn's East New York neighborhood, Marcia appeared from the walkway between public housing buildings. We made eye contact, and she walked over to me, leaning over to give me a hug. I responded, saying, "We finally get to see each other face-to-face!" It was four days after her first phone call inquiring about an interview. Marcia laughed and agreed. During those four days, the New York City homeless shelter intake center had found her ineligible for shelter placement, forcing Marcia to focus all of her attention on reestablishing temporary housing. We walked and talked as we made our way between the tall public housing buildings. Upon approaching an apartment door, she knocked on it using the door knocker, then proceeded to take off her sneakers while standing on the doormat in the hallway. Following her lead and respecting house rules, I stepped onto the doormat and removed my shoes as well. It became clear that her knock on the door was a notification to others inside that we had arrived, seeing as the apartment door was already unlocked. She opened the door, extended her hand to grab my shoes, and placed them under a nearby wheelchair. Picture frames with family photos filled the living room area, hung across the walls and located on each table. We entered a three-bedroom apartment: one bedroom for Marcia's mother-in-law, a little girl's room for what looked like two girls, and the third room, where her sister- and brother-in-law were relaxing with their 5-month-old baby. Marcia described her mother-in-law's apartment as a comfortable place for her. It was clear why; it felt like a cozy, family-friendly environment while spending time in the apartment myself. Unfortunately, the apartment did not have enough room for Marcia, her husband, or her children. She was staying in the El Camino shelter, which is infamous for its poor living conditions.

Marcia was a mother of four children who were all under age when I met her. Marcia did not have custody of or live with any of her children. Marcia's oldest daughter, who was 15 years old, had been adopted at age 1. Marcia's 12- and 9-year-old sons were in their father's custody. As Marcia explained, her sons were with their father "not through the system or anything—[but] by choice." Her 6-year-old daughter was in the custody of Marcia's mother. Even though she believed the child welfare system made a "big error" in removing the parental custody of her youngest child, Marcia was relieved "that error came out [with a] good outcome" because her daughter was with her own grandmother. Turning around and pointing out the window, Marcia showed me that her youngest daughter also lived right across the street from where we sat in her mother-in-law's apartment. She paraphrased a West African proverb, noting that "it doesn't only take one person to raise a child, it takes a whole community." This proverb recognizes the collective strengths of "shared mothering," in which others help mothers carry out essential tasks to share the mothering labor and ultimately support mothers through navigating motherhood. Thus, the living and custodial arrangements of Marcia's children were not, in and of themselves, considered bad mothering. As with Marcia, mothers viewed shared mothering positively and as a critical feature of overcoming obstacles as criminalized women of color,[16] allowing them to combat negative assumptions about nonresidential and noncustodial mothering.

When asked to describe things she did as a mother, Marcia responded:

> I'm very active in my kids' school shows, um, graduations, plays, birthdays, activities, when they call me for homework, when they need advice as a friend, for everything. I do all the stuff, all the stuff a real mom is supposed to do.

I pointed out, "So, you said 'a real mom.' What's your definition of a real mom?" Marcia clarified: "A mom: someone that's there, not only financially but for the most memorable days of the kids' life—that's a mom. Or, someone that you wanna be like; someone you could look up to." Regardless of the nonresidential and noncustodial arrangements, she described still "being there" for her children, which she accomplished through her attendance at important events and by being available to talk during times of need. Her adopted 15-year-old daughter had found her just a year before on Facebook. "And from there on, we cool every day—*every* day. . . . When she comes out of school, she calls me, I call her—every day." These examples illustrate the caring labor of motherwork that often goes unnoticed or remains ignored when the public depicts formerly incarcerated women as bad (m)others. Performing these behaviors was extremely meaningful to Marcia as a mother, because according to her, "a good mom is the one that's there whether you're up, down, sideways, high." In fact, she considered herself a good mother based on this very emphasis on "being there" for her children. In this way, Marcia's personal ideals and understanding of good mothers aligned with gendered notions of mothering, despite social assumptions about her criminalized status and her nonresidential and noncustodial arrangements. Smiles came across her face, showing pride and joy as she discussed her motherwork and the positive response from her children:

> They say, I'm the greatest mom: "My mom is the best! My mom is the funniest! My mom is the coolest!" And *that* makes me feel so overwhelmed [with joy] to know that at least I fulfill that place in my kids' life. . . . I don't need to prove to nobody that I'm a good mom; my kids know I'm a good mom.

"I'm a prime example," she said of herself as a good mom. "I would be glad to teach a lot of mothers what's an example of being a good mom when kids are not in your custody."

Natalie, another mother, was originally from Virginia, but she had traveled to New York City with hopes of getting access to more housing opportunities. When I met Natalie, she was staying with an aunt in Harlem but was hoping for something more permanent. Natalie had three children. Her 12-year-old daughter and 11-year-old son were under the full custody of their father in Virginia. Despite the nonresidential arrangement and the physical distance from them, Natalie's motherwork entailed communicating with them via Facebook. Natalie's youngest child, her 4-year-old daughter, had never been in her custody. Due to a positive test for cocaine, Natalie was unable to leave the hospital with her daughter when she was born. Her daughter was taken into the foster care system and eventually adopted by her foster mom. Fortunately, Natalie's daughter lived in Harlem, only four blocks away from where Natalie was staying at her aunt's home. "She just stay right around the corner" she said figuratively, highlighting that four blocks was really close for their relationship. For Natalie, motherwork entailed visiting her daughter on the weekends to braid her hair, guaranteed time to interact in person on a weekly basis. She also described calling her during the week to check on her whereabouts. Her description of good mothering was not limited to custodial rights or joint living arrangements, but generally consisted of being involved in her children's lives and knowing where they were even while separated. Specifically, Natalie believed "a good mom is somebody that know where they kids at, all the time. No matter whether the kids with you or not, you still in they life." Like Marcia, Natalie described a good mother in a way that was linked to her own actions and, by doing this, she upheld her involvement in her children's lives as good mothering. She didn't believe living with children automatically made women good mothers since they could be "stranger[s] living in the same house. They just see each other in passing." On the contrary, even though she was living apart from her children, she described remaining involved: "I just tr[y] to keep in contact with my kids and let them know I love them. . . . As long as I could hear they voice or see or know that they doing all right, I'm fine."

As evident with Marcia and Natalie, formerly incarcerated women often viewed themselves as good mothers despite their criminalized status and the social stigma about them as (m)others. Marcia highlighted that nonresidential and noncustodial arrangements are not necessarily bad since it takes a village to raise a child, and a mother can still "be there" in these circumstances. Similarly, Natalie highlighted that living together and having custody did not necessarily mean "good" either because mothers can still be strangers under the same roof as their children. Instead, across my interviews, I found that "good" mothers were most commonly described as women who were "always there" for their children by providing unconditional love; putting children's concerns before their own interests; and being available to listen, talk to, and advise them during times of need. These narratives of good mothering practices coincide with normative constructions of motherhood, suggesting that their *views* are no different than those of others who are beyond the grasp of the criminal legal system. Still, they reframed notions of good mothering practices by emphasizing certain meanings when they were practical realities post-incarceration. For instance, the mothers described "being there" by giving their children attention, which was broadly defined, and taking care of maternal responsibilities in some way. This understanding allowed them to view themselves as good mothers when they did not have custody of or live with their children and to remain resilient against negative labels as so-called bad (m)others that tainted their visibility in society.

Mothering without Contact

Narratives about good mothering behaviors were the most complex for formerly incarcerated women who had no contact with a child. These mothers at times simultaneously met their own maternal ideals as good mothers while also contradicting them, yet they maintained positive views of their mothering despite unfortunate circumstances like not being in touch with their children. Doing so allowed them to disassociate themselves from "bad" mothering in a number of ways.

Two mothers did not have contact with their only child. Jesenia was one of them. Four months had passed since Jesenia had communicated with her 5-year-old son, who was not in her custody and who lived with his father and paternal grandmother. In some ways, Jesenia was unable to fulfill the behaviors she associated with good mothering: at least some form of communication, which she did not have. For instance, according to her, a good mother is responsible for "making sure he's up to date on his shots and he's getting the medical [check-ups] that he needs. That he's doing schooling. And . . . just being there for the job when the child needs assistance with homework and stuff like that." This demonstrates some disconnect between her idea of good mothering practices and the actions she was able to perform at the time. Though some may argue that her lack of contact and the inability to perform some of these tasks are grounds for considering her a bad (m)other, Jesenia viewed things slightly differently. "I know where he lives," she said. Jesenia would mail her son clothes, shoes, and leisure items like Hot Wheels toys and books in Spanish and Italian. In doing so, she described mothering from a distance, a concept often applied to mothers without custody and to transnational mothers who live in different countries from their children, but which is also a reality for mothers in the criminal legal system.[17] According to Jesenia, "A good mother is somebody that puts [the] child's concerns—like their health, their wellbeing, the environment they're in—first before anything." This description is consistent with notions of "intensive mothering" as being child-centered.[18] Also in line with gendered expectations of women, she emphasized her responsibility to raise her son to be a respectful man and to be a positive role model for him:

> As a mother, what's expected of me is to be a positive role model for my child. Show my son what is proper for him growing up as a man and what a man should do as far as being respectful to women, showing women respect, not cursing—like his grandmother does—and, you know, learning how to communicate without yelling. And, that's something he lacks in that environment.

Jesenia did not believe living with his father and paternal grandmother was best for her son because they did not display the respect that she wanted to instill in him, and she did not believe they were positive role models for him. Jesenia understood her own anger management and recovery from substance use as efforts in self-development to regain custodial rights. She believed doing so would help remove her son from a toxic environment and considered her personal endeavors as ultimately being for her son, "because the more you benefit yourself, the more you're gonna be able to benefit your child." In this way, Jesenia was able to make broad connections between her role as a mother and her everyday activities post-incarceration, arguing that these actions were, in fact, child-centered. This very focus on being child-centered and putting her child's concerns first allowed her to make sense of life after incarceration as a good mom. In other words, she saw herself as a good mother by attributing her personal endeavors to the best interests of her son, despite having had no communication with him in the last four months.

Though Jesenia was 1 of the 2 mothers who did not have contact with their only child, 7 mothers did not have contact with at least one of their multiple children. Bernadette, a 63-year-old mother of six, did not have contact with two of them, her middle son and middle daughter. Bernadette's mother "stepped in" to help her raise these two children at a time when she could not do so herself because of her previous substance use. Nevertheless, not being there at a critical time in their lives contributed to the ongoing lack of communication with these two children. When asked to describe a "good" mother, Bernadette responded: "A good mom stays with her kid and take care of it, and do the things they suppose to do as they grow." Although some may argue that Bernadette's actions with her middle son and daughter did not coincide with her descriptions of a good mother (i.e., someone who stays with their children), Bernadette still did not consider herself a bad mother. She managed this discrepancy between being a "good" or "bad" mother by emphasizing her feelings that she "loved all of them" and by rationalizing her behaviors given the circumstances. She believed the previous arrangements of shared mothering were necessary due to her previous substance use and were therefore the best option for her children. In other words, these arrangements were made with good intentions but sometimes resulted in the women losing communication with their children.[19]

Like Bernadette, Paloma was a mother of multiple children who did not have contact with some of them. "How many kids do you have?" I asked. "I have ummm many of kids," she said with an uncomfortable laugh. "Yeah ummm . . . I have 10 children." "How old are they?" I probed. Taking long pauses in deep thought, Paloma struggled to provide the ages of three of her children. Paloma had ten children but did not have any contact with the majority of them; seven children were taken at birth due to positive toxicology tests for drugs. She believed a good mother was someone "taking care of responsibilities" such as having food available in the home. When asked specifically about her actions as a mother, Paloma only spoke of her youngest child, her 3-year-old son, whom she had custody of and with whom she lived. In fact, she became emotional and a large smile would shine across her face when describing her actions as a mother to her youngest son. Paloma's focus on her youngest child appeared to be a protective function. She diverted attention away from her maternal disengagement with her older children and instead directed our discussions toward examples in which she was meeting maternal ideals. This was a protective measure of highlighting positive maternal relationships, which allowed her to view herself and to present herself as a good mother, regardless of her past and the disconnect with seven of her children. "I've been in both places. I've been a bad mom and I was a good mom." As for Paloma, the dynamic nature of "good" and "bad" mothering allowed mothers to compensate for their past and for not having contact with at least one of their children. Specifically, when they had multiple children, they were able to concentrate their motherwork on those children with whom they could "try again" to demonstrate good mothering.

It is important to note, however, that this notion of having been both a good and a bad mother was not common among all the women in the study. Some did not view themselves as "bad," arguing that bad mothers do not exist. As one mother explained, "I really don't think there's a good and a bad when it comes to being a mother. You're a mother and you're just trying to deal with that responsibility on its own." Motherhood, in and of itself, is not always a walk in the park. Dealing with maternal responsibilities in general can be difficult for any mother, which is why there is a market for mothering books and guides that cater to helping women navigate things like pregnancy, working full-time outside the home, managing single motherhood, and balancing motherhood with intimate relationships.[20] Combined with the fact that they were of African American, Latinx, and West Indian background, the women faced racialized stigma and oppression as mothers of color that they needed to tackle head on. They stressed that instead of being bad as individuals, some women simply made bad decisions during this process. "I just don't think there's 'bad mothers,'" said Josefina. "I just think they make bad decisions and sometimes you're just at the wrong place at the wrong time." Similarly, Henrietta noted, women are "not really bad mother[s]; it's what they do that's bad." However, even this notion of making bad decisions is subjective and disproportionately policed in communities of color. "Everyone makes mistakes. *Ev-ery-body*. Some make a little bit more difficult mistakes. I say everyone's broken the law. Some get caught, some don't." These narratives demonstrate that mothering is complex and often too complicated to put into binary labels of good or bad, especially for mothers of color, who are rendered invisible mothers during times of need yet criticized as visible (m)others when perceived as being flawed.

Their circumstances and experiences were so complex that the women believed others should not judge their character based on their criminalized status or according to normative conditions such as having custody of, having contact with, or living with children. Instead, they believed they deserved recognition for their motherwork, especially as a marginalized group after incarceration. They were able to perform motherwork by mothering from a distance. Marcia spoke with her adopted daughter every day after school and made sure she was present at her children's most memorable occasions, even though she did not have custody of them. Natalie used social media to remain in contact with her children in another state and visited her nearby daughter on a weekly basis to braid her hair. Jesenia mailed things to her son even though they had not been in contact recently. By highlighting this mothering from a distance, they emphasized actions that were in line with good mothering ideals and, in essence, dissociated themselves from being bad (m)others.

It is possible that mothering from a distance is also somewhat normalized by the shared mothering among African American, Latinx, and West Indian communities. I found that shared mothering helped the mothers overcome the impact of state control and surveillance and, despite individual setbacks, allowed some to maintain maternal relationships. However, noncustodial and nonresidential arrangements sometimes resulted in a lack of communication with children. In these circumstances, the mothers highlighted that the original distance was in their children's own best interest, explaining that prior arrangements had been made with good intentions but sometimes resulted in troublesome relationships with those children. When the women did not have contact, I found that they often stressed how their everyday personal endeavors and goals were still motivated by their maternal ideals to be "good" mothers. In other circumstances when they had multiple children, they were also able to account for perceived inadequacies as bad (m)others by focusing their motherwork on subsequent children as somewhat of a second chance to do better. Finally, and more broadly, many disagreed with the general notion of being bad people and believed they—and other mothers like them—had simply made bad decisions, framing themselves as good mothers overall despite social perceptions of them to the contrary.

THE UNSEEN POST-INCARCERATION MOTHERWORK

Public assumptions about mothers in the criminal legal system render them as uncaring and expendable. Contrary to such assumptions, research finds that motherhood is a great source of motivation for women during and after incarceration.[21] Maternal concerns and responsibilities, however, introduce an array of obstacles for formerly incarcerated mothers that the public is simply unaware of or chooses to ignore. As one mother explained, "It's hard enough trying to get your life together not only for yourself, but for one, two, three, four, whatever kind of kids you got." She continued, "The woman who comes out [of incarceration] who has children has to worry about getting her children back, being able to provide for herself and her children, [and] being able to be independent while still providing for those children." This account demonstrates how the mothers largely believed that, compared to women without children, they encountered *additional* obstacles whether they had underage children or adult children.[22] The following discussion examines how penal control has severe consequences for mothers of color and how, even amid these obstacles that are invisible to the general public, the mothers engage in motherwork that largely remains unrecognized.

From "Losing Place" to Gaining Positionality

Confinement behind jail or prison walls often results in people losing touch with the transitions of society. For instance, many who are released from incarceration are unfamiliar with the newest technology, the average price of common goods, and the updated and often complex public transportation systems, as well as with minor factors like recent songs or popular dances. Yet penal control also has gendered consequences, since women tend to be the primary caregivers of children before incarceration.[23] Incarceration forces maternal care and responsibility to fall on others on the outside while carceral systems keep mothers confined behind bars. As a direct result of penal control, mothers may "lose place" with their children during confinement through their diminished involvement as caretakers and their weakened role in maternal authority as children grow and develop in the mothers' physical absence. Family support may help offset mothers' "losing place" with their children when they are able to see their children during visits or speak with their children through phone calls. The financial burden of expensive prison calls and the long, stressful process to visit faraway prisons, however, mean that mothers still face the reality of "losing place" with children. In fact, the mothers with whom I spoke discussed many adjustments in increasingly taking over the mothering role after "losing place" during their incarceration.

Many mothers I met were still learning how to regain their maternal place in their children's lives. One way they tried to accomplish this was by reacquainting themselves with their children. Research shows that after a stint of incarceration, formerly incarcerated women commonly find the need to learn about their children post-incarceration.[24] During Donna's incarceration, her son lived with Donna's brother, who had temporary custody of him. Her son, who was 11 years old when she was incarcerated, was 14 years old upon her release. With the support of his uncle and the inevitable growth that comes with age and time, Donna's son had developed independence and gained some household responsibilities in her absence:

[B]efore I left, I was ironing his clothes, I was washing his clothes, *I* was taking out the garbage, *I* was washing the dishes. I come home, *he's* ironing his clothes, *he's* taking out the garbage, *he's* washing the dishes. So, you know, he really learned a lot from my brother and he became more independent.

Even though she was proud of her son, Donna experienced some conflict since she expected and desired the little boy that she was accustomed to before her incarceration. "He's just trying to show me that he has grown through the years but, you know, I still want that little boy." By the time she returned from prison, her son had had three birthdays without her, grown facial hair, begun playing basketball, and developed a new interest in fashion and sneakers. Her son, who had behaved like a "small child" before she was incarcerated, had grown into a teenager who wanted to "be a man." Two and a half weeks after her release from prison, she was still learning about her son's newfound interests.

While Donna was still getting reacquainted with her son two and a half weeks after her release, another mother, Marie, had already spent seven months in the community after her release. "Losing place" with her son was also a reality for Marie but, unlike Donna, more time had passed for Marie to begin regaining a place in her son's life. Prior to her incarceration, Marie had lived with her mother and her only son. During her incarceration, Marie's adolescent son stayed with his maternal grandmother because he was already living with her. Although this prior arrangement was beneficial in managing responsibilities during Marie's incarceration, shared mothering did not protect Marie from "losing place" with her son. Marie explained to her son that when he wanted to engage in any leisure activities during her incarceration, he needed to ask for his grandmother's permission. Eventually, he realized that his grandmother "was in control" during his mother's incarceration. In fact, his grandmother played a major role in raising him throughout the majority of his young life. During the seven months after her release, Marie had shared custody with her mother but did not live with her or her 13-year-old son. He continued to seek his grandmother's advice and permission instead of seeking it from her. Marie had previously advised her son to take this approach during her incarceration, but "losing place" took an emotional toll on Marie; she was saddened that she had lost some influence in her son's life. "I felt some kind of way. It caused feelings in me."

Initially upon her release, Marie took an authoritarian parenting approach. When her son stayed with her temporarily over the summer school break, she was "really on him" about household responsibilities. She imitated herself speaking to her son: "Clean your room. Do your laundry. You have to pass inspection so we can give you your allowance." Eventually she realized that this parenting approach "was not working" for her or her son, who felt incompetent and smothered by her actions. She found that her son valued simply staying inside so they could "lay on the bed and watch movies together." Marie then adjusted her mothering behaviors, distancing herself from the authoritarian approach. She began visiting her son on the weekends "just to spend some time together." This new approach in her nonresidential mothering after incarceration focused more on quality time, which she believed allowed for better and open communication with her teenage son. "I took the time and made some changes and I see that this is working better for us, you know, communication." Marie explained that by the time of her interview—seven months after her release—her son would seek her advice: "He calls me like at a major crisis." This was a drastic change in their relationship, demonstrating improvement as she gained some position in her son's life.

Making Up for Lost Time

The notion of "losing place" with children is intertwined with the concept of "lost time": time apart from children in which mothers miss things like interactions, opportunities, mental and physical growth, and life transitions. This is common among mothers who spend or have spent time apart from their children. For instance, some mothers spend numerous hours working outside of the home, others may live in different regions or countries from their children, and military mothers may deploy for months or years at a time. In these circumstances, mothers may try to make up for the "lost time" while apart from their children.[25] The same was true for the formerly incarcerated mothers I interviewed. The length of their last incarceration ranged from seven days to as long as five years, with the average "time lost" being one year and three months. Moreover, most mothers experienced multiple incarcerations, which allowed lost time to accumulate.

Some formerly incarcerated mothers tried to make up for the lost time by trying to "do everything" for their children. This involved efforts to "buy them everything," particularly things that were unnecessary. Mothers' efforts to buy their children everything they wanted was a way to initiate interactions and try to please their children. Efforts to "smother them with your love," "to be with them all the time," and to give them too much attention were other ways mothers tried to reclaim lost time with their children. Whether consciously or subconsciously, formerly incarcerated mothers sometimes engaged in these actions with the hope of earning back the time that was lost with their children because of incarceration.

Kerry-Ann, for instance, was incarcerated for two years and six months when her oldest son was approximately 6 years old. She explained the thought process that motivated her to try to "do everything" when she was initially released:

> I'm thinking: "Too much time has gone already and I got to get things right and [my oldest son] gotta get things right.". . . You come out and you want to do *everything* and you're racing. It's like a race against time because you lost that time and you're trying to get it back.

At times these actions were described as "overcompensating." In general, overcompensating can be a potential recipe to fall into crime to keep children happy.[26] The mothers wanted to provide their children with material items, but they understood that committing a crime to accomplish this goal would ultimately jeopardize their freedom and hurt relationships with their children. To avoid more complications post-incarceration, the mothers stressed the importance of giving their children the best resources that they already had accessible or that they could obtain legitimately.

Instead of trying to make up for lost time, some women suggested a softer approach to reuniting with children. As Kerry-Ann acknowledged, because of her concentration on the lost time during incarceration, she was "moving full speed ahead" upon her release. "You sort of want to come back out and make up for time lost, but you can't. So, that's hard. . . . [Y]ou can't get [the time] back, so you shouldn't try to." Now, looking back ten years after her release, she believed that trying to make up for lost time was not the best approach because she "didn't stop and think, and analyze the situation." Instead, she suggested that other mothers "should just try to come out and see what's going on and see how you fit in." This approach, however, was also equated to trial and error, in which "you sort of keeping failing and then you get it right after some time." Given this trial and error in post-incarceration motherhood, the mothers stressed the importance of taking things "little by little" to overcome any setbacks and to reinforce their maternal position.

Undoing the Learned and Securing Children's Improvements

I attended a support group in the South Bronx for women in the criminal legal system. A handful of women attended the meeting, representing the racial-ethnic makeup of the surrounding community, which is predominantly people of color. Like myself, the program coordinator was Latina. To my surprise, the support group did not use the circular seating arrangement that typically avoids a hierarchical undertone and allows everyone to see each other while they discuss topics of concern. Instead, the program coordinator ran the support group as more of a classroom setting, with a lesson plan for their discussion. She stood up in the front of the room, by a whiteboard, while the women remained seated facing her, like students. The topic of the day was motherhood. She would pose questions and write the women's responses on the whiteboard. In her responses to the women, she focused on telling them to take personal responsibility for their actions and to change their behaviors to fix things in their lives. At one point, the program coordinator brought up the idea of children being bad, arguing that this resulted from their home environment and bad parenting. One woman, seated close to me, did not appear to like the conversation. She kept quiet for the majority of the "lesson" but occasionally made faces of disagreement as she listened. Eventually she spoke up, saying that despite her past, she was not a bad parent. Even though the program coordinator was suggesting that children engage in bad behavior because they are missing something and they are not taught otherwise, this woman stressed that even though she "did [her] wrong," her son still had manners and was respectful of his elders—overall, not a "bad" kid.

What I observed in this support group is not rare but rather the norm. Penal control removes mothers from the home; restricts their access to and communication with children; and then blames mothers if children are not performing well in school, if they appear aggressive, withdrawn or anxious, and if they show any hint of mental illness. In doing so, society attributes children's "behavioral problems" to the mother's absence—mother blaming at its best, seeing as social-structural disadvantages before mothers' incarceration likely influence these "behavioral problems."[27] I found that support groups for formerly incarcerated women often forced them to accept personal responsibility for their children's actions and, in other words, to internalize the mother blaming from society. This is consistent with research by various scholars who have acknowledged such gendered penal governance and the unique consequences of penal control for women, especially women of color.[28]

Based on gendered expectations, society dictates that women should be the primary caretakers of children; if anything goes "wrong" with children, the mother is to blame. As long as systematic disempowerment of women of color persists, motherhood as an institution will remain a stratified entity in which social status determines the available resources and women of color remain invisible as worthy recipients of support.[29] As a result, women of color are disproportionately under state surveillance and control as "unfit" or bad (m)others. This was evident in the support group I visited: a group of criminalized women of color who were being "taught" that "bad" children are a result of bad parenting and that they, as mothers, must take responsibility for their (and their children's) actions.

All things considered, however, the mothers I interviewed rarely put all of the blame on themselves but highlighted how their children's behaviors were affected by the wide grasp of punitive carceral systems. They described a clash between how they wanted their children to behave and the habits their children acquired while their mothers were under penal control. Makayla explained that her 11-year-old son was not brushing his teeth before bed and "was very come-home-from-outside-and-in-the-frig," which she believed indicated a loss of manners during her absence. "It is a problem when you're reuniting with your child and they have one system and you have to give *your* system," Makayla explained. This clash was a challenge mothers often faced upon their return from incarceration. Makayla continued, "You have to stay consistent on changing the rules back to how *you* want things as opposed to how they were before." Mothers described undoing the learned behaviors their children had acquired during their incarceration, like being disruptive, and working with their children to instead make improvements in these areas.

Like Marie and Donna, described earlier, Madison's family also took in her children during her incarceration. Although Madison's 6-year-old son and 4-year-old daughter lived with their maternal grandmother during her incarceration, they lived with Madison after her prison release. Even after she found housing with her two children, the hardest aspect of her reentry as a mother was "not having control over the past couple of years." Madison believed that her children had lacked structure while they lived with their grandmother. She believed her children's behaviors upon her release were not reflective of her mothering and were not be-haviors that she, as a mother, wanted her children to display. "All the effect that it had on your children is the hardest part for me. I felt like, 'What the fuck? This is not how I want my children to be.'" Madison continued, "But I can't be mad because I wasn't around to mold them how I want them to be."

This clash between how Madison wanted her children to behave and how they behaved upon her release introduced additional ob-stacles in repairing the harms of penal control and also shaped her reentry goals: to teach her children to behave in ways she would be proud of as their mother. Madison tasked herself with teaching her two children that certain behaviors they had learned with grandma were unacceptable, like waking up at 6:00 a.m. and turning on Netflix. "G-momma let us," her children said, explaining that TV was okay at their grandmother's home. "Okay, well this is mommy home. Like, we are home again. So, this is not gonna happen," Madison responded to them. "I don't agree with sitting around watching TV," she explained. Madison did not believe that children should rely on television to pass time in isolation, which is what they had become accustomed to in her physical absence. Madison described working to correct this habit and trying to get her children acquainted with what she believed were healthier routines. Rather than allowing them to watch television, she preferred shared activities with her children like coloring, painting, or cooking together "to make our own pizza." But if they *did* engage in individual work or screen time, she tried to ensure that it was some-thing educational. "So, we have the iPad where it's mostly learning activities." Madison also made sure to give them positive reinforce-ments when they made changes in their behavior. "I do the positive reinforcement like, 'Ohh you behaved! Oh, party-time on Friday!'" Continuing, she related:

> Umm encouragement is very important also. Like, they need to know that what they're doing is good; and if it's not good, a better way they can go about doing it. I feel like that's very important also because that's what my kids thrive off. They thrive off encouragement like "Ohh good job!!" . . . And now, I see a big transformation like affectionate[ly] with them too. They wasn't very affectionate.

Though she found it difficult correcting her children's behaviors, Madi-son noted that the most rewarding moment as a mother since her release was being able to see the progress her children were making in their behavior and their education. To her, this was a sign that her children were "going to be fine" and that her motherwork was having a positive impact on her children despite the consequences of penal control.

Mothering through Troubled Relationships

Even though the women believed being there, broadly speaking, was a basic component of mothering that they were able to do, this was often fraught with emotional wounds that made it difficult. Children expressed feelings of abandonment, betrayal, and bitterness as a result of their mother's incarceration and behaviors leading to their incarceration, like substance use. Such feelings contributed to the difficulties mothers faced in rebuilding these relationships post-incarceration and "getting that bond back" with their kids. Bernadette noted the difficulties in creating this maternal bond upon release:

> You don't know where to begin at. You don't know what to do. And you don't know how to bond with a child if you just came out of jail because they have a resentment to[wards] you about being in jail.

Even though the women believed that they had to "deal with" their children's emotions to rebuild mother-child relationships, this was especially difficult when they did not know *how* they should address their children's feelings. Such uncertainties about the best approach were often troubling for mothers as they tried to address the discrepancy between what they had hoped for after release and what was occurring in reality.

Some mothers made suggestions about how to address their children's feelings. Common remarks were that their children were "entitled to [their] feelings" and "entitled to respect." When I met her, Francesca had a 19-year-old son who had been in elementary school when she was incarcerated for grand larceny and organized crime. Even though she had been released from incarceration 11 years before I met her, she recalled the emotional stress that her son had experienced during her incarceration: "he was abused, he was hit [and] he was mistreated" by his temporary caregivers. She believed maternal incarceration was especially difficult for children because "the system is taking you away" from them, stressing children's feelings of abandonment and betrayal from "not having [their] mom there."

I tell you: being a mom is not *easy*. . . . But it's tough on a mother that went to jail because your kid—remember—feels abandoned, feels betrayed. And when you leave your child for an extended time and come back into your child's life, it's not gonna be easy to win him because he feels abandoned, he feels betrayed.

Even though these negative emotions from children was hard for mothers after incarceration, Francesca argued that mothers "have to deal with it" by giving their children time and space to heal. Francesca continued, "It takes time; Rome was not built in a day so don't expect the child to be loving you in one day. You was out of his life for whatever bout of time." Given the impact of incarceration on children, mothers believed that children are "entitled to be heard" and that formerly incarcerated mothers must view things from their children's perspective and be respectful of their "boundaries" and of "what they want." Just as mothers were tasked with viewing things from their children's perspective, Francesca thought children would eventually come around to understanding their mothers' perspectives as well. "They gonna grow up, they gotta understand, and by you talking to them—little by little." The mothers believed their children would eventually "grow out of it," meaning, that children would eventually lose those feelings of resentment and anger about their incarceration. Considering the time necessary for children to come to terms with the effects of maternal incarceration, the general consensus among the mothers was that "you can't rush them into nothing," and mothers must therefore "take it one day at a time" and be patient while their children make this transition.

Despite these expectations that children would eventually "grow out" of these feelings given time and space, mothers clearly expected their adult children to have already grown out of them. Wyndolyn was 48 years old when I met her. Even though she had been in the community for two weeks since her last incarceration, Wyndolyn had been incarcerated five times over the last thirty years. According to Wyndolyn, her 28-year-old daughter had a "real nasty ass disposition," speaking to Wyndolyn in a disrespectful manner:

I told her that: "Regardless of how many times I go to jail or how many times I relapse or something like that, you're gonna talk to me like I'm your mother. You're not gonna disrespect me, you're not gonna talk to me how you wanna talk to me."

Wyndolyn recognized that "it *could* be that she was still hurting." However, she believed her daughter should have grown out of those feelings already. "I think that she should've been old enough to grow out of that by now." At the time of her interview, Wyndolyn was not speaking to her daughter.

Like Wyndolyn, Laura did not have contact with her daughter, who was 20 years old. When her daughter had graduated from high school at age 18, Laura had attempted to surprise her at the graduation. Laura gently touched my arm during her interview, demonstrating how she "touched her gown" at the graduation and said to her daughter, "It's mom." But she was shocked at her daughter's response:

> [S]he looked at me. She looked like she saw a *ghost*. . . . And she took off. She looked like she was trying to zigzag [through the crowd], and get away from me. . . . I didn't follow her because it was such a rejection.

Speaking in a low voice, Laura then stated, "I thought she was gonna grow up by then." In a sense, the mothers expected a process of healing within their adult children. When this healing did not happen as hoped and expected, mothers risked losing contact with these children, as seen with both Wyndolyn and Laura.

Mothering the Third Generation

Over one-third of the mothers were also grandmothers or expecting a grandchild. For these women, motherhood was not limited to their children but also applied to their grandchildren. When asked what they did as *mothers*, they noted babysitting and taking care of grandchildren, often done in a maternal effort to help their children. In this way, the caring labor of motherwork extended to their grandchildren.

Racial-ethnic interests in mothering grandchildren may exist. Though this connection was not directly mentioned by mothers during our conversations, research demonstrates the substantial role of grandmothers and extended family among African Americans, Latinxs, and West Indians.[30] For African American, Latina, and West Indian grandmothers, their caregiving of grandchildren is "not merely a response to economic circumstance but a reflection of cultural beliefs in the centrality of family, and cultural practices in sharing responsibility for childrearing."[31] Not only are they potentially more inclined to *want* to mother their grandchildren—as they are often raised by grandparents themselves—but they benefit emotionally from this involvement. For instance, compared to white grandmothers, Black grandmothers are less likely to describe burdens on their social life, and they feel more self-esteem when raising grandchildren.[32] Consistent with this research, grandchildren clearly brought great pleasure to the mothers I interviewed. They referenced their grandchildren when describing their most rewarding moments as *mothers* after incarceration. Over a quarter of the grandmothers considered these rewarding moments: becoming grandmothers, seeing and bonding with their grandchildren, and being able to "shape" grandchildren and watch them grow.

Once the women had grandchildren, maternal focus shifted in two ways. First, when women had multiple children, they sometimes focused their attention on children who had borne grandchildren. As Lucinda explained: "I love my children, but my focus is on my daughter because she has my grandson." Lucinda's daughter and 10-year-old grandson lived just outside of New York City, and the three of them met about three times a month and spoke on the phone frequently. In addition to giving her daughter advice about intimate partners, Lucinda also used these phone calls to give her daughter advice about her grandson. "[W]e talk on the phone more than I see her. And, it helps me shape my grandson." Second, some grandmothers shifted their attention from their children to focus on their grandchildren. At the time of her interview, Karen had two children, a 21-year-old son and a 20-year-old daughter. She noted that because her two children were older in age and presumably "grown," she would remain available for them but was focusing her child-rearing efforts on her grandson. Throughout Karen's interview, she would cheerfully incorporate her grandson's name when discussing her reentry progress. With a large smile, she would say things like, "it's about [my grandson] now. All about [my grandson]." Overall, the formerly incarcerated women described trying to be involved in their grandchildren's lives and having pride in these relationships when they were present.

I found that grandchildren not only provided mothers with pleasure but, after facing difficulties mothering their own children, grandchildren sometimes represented second chances. Some mothers tried to make up for lost time and losing place with their children by directing their attention to grandchildren and being actively involved in their lives. As a result, relationships with grandchildren tended to be healthier than those with their own children. As Bernadette admitted, she got along better with her grandchildren than with her own daughters. Bernadette began to show me pictures in her phone:

> See, this is me at BBQs with my granddaughters. See, I have fun with them. The 13-year-old and 19-year-old, we go out sometimes. We have fun. I get along with them better than my daughters; I get along with them good.

Even though Bernadette admitted that she and her daughter "butt[ed] heads," she was "really close" to her daughter, and their relationship was actually closer than it had ever been.

Unfortunately, while mothers may have considered mothering the third generation as a second chance, their children did not always take this so well. Attempts to build relationships with grandchildren or give advice about their grandchildren were sometimes met with hostility from their own children who still held resentment. Wyndolyn, for instance, had three adult daughters who were 25, 28, and 30 when I met her. Between her eldest two children, she had three grandsons who were 6 years old, 2 years old, and 7 months old. Wyndolyn described babysitting her grandsons whenever her daughters needed her to: "Whenever my children *needs* me [to babysit], I drop anything [that] I'm doing at the [drop] of a hat and I'm on my way." Yet Wyndolyn's greatest challenge as a mother was that her daughters were not receptive to Wyndolyn's mothering advice because of her lost time in their childhoods.

> *JGH:* Okay, so what's been the greatest challenge for you as a mother since you came home?
>
> *Wyndolyn:* Just them accepting my opinion about raising their sons. They was like: "You wasn't even here to raise us. How you gonna tell us how to raise our sons?"
>
> *JGH:* How do you feel about that?
>
> *Wyndolyn:* Bad

Thus, even though the women took great pleasure in having a role in their grandchildren's lives, this involvement did not always reconcile mother-child relationships that were still troubled, a reality for about 3 of the 13 formerly incarcerated mothers who had grandchildren.

CONCLUSION

Overall, this chapter demonstrates how the hypersurveillance of communities of color, gendered consequences of incarceration, systematic constraints of parole supervision, and stigma as "bad" (m)others all worked in unison affecting mothers' lives post-incarceration. I argue that despite their marginalization and stigmatized visibility as criminalized (m)others, mothers of color are "winning in the margins" of the carceral state that surrounds them. They engage in practical mothering behaviors that are suitable for their realities post-incarceration, which allows them to remain resilient against the stigmatized labels that incarceration attaches to them.

Generally, opportunities to perform motherwork differ across social groups, with those most marginalized and stigmatized facing substantial social and structural barriers. The role of racial-ethnic background is inescapable in a stratified society that marginalizes underrepresented groups. State and public systems like the child welfare system often deem mothers of color "unfit" and as a threat to their children, but the mothers saw the carceral state as the true perpetrators of harm to their children. For instance, hypersurveillance in communities of color introduced concerns about protecting children in a society that judges and condemns others based on physical appearance, then acts on prejudices that expose children of color to social and physical harm, even from law enforcement. Consistent with research on resiliency and resistance in Black communities,[33] the formerly incarcerated mothers expressed maternal responsibilities of protecting their children from racial-ethnic discrimination. Interestingly, even though public discussions and existing research typically focus on race, the mothers' narratives suggest varying maternal needs for protecting their children based on ethnic nuances in social treatment. This is in line with research arguing that parents prepare their children for discrimination according to its anticipated presence and impact in their lives.[34] Yet criminological research examining these types of ethnic nuances is limited.

In addition to these ethnoracial nuances, programmatic efforts must account for intermingled gendered experiences when helping formerly incarcerated mothers of color. The "baggage of the [prison] system" complicates how women navigate motherhood after incarceration. Society dictates that women should be primary caregivers for children, and yet the mothers believed incarceration—and state control more generally—created numerous stumbling blocks that affected mother-child relationships. For instance, the carceral state regulates motherhood via parole policies that function as an added form of scrutiny, placing additional hindrances on their maternal relationships as they deal with curfews, communication restrictions, required permissions, and more. The mothers also described "losing place" in their children's lives; "losing time" with their children; witnessing negative behaviors children acquired during their incarcerations; and having challenging interactions with children who felt abandoned, let down, and upset. The mothers tried to address these circumstances by making efforts to gain positionality in their children's lives, making up for lost time, reacquainting their children with healthier routines, and providing for their children and grandchildren in whatever way possible. In these ways, the formerly incarcerated mothers worked through the collateral consequences of penal control to carry out motherwork.

Normative descriptions of motherhood typically entail intensive mothering behaviors like spending a great deal of money, sacrificing one's time, and wholeheartedly adhering to others' recommendations.[35] Groups such as employed mothers or transnational mothers may reframe such notions of good mothering based on their circumstances.[36] I found that the same was true of the formerly incarcerated mothers I interviewed, who rarely emphasized labor-intensive and financially expensive behaviors typically associated with intensive mothering; instead, they reshaped what good mothering looks like within the face of carceral oppression.

Good mothers were described as women who were "always there" for their children, but "always being there" was broadly defined to represent their realities. They did not need to live with their children, have custody of their underage children, or even have contact with their children to "be there" for them or perform good mothering behaviors in some way. Rather, they emphasized attending important events when able, visiting occasionally, and remotely sending money or relevant items, as well as listening to, talking with, or giving advice to their children, actions that were often possible because of the collective strengths of shared mothering. Thanks to others' help, shared mothering often provided a bridge for these women to mother from a distance. In addition, when mothers did not have communication with at least one of their children, they described attributing everyday personal endeavors in their reentry (like anger management and maintaining their sobriety) to being in their children's best interests. When they experienced a lack of contact with older children, they sometimes focused their efforts on younger children or grandchildren as "second chances," highlighting these actions and relationships as representations of them as mothers. Even when they had difficult or nonexistent relationships with their children, some mothers did not allow these negative situations to dictate how they saw their overall character or role as mothers. All things considered, these formerly incarcerated mothers saw themselves as good mothers so long as they were engaging in motherwork to their best ability within their circumstances. They reframed maternal ideals in the post-incarceration context, and their broad definitions of "being there" allowed them to emphasize meanings of motherhood associated with *practical* actions they performed, a form of resistance against gendered and racialized labels as bad (m)others.

This chapter reveals some of the many ways formerly incarcerated mothers of color engage in motherwork by working around common constraints. Unfortunately, this motherwork remains largely invisible to the public and goes unnoticed by those who view mothering as a uniform experience and who hold restrictive notions of what motherhood should look like. Reentry programs should meet the mothers where they stand by looking beyond socially constructed understandings of what motherhood is *supposed* to entail. Instead, program personnel should recognize the positionality of women of color in broader society and acknowledge the women's motherwork within their post-incarceration realities. This recognition would help provide a more adequate account of the women's mother-child relationships, their experiences under parole supervision, and their endurance through punitive carceral systems, as discussed in this chapter. As argued in *Unbecoming Mothers*, "Recognizing mothers' positionalities is key to rejecting the construction of a single, objective, neutral truth about mothering and motherwork."[37]

CHAPTER 2

Custody and Housing

"I Just Want My Baby Back"

"They arrested everybody in the house," Donna said as she remem-
bered the events leading up to her incarceration. Donna's incarceration coincided with the incarceration of her husband and her mother,
leaving no one in the household to care for her 11-year-old son, who
was present during the arrests. While the NYPD arrested both parents
and the grandmother, Donna was able to suggest a preferred placement
for her son. "One of my neighbors came down," she said gratefully.
"So I didn't have to go through ACS [Administration for Children's
Services]—thank God."[1] Arrests may draw the attention of the child
welfare system when underage children are present, and these children
could eventually be placed in foster care if there is no one to care for
them. Donna's brother was able to get temporary custody of her son,
a custodial arrangement she was pleased with because her son "could
have been in foster care, being with somebody he didn't know," which
Donna described as "a lot worse." Donna's son dodged the intrusion
of the child welfare system and the wide grasp of foster care, but other
children experiencing maternal incarceration are not so fortunate.[2] The
overlap between children of color in foster care and their mothers in
the prison system is evidence of the systemic punishment of mothers
of color.[3] In this chapter, I present the mothers' accounts of navigating
motherhood within the seemingly opposing, yet overlapping, criminal
legal system and child welfare system.

The guiding principle of the child welfare system is to act in children's best interests to keep them safe.[4] Under the pretext of this guiding principle, professionals have a duty to report any perceived cases of child neglect or abuse to arguably "save" children by removing them from the parent's custody. While the objective of saving children may appear noble, in practice the child welfare system often punishes the most stigmatized and marginalized mothers and operates as a form of social control. Since mothers are expected to be (and often are) children's primary caregivers, they are the first to be accused of neglect when they somehow contradict normative middle-class standards of intensive mothering. Determinations of neglect are essentially living conditions that are synonymous with living in poverty. Insufficient income can severely hurt the ability to always have sufficient food in the home, to consistently buy clothing for growing children, to stay home from work on snow days or when a child is sick, or even to pay for regular or unexpected medical expenses if a paycheck is almost entirely spent on day-to-day costs. African American, West Indian, and Latina mothers battle racialized marginalization as invisible mothers that puts them and their children at risk for diminished resources like finances and health care. By navigating systematic oppression as mothers of color, they become disproportionately susceptible to increased state exposure and surveillance, especially when seeking support.[5] This heightened visibility as struggling (m)others is then used against them to justify interventions by the child welfare system to strip parental custody to "save" their children from neglect. They are especially susceptible to racialized and classist accusations of neglect because Black families are stigmatized as being disorganized and unstable,[6] reinforcing a biased visibility as unfit or bad (m)others while blurring public visibility of their motherwork, as discussed in chapter 1.

A common theme among the formerly incarcerated mothers was a desire to reunite with their children. In fact, research shows that as many as 88% of mothers plan to live with their children upon their release from incarceration, and 59.5% expect to have custody of under-age children.[7] Yet in this chapter I argue that in trying to "save" children, the child welfare system pathologizes mothers of color and their post-incarceration motherwork as being inferior and the epitome of "bad" mothering. By devaluing their motherwork, the system presents additional barriers to mothers of color and complicates their chances of regaining custody. After serving their time, they must still have to fight against social constructions of motherhood to shift the nature of their visibility and prove themselves worthy of having custody. Yet once in foster care, African American and Latinx children are less likely than white children to reunify with birth parents, and they reunify at a much slower rate.[8] This suggests that the child welfare system is not an unmitigated force for good for minoritized mothers, forcing them to view it with a critical eye.

After nearly three years incarcerated, Donna hoped to live under the same roof as her son again. "I'm hoping to unite with him after this year. . . . He's fine where he is, but I just want my baby back." When I met her, she was living in a residential reentry program for women. She believed her son was content and well taken care of while living with his uncle, but her goal was to be "standing on [her] own two feet" with proper housing so they could live together again. As Donna surmised two and half weeks after her release: "I know we got to crawl before we walk; I just plan to walk fast." As Donna did, the other mothers described taking things "one day at a time" and "one step at a time," yet they still hoped to move quickly to meet their maternal goals of reuniting with their children. In light of mothers' hopes and efforts to reunite with their children, they shared interests in creating a home environment. Establishing a home was important for mothers seeking custody, for mothers with custody but whose children lived with other family members, and for mothers seeking better living arrangements. This chapter examines the various barriers they faced in creating a home post-incarceration, whether or not this home environment included their children.

THE ROLE OF FAMILY AND COMMUNITY IN SHARED MOTHERING

As mothers of color endure systematic oppression within a patriarchal and racialized society, their family unit and community network often help offset the negative impact on them and their families. I found that one way family and community members supported mothers through carceral hardships was through *shared mothering*, which entails the act of taking on and sharing mothering responsibilities. Embedded within the cultural foundations of African Americans, Latinxs, and West Indians, shared mothering practices are typically a way for family members and community members to help one another overcome systematic oppression by providing childcare when biological mothers are unable to do so.[9] Shared mothering can be especially helpful when mothers of color are arrested, detained, incarcerated, and adjusting to their circumstances post-release. More specifically, by accepting some of the mothering labor, these familial or community othermothers can support blood mothers through difficult times in the criminal legal system and help prevent, or at least fight against, state interventions that remove their children.[10]

Biological Family as Othermothers

Research describes a strong family and community bond among marginalized racial-ethnic groups.[11] In line with this research, common terms the mothers used to describe themselves and other African Americans, Latinxs, and West Indians were *close*, *united*, and *family-oriented*, with a "strong obligation to family."[12] They considered unity and collective efforts to be protections against obstacles thrown in their way. "We always have that extended family," Kerry-Ann, a West Indian mother from Jamaica, explained. "Us, we take anybody in. 'You don't have no mother? Come live with us.'" She continued, "We believe in a home; not just a house, a home. So, we believe in making it a home." Kerry-Ann's account demonstrates how a willingness to take anybody in is grounded in a larger mission to ensure that children's needs are met and that they have a place to call home.

Qiana was a Latina and African American mother. She described shared mothering as a cultural protection, distinguishing families of color from white families in how they accept childcare labor when loved ones are in need. Compared to white families, she explained, "I just feel like with African American families and Latina families, I think they're more family-orientated and more closer knitted." She continued:

> I feel that they're the type that just take on the role of taking care of any and everybody, especially when it comes to family and kids. I just feel like they just have that gene in 'em that when something goes wrong, it's about the child. . . . [W]here there's a *child* involved, it's like: "Okay, well, listen, you got your own thing going on, but bring the baby over here, bring they stuff here, and I got 'em."

This was Qiana's experience with her family serving as othermothers to her son. "My son *has* the love that he *needs*," said Qiana, as she explained that her son was living with her aunt during an open case with the child welfare system. "My aunt is there. My grandmother is there.

My mother is there [and] my brothers. . . . I'm very family orientated, so my family is like a tribe." In speaking about the impacts of incarceration, Qiana reiterated the West African proverb "it takes a village to raise a child" and noted that because of this, her son still "has love all around the board."

In normative expectations of family accountability, grandmothers are the next in line after fathers to care for children; in reality, grandmothers were often the first choice given the prevalence of single motherhood and the cultural importance of grandmothers' involvement. Of the 37 formerly incarcerated mothers, only a quarter had at least one child stay with a father or stepfather as the primary caregiver at any point before, during, or after the mother's incarceration. This was common across all three ethnic groups. The mothers explained a number of potential reasons that African American, Latinx, and West Indian children were not likely to stay with their fathers when the mother was in the criminal legal system. They highlighted the nature of the parents' relationship, the criminal involvement of the father, the openness of the father to care for children, and the fathers' financial ability to actually take on this responsibility if willing to do so. Grandmothers often compensated for these absent or disengaged fathers by taking on the bulk of shared mothering and nurturing the next generation as othermothers.

Of the 37 mothers, at least 19 (51%) had their children cared for by grandparents at some point before, during, or after incarceration, with an additional two mothers who had their children raised by great-grandparents. "African Americans have a lot of single parenting," explained Rashida, an African American and West Indian mother. "So, you figure: the mother that raised you—who else would be perfect to raise your children?" Donna, an African American mother, also reiterated the prevalence and importance of grandmothers' shared mothering:

> I think with African American women, I just think that like grandma is always like "ma" to kids. Whether we're in jail or we're in the street, like, if we leave today [or] tomorrow, grandma is gonna take that baby, you understand? And that's just how it is.

Donna then noted the role and impact of shared mothering in her personal life, encouraging a close relationship between her mother and her son. "It's nothing that she wouldn't do for him, and I know that. And, it just seem that I had him but that's her child." By accepting some maternal labor during times of need, grandmothers were often the glue holding families together while mothers were in the criminal legal system.

Francesca, who identified as African American and Latina, stressed family's obligation to care for children and protect them from state intervention and control. "Us—Latinos and Blacks—it seems like we take from the grandmother taking care of the kids and it's our job; if not, the niece; if not, the sister. Somebody's gonna take care of your children and babysit." She continued, "That's our obligation as a family. . . . In the family, we count on one another to raise our kids because we're not trusting [other] people to take care of our children." Here, Francesca hints at the distrust of the state and of strangers raising their children. This was shared by Ana, who imitated African American and Latinx grandparents saying, "No one's gonna raise, [or] take my grandchild." Strangers and the state were often overlapping bodies that could not be trusted with minoritized children since they could "label them as 'troublemakers'" and "discard those kids," as Natalie, an African American mother, explained. In fact, children in foster homes may experience abuse and neglect, the very conditions that the child welfare system tries to "save" children from by removing them from their homes. They are then essentially discarded once they age out of foster care and are left with high rates of homelessness, victimization, unstable employment, and insufficient income to live on their own.[13] While some children in foster care may potentially benefit from some aspects of a new environment, the assumption that nonkinship foster care may serve as a saving grace for all of these children is flawed.[14] Thus, family members worked collectively through shared mothering to avoid losing children to state intervention. In this way, the collective value within shared mothering helps minimize the carceral impact on mothers of color and their children.

Community Members as Othermothers

Since kin networks upheld the principle that it takes a village to raise a child, the responsibility of caring for minoritized children was not solely restricted to biological family. African American mothers described also relying on othermothers, who were members of their community that supported them before, during, or after incarceration.

Lucinda was an African American mother who lived in Spanish Harlem. As I sat on her living room couch and listened to her life story, Lucinda pointed to a nearby photo. "That lady on that picture right there," she said, "that's my 'New York mom.'" In the absence of her biological family, who lived in Washington, D.C., Lucinda had developed a family-like relationship with a woman who became known as her "New York mom." When Lucinda was arrested shortly after having her son, her son's father "didn't know what to do with the baby." He told Lucinda's friend about the arrest, and this friend took the baby to her own babysitter. Lucinda explained, "That's how she [New York mom] came into my life, and she raised [my son]." Even in the absence of a biological connection, her New York mom was a woman in the community who was willing to help others in need, including Lucinda. "She didn't have any children, but she raised everybody else's kids." At least when it came to her son, Lucinda was able to avoid state intervention because of shared mothering with a member of her community. Her New York mom had since passed away, but Lucinda still reminisced about her "grandma *aura*" and "grandmother instinct" for caring for other people's children.

Bernadette was another African American mother who discussed the role of othermothers in raising her children. When her children were young, Bernadette battled with substance use, and Bernadette's mother communicated these battles with a "lady that live around the corner." This woman could not have children of her own and wanted to help raise Bernadette's middle daughter "from a little girl up." Bernadette explained, "I said, 'all right' 'cause I couldn't take care of [her] at that time so she raised her." Even though Bernadette "always loved her," she believed that she was not in a position to raise her daughter. The woman in her community was willing and able to do so and, as Bernadette shared, "I think she really love her."

Although the presence and importance of shared mothering was discussed by all three ethnic groups of African American, Latina, and West Indian mothers, it was relatively less common to hear mothers talk about community members who functioned as othermothers. In fact, the role of community members in shared mothering practices was only discussed by African American mothers, as seen with Lucinda and Bernadette. Explanations for this nuance across the three groups are unclear, but the work of Patricia Hill Collins suggests that African Americans, in particular, have historically endorsed community-based childcare and favored community othermothers to overcome their racial oppression during and since slavery.[15]

All in all, the mothers' accounts show how biological family and community members can help fight against state intervention in families of color and avoid (or delay) children being "lost to the system." These othermothers upheld a collective value for the blood mothers in navigating the punitive effects of the criminal legal system.

The Last Resort

When the women's children *did* enter nonkinship foster care, this was typically in the absence of extended family members who could serve as temporary caregivers. This is consistent with research that shows mothers of color are likely to leave children under grandparents' care, and they lose custody only after preferred family arrangements are unavailable.[16] When police officers arrested Valerie, her sons were 15 and 16. The arresting officers asked Valerie if her mother could "get there before they pulled out the driveway" so Valerie's children would not be left unsupervised. This, however, was an unrealistic request for Valerie since her mother and other family members lived in a different state. As a result, Valerie's children were taken into state custody, where they lost contact with their mother over time and had no communication with Valerie three years later when I met her. Mothers like Valerie are essentially penalized when physical distance from relatives excludes them as viable caregivers.

Before her last incarceration, Carolina was a single parent raising her 1-year-old son and her daughter, who was almost 4. "They were taken away because I had to go to prison and I didn't have [any]body to take care of them." Although most women relied on shared mothering with their parents, Carolina's parents had passed away before her incarceration. Carolina had one sister; this sister tried to get custody of Carolina's children but was found ineligible because she was classified as a disabled person and was receiving Supplemental Security Income (SSI) after hip implants. The child welfare system would not allow her to be the children's guardian. The child welfare systems claims that whenever possible, it tries to keep children with family or friends and only places children in foster care when loved ones are absent or unable. However, Carolina believed her sister was "functional" and physically capable of taking care of her children: "They made it seem like she can't move or run around after them." Four and a half years after her surgery, "they still said no because she's on disability." In essence, evaluations of fitness are not limited to parents but extend to family members hoping and trying to obtain guardianship. Once the state has intervened in the lives of families of color, systematic restrictions can block family from shared mothering by way of legal guardianship. "She feels bad that she can't have them, that they had to go with strangers instead of staying within the family. But there's nothing that we could do."

NEGOTIATING "FITNESS" AND RECOVERING "SAVED" CHILDREN

When children are "lost" to the child welfare system, mothers are forced to negotiate "fitness" to regain custody and recover their children who were supposedly "saved." They have to validate their motherly roles in the eyes of the child welfare system, but the mothers I interviewed believed that determinations of parental fitness were weighed against them due to unfortunate circumstances deemed to be "neglect," their social position as mothers of color, and reentry barriers to establishing housing and navigating parole stipulations.

At least 11 mothers (30%) had children who were in foster care or had spent some time in the foster care system. For 6 of these mothers, their children were born with a positive toxicology test for drugs, prompting child welfare personnel to become involved and initiating an investigation. Substance use histories posed challenges for several mothers in maintaining and regaining custody of their children. Of the 37 mothers I interviewed, 70% had a history of substance use. Substance use among women often develops as a coping mechanism against verbal, physical, and emotional abuse.[17] The child welfare system argues that substance use alone does not serve as evidence of child neglect in New York State, and that it requires "misuse" of substances that arguably impair the ability to care for a child.[18] Yet in practice, state law requires medical providers and social workers to report *suspicions* of child neglect. These mandated reporters within clinics and schools, for example, become complicit in the state control of women's bodies, disproportionately exposing mothers of color to investigations for substance use. Jesenia believed social systems viewed these mothers collectively in a negative light as perpetrators who were intentionally causing harm to their children, rather than understanding them as victims of their circumstances. As a result, she argued, "It's a lot more difficult to get information on your case and how you can get through it because they're just viewing you in one perspective. They view you as the victor, [rather] than the victim." Instead of providing services and support to them as women dealing with a disease, social systems ostracized them, criminalized them, and stripped them of their maternal custody.

Throughout the United States, conditions of "neglect" are the most common reason child welfare systems remove children from their homes.[19] Such conditions can include a lack of adequate housing, education, medical care, food, and hygiene, among other things. These living conditions are synonymous with living in poverty. Based on standards of neglect, child protective specialists within the child welfare system can label mothers as unfit parents as if their *circumstances* define who they are as *individuals*. Instead, systematic determinations of parental fitness should be understood within the context of the marginalization that shapes their everyday obstacles.

Of the 11 mothers who had children taken into foster care, as many as 7 had children who were eventually adopted (3 by family and 4 by nonfamily), including 1 mother who had an additional child awaiting final adoption by her maternal grandmother. Two mothers had children who were still in foster care. Two mothers, including Priscilla, had regained custody. As Priscilla summed up: "It's so easy to get your children removed, but it's so difficult for you to get them back." Parents and guardians must demonstrate a steady source of income to support daily costs, but working or interning introduces another area of inquiry about day care while outside the home: "Who's gonna watch the kids?" Day care can be expensive and also limited if caregivers are looking for the most affordable option. In addition to concerns about day care, the child welfare system evaluates the living arrangements and living conditions to determine if they are suitable enough for children, according to agency standards. Priscilla explained:

> You have people telling you: "Oh, You gotta prove you have housing—an apartment for them. Every room has to have a window. They have to have guards on the windows." All this and it's like pressure: "How I'ma do all this? I don't have $10,000 on my hands!"

Priscilla described these requirements, like window guards, as the "little things" that justified refusal to regain custody, which took an emotional toll:

> It just felt so helpless that you feel that you got no hope in life, you know, that you never gonna get them back. You're fighting the city. . . . [A]nd they'll go and check: "No, we don't want this. This is not good enough for the children."

Even when mothers were able to obtain housing, they faced the reality that this progress was sometimes still not enough to regain parental rights to their own children. The child welfare system claims that it tries to keep families together, but definitions of what is good enough—as the child protective specialist told Priscilla—are based on social constructions of motherhood that inherently make it difficult to regain and maintain custody.

Priscilla believed that through disproportionate opportunities and unfair evaluations of fitness, Black and brown mothers had a far more difficult time regaining custody than white mothers:

> I think that society still has . . . a very weird way of looking at certain people and judge them by their ethnicity. I believe that we are considered minorities and we get the [shorter] end of the stick. I believe that—and I truly believe that—a white person has more access and a better chance in recovering their children than a Black person or Hispanic person would, just in my own experience.

Her children's father was also Latinx, and she believed the child welfare system intentionally "gave him a very hard time" when he tried to get their children back. "Him as a *Spanish* male was two *years,* and he wasn't getting high or nothing, and he couldn't get them!" Her husband was only able to get custody after receiving housing assistance from a local agency called HourChildren. Founded in 1992, HourChildren is a prominent program in New York that provides prison-based and community-based family services for women in the criminal legal system and their children. The program's name highlights "the key hours that impact the life of a child with an incarcerated mother—the hour of her arrest, the hour of their visit, and the hour of their reunification." Founded by a white nun, HourChildren functions on the beliefs that "change takes time" and "love makes the difference." It was because of this program that Priscilla and her husband were able to regain custody, but she wondered, "What about the person who doesn't have that opportunity and loses their children for good?" Overall, when it came to regaining custody, the mothers believed they needed to "fight for [their] rights" because of the social and structural barriers stacked against them as African American, West Indian, and Latina mothers, coupled with having criminal records.

Mothers believed the child welfare system and Family Court judges used their criminal records against them as a generic portrayal of their overall character, without considering underlying information about their personal experiences. Francesca stated: "[They] throw back your criminal record in your face. Isn't that sad? Your criminal record: they throw it at you." Because of this, she described the system as being "so freakin' corrupt," using a mother's criminal record against her in determinations of maternal fitness. The child welfare system essentially renders mothers as unfit until they abide by a "service plan": a list of tasks to show they are "fit" enough as mothers to regain custody. Common aspects of the mothers' service plan included mental health evaluations, anger management classes, parenting classes, and programs for substance use, each of which often took weeks or months to complete. These made up a combination of individualistic conditions to "fix" (m)others. In trying to "save" children, the child welfare system was pathologizing the mothers as being inferior and pathologizing their motherwork as the epitome of bad mothering. Yet as law professor Annette Appell argues, "Making children linger in foster care is unconscionable when what they are waiting for is so subjective: turning 'bad' women into 'good' ones."[20] Vera argued that many of these requirements were unnecessarily included as hurdles merely because of the mothers' involvement in the criminal legal system:

> I just think that: sometimes the hurdles—they want them to jump over and walk in a straight and narrow and kiss they ass. . . . Don't put us all in one category because, okay, I may have went to jail or I may have been arrested; we're still not all the same. You gotta meet each individual for who they are.

She believed the requirements to reunite with children should be catered to each mother without prejudice based on her criminal record. Instead, the mothers viewed the demands to regain custody as being more destructive to them as mothers than they were helpful to their children.

Carolina was still fighting to regain custody of her children after they were taken by child welfare at the time of her arrest. She was incarcerated for three years at Albion Correctional Facility, which is approximately a seven-hour drive from where her children lived in New York City. Six months into Carolina's incarceration, her children started to visit her through a program called the Children of Incarcerated Parents Program (CHIPP). The program, run by child welfare, provides transportation so children can visit their parents in the local city jail or in federal and state prisons throughout New York State, like Albion. Despite the 400 miles between her and her two children, this program allowed her to receive monthly visits and to have a relationship with her children from behind bars. "My relationship, really, with my son started in prison because when I left him, he didn't know much, he didn't even walk. So, like he got to know who mommy was through my incarceration visits." At first, her 1-year-old son was distant during the prison visits and did not want to be held by her. Over time, however, her son grew comfortable with sitting on her lap during the visits and wanted to remain with her. As Carolina described, he became close. "He runs to me like 'Mommy mommy mommy.'" Her daughter, who is three years older than her son, had no problems remembering who mommy was on the first prison visit. "My daughter just was all over me from day one. Like, from day one, like: 'Mommy mommy mommy!' 'Cause she was very close to me; she slept with me every night. You know, so she miss[ed] mommy. She was just like waiting for that visit."

A month and a half after her three-year incarceration, Carolina found herself still trying to regain custody of her two children. Her service plan from the child welfare system included random drug testing three times a week, a certificate from a drug treatment program (which lasted six to nine months), monthly visits with a psychiatrist, a certificate from a fourteen-week anger management program, and employment.

> I have my children in the system. . . . I have to do x, y, and z to get them back. . . . So it's a lot, it's a lot for a mother that was incarcerated to just come home for all this to be on their plate.

She described working on each of these requirements all at the same time, sometimes feeling overwhelmed as if she were "running like a chicken with no head." As with Priscilla and Carolina, the formerly incarcerated mothers commonly felt overwhelmed by the requirements to regain custody. Marcia, for instance, described adhering to the tasks of her service plan to reunite with her daughter, but making little progress in the eyes of the agency:

> I got stressed out. . . . I couldn't take it no more. I started feeling closed in. I started feeling too much pressure. I'm not good under pressure. "You making me do all these things and I'm bring[ing] in week-by-week certificates, papers, doing this, reports, no drug testing—everything, everything, everything." I did everything for her.

As another mother explained, "A lot of women go through *shit* because the city takes their kids." It was common for mothers to feel defeated by this process and wonder: "Why is my child not with me yet?" This demonstrates how, after serving their time, they must fight against social constructions of motherhood to prove themselves fit as mothers—a process that can further disempower them in this battle with the child welfare system to "save" their children.

As discussed in chapter 1, parole stipulations like travel restrictions and frequent reporting to parole officers can cause more harm than good for navigating motherhood post-incarceration. Research shows that mothers often feel forced to decenter motherhood in their lives to meet parole requirements and avoid technical violations like not reporting to their parole officers.[21] Yet decentering motherhood to fulfill parole obligations can hurt assessments of their fitness and shape their visibility as (m)others. Even though Vera's children were "already older" when she was incarcerated, she described seeing parole officers threaten to call child welfare on other mothers: "Well, we gonna call ACS," Vera said, imitating parole officers. This threat of reporting a mother to the child welfare system is a form of social control in which parole officers may "use" the system to show authority and demand compliance. Vera continued, "It's something always hanging over them to actually make them act accordingly." This demonstrates that when trying to regain custody, the punitive nature of parole supervision and the extensive parole requirements further complicated assessments of mothers' fitness.

Overall, the mothers' experiences demonstrate tensions between notions of care in the child welfare system and notions of justice in the criminal legal system, presenting a double-edged sword at the intersection of both systems. Mothers who lose custody of their children must demonstrate their fitness as mothers while negotiating custody of their own children—a process that, as shown here, can be long, troublesome, classist, and racialized. The mothers believed the child welfare system should improve this process by adjusting the service plan to avoid penalizing mothers of color for their motherwork amid systematic oppression. They also stressed necessary changes in how public agents view and treat them because of their criminal records, noting that parole officers should not use custodial arrangements as threats for compliance. In general, the women observed some disconnect between requirements imposed upon them and the available resources to meet these requirements. As a result, the mothers suggested more programs were needed specifically devoted to helping them regain custody of their children post-incarceration.

In Carolina's case, she took advantage of the CHIPP, but such programs do not supersede formalities to regain custody. Approximately one month after her release, she started to see her children but could only do so under the supervision of a child protective specialist. By two months after her release, Carolina started to have unsupervised visits with her children. She believed her daughter displayed more joy when their visits were not supervised:

[A] lot of difference in her [daughter's] actions in her happiness . . . the way she *acts*, the way she *throws* herself at me and you see her *running*, you see the excitement in her. . . . [B]ecause when they supervised, you have some-body stand sitting there watching everything you're doing with your kids.

Although supervised visits are intended to protect children and to pro-vide assistance if necessary, the mere absence of a watchful eye may stimulate a more natural and comfortable interaction. The child pro-tective specialist allowed Carolina to interact with her children with-out supervision only after complying with an allocated service plan and seemingly posing less of a risk. The transition from supervised to unsu-pervised visits is permitted only if a mother is increasingly adhering to agency standards of motherhood. While prison visiting programs like CHIPP can be helpful in maintaining or building a relationship with children during incarceration, agency determinations of progress remain grounded in social constructions of maternal fitness that mothers must demonstrate through stipulations like anger management programs, par-enting programs, and regular psychiatrist appointments. Until mothers successfully complete these expectations to seemingly fit normative stan-dards of motherhood, prison visiting programs alone may be insufficient in helping them recover "saved" children.

PLEASING (TEMPORARY) CAREGIVERS AND CHILDREN

In addition to the barriers in dealing with the child welfare system, navigating motherhood post-incarceration is also shaped by caregivers' interests, the degree of communication with children, and children's re-ceptiveness to their mothers' efforts. In hopes of finding housing for themselves and their children after incarceration, the mothers searched for ways to shift their children from previous living arrangements. This, however, not only called for the mothers to have comfortable living conditions and reentry circumstances, it also required them to negotiate with the temporary caregivers and to potentially alter their children's routine or way of life.

(Temporary) Caregivers

Shared mothering played an important role for mothers as they relied on others before, during, and after their incarceration. At times, however, dealing with family members complicated mothers' efforts to reunify with children because caregiver "relationships dictate how involved the mothers are allowed to be in the raising of her children."[22] Family was instrumental in raising children during mothers' physical absence, but family also played a large role in whether and how mothers reunified with children.

On occasion, mothers encountered problems when family hoped to make temporary custody arrangements more permanent without the mothers' full consent. Prior to Josefina's incarceration, her youngest two sons were in the temporary custody of their paternal grandmother. When Josefina was released, she learned that their paternal grandmother had proceeded with obtaining full parental rights during her incarceration. Josefina felt betrayed by someone she trusted to care for her sons during her incarceration but who, essentially, "went behind [her] back" to seek full custody. When I met her about ten weeks after her release, Josefina was no longer in communication with her 10-year-old and 15-year-old sons. "She doesn't let me talk to them anytime. . . . She separated everything." As a result, Josefina relied on Facebook pictures for visual updates about her two sons. Formerly incarcerated mothers may be confronted with relatives who are not willing to relinquish their temporary role as primary caregivers and "relatives assuming sole 'ownership of mothering.'"[23]

Ana's daughter was over 18, but Ana's parents had temporary custody of her two underage sons. Ana described not wanting to "uproot" her sons from the stable environment they had established with their grandparents in Las Vegas, to then expose them to residential instability upon her release. Since she did not want to rush her children into unstable living arrangements, Ana tried to create a "stable environment for a home" before making plans for her three children to join her in New York City. Ana's parents, however, disagreed with her about the best custodial and living arrangements for her sons after her release. Ana's father wanted his grandchildren to stay with him because he was accustomed to their company, and Ana's mother believed the boys were "better off" with their grandmother. Ana stressed her maternal role and responsibility to take care of her children, even during difficult times.

The disagreement with her parents introduced a clash over what Ana believed was best for her own children as their mother. "[My mother] wanted me to keep them there. I'm their mom, they're coming with me. Simple as that and I think she has a problem with that." By having her children live with her and away from their grandparents, Ana described standing her ground against her mother, who "wanted to take control." Notably, Ana believed she was misunderstood as a mother and that this contributed to her mother's assumption that the children were "better off" staying with their grandparents.

It bothered me to see that, that she really felt that I was just gonna leave them there and forget about my kids because she felt I thought it would be easier. Why would you think that of me? Why would you ever have that impression of me when all I do is fight every day to provide for my kids and be with my kids? . . . I think she misunderstood me as a mother.

Unbeknownst to Ana's mother, Ana switched temporary custody over to her adult daughter so that she was legally able to pick up her younger brothers from their grandparents' home in Las Vegas and drive them to New York City, where Ana was living in a single-family transitional housing unit. Unaware of the shift in temporary custody, Ana's mother threatened to call the police on Ana's daughter for kidnapping. This threat against her daughter was the main reason Ana believed her relationship with her mother was "damaged" and could not be recovered. Though Ana was content with her decision and pleased to live with her three children post-incarceration, this decision ultimately resulted in a strained relationship with her own mother, as they cut off all communication and were still not speaking approximately ten months later.

Despite the mothers' attempts to maintain full custody or to find housing for themselves and their children, they were forced to negotiate housing and custodial arrangements with temporary caregivers. For mothers like Josefina and Ana, family may disagree about what is best for the children when mothers are in reentry. As shown in Josefina's case, negotiating with temporary caregivers may affect mothers' reunification with their children and impact mother-child relationships. In this way, custodial and housing arrangements are a function of broader family matters and may complicate mothers' experiences.

Children

Though formerly incarcerated mothers often had hopes that their underage children would reside with them post-incarceration, this required their children to transition from previous living arrangements. Mothers varied in how they confronted this change and brought it to their children's attention. For instance, even though Donna's 14-year-old son and Marie's 13-year-old son are only a year apart in age, the mothers took different approaches in determining if they should change their children's living arrangements and when to do so. As Donna explained:

It's not just getting them back because he's at that teenage year where I might want to make a decision but the decision might not be good for him. So, I have to like ask him a lot of things like, "How do you feel about this?" or "Do you want to finish school where you're at?" or "Are you ready to come here and finish school?"

Donna took a collaborative approach in asking her son what he wanted and allowing him to participate in the housing decision. Marie, however, viewed herself as the sole decision maker. Marie explained to her son that his grandmother was only a temporary caregiver and he would eventually need to reside with Marie as his mother. Marie described their dialogue:

He like, "No. I am staying here with grandma where it's safe. Come stay with us 'cause I have memory in this house, mommy. I'm with ma- grandma, you know. You can come here." I am like, "[Son], I can't come live with mommy anymore. I have to live on my own. You weren't meant to live with ma forever."

Marie's son wanted to remain in his grandmother's house, where he had lived with Marie before her incarceration, when she was battling substance use. Their dialogue suggests that he was open to living with his mother again, but under the condition that they were both living in his grandmother's home, a place he considered "safe" and filled with memories.

According to Marie, children of formerly incarcerated women "need to be enticed" by showing them that the mother is stable and that prospective living arrangements would also be stable. This was consistent with other mothers who wanted to reunify with their children; apart from their children having stable living arrangements, mothers believed they needed to reassure their children of stability. Seven months after Marie's release, however, her son was still residing with his grandmother. "I want him to live with me, but I don't have a place to put him to live with me," Marie said. She was living in transitional housing, which she shared with three other women, two of whom had their children living with them. While her room was sufficient for her, it was not enough for her teenage son to comfortably live with her: "I don't want him to come and I am in a program and we sharing the same room."

Even when the mothers *did* reunify with their children, living together was not free of complications. Most of the mothers aimed to live in an apartment with their children after incarceration, yet this transition sometimes introduced unexpected obstacles for children, especially when they were accustomed to previous living arrangements. Like many formerly incarcerated mothers, Madison lived in transitional housing that consisted of communal living with other formerly incarcerated women. After about six months living in HourChildren's communal housing with her children, Madison transitioned to a single-family apartment under the same program. Although this transition was a sign of progress in housing, her 6-year-old son and 4-year-old daughter preferred the communal living style over the single-family apartment. According to Madison, "moving to an apartment was actually harder than living in the communal living for them." Her children were not accustomed to living in "such a little space," unable to "run around" and play with other children, something they were able to do in the communal housing, which more closely resembled living with their grandmother during Madison's four-year incarceration.

This housing adjustment for Madison's children was similar to the adjustment Ana's children underwent. Even though Ana was happy to live with her three children in transitional housing, she believed it was particularly difficult for her eldest, her 21-year-old daughter. Ana admitted that her transitional housing unit was a "small apartment" for the family of four. Ana's daughter had been living on her own for two years and was not accustomed to residing with her two younger siblings before the three of them moved to New York City to live with their mother. As Ana shared, "Even though I don't put the rules too much on her. But living with her brothers: sibling rivalry." Ana believed the transition to live together was "a little difficult for her" daughter and "a little overwhelming at times." I had the pleasure of meeting Ana's daughter, Zoe, a few times in Ana's reentry program and at their transitional housing location. At 21 years old, she was only a few years younger than me and seemed comfortable speaking about her experiences. Zoe believed her mother, Ana, had a fear of "being too strict" on her sons, thinking that if she were, her sons would want to leave her care. Yet Zoe believed "stricter actions" were necessary to prevent her brothers from becoming "street thugs." As their older sister, she took on some of the disciplining that her mother was reluctant to execute. "I know my brothers feel that I try to butt in when it comes to disciplining them. . . . [T]hey feel like, 'Oh, look, we have two authority figures now. And, not too long ago, we didn't have one.'" Even though Ana believed her daughter, Zoe, found it difficult and overwhelming to live with her siblings, Zoe made light of these difficulties. Zoe explained to me that "every family has their good times and bad times," which may include arguing, but "overall, we love each other."

HOME SWEET HOME?

After incarceration, the mothers generally hoped to have a place they could call "home." A home is a place they can call their own. A home is independence: owning keys that can open the doors to their own living quarters. For them, a home affords them privacy from strangers, unlike what they experienced during incarceration. In a home, they have the freedom to do things that others take for granted, like playing music, having a gathering, or even smoking a cigarette. In a home, they are not restricted from having visitors when or if they please. When mothers had contact with their children, they often hoped to establish a home where their children could eventually live with them, whether they were underage children or young adults. A home is stability for themselves and their children in which mothers can "give them a roof over their head" and know that "they [are] gonna be safe in a secure place." As explained by Marcia, "I need my own space, my own room, my own apartment so when my kids do choose to come to spend [time], they have their own room [and] they could do what they do and I don't have to have nobody tell me what to do or what to do with my kids." A home with their children would give them the freedom to be mothers without patronizing state oversight of their motherwork.

This section discusses the practical barriers formerly incarcerated mothers face in establishing a home. It demonstrates how the shelter system contradicts notions of a home and complicates mothers' efforts to maintain and enhance maternal relationships. This is followed by a discussion of mothers' goals to overcome housing barriers and create a home with dependent children—that is, children under 18 as well as adult children still in need of support. Finally, I briefly highlight nuances in how mothers described their housing goals in relation to their adult children who were dependent versus adult children who were self-sufficient.

Practical Barriers in Establishing a Home

Despite common desires to establish a home post-incarceration, only four mothers described having their own homes, whereas fourteen mothers lived in transitional housing units, nine lived in shelters, and five lived in the apartments of family members. The remaining five were in a variety of living situations, including a residential drug treatment program, an apartment with a roommate, a room that a stranger was subletting, homelessness, and one mother who lived with her husband but whose living situation (e.g., apartment or shelter) was unclear.

The mothers understood that establishing a home would require them to jump through various hoops. Apart from having a criminal record, women of color in general face institutional exclusion from housing opportunities.[24] Women of color often encounter housing discrimination during or after in-person contact, when housing authorities make visual assumptions about their race or ethnicity and make decisions based on prejudices about them. For instance, housing authorities presume women of color to be single (m)others supposedly on welfare, with unruly children and messy homes. They may then act on these prejudices by restricting women of color to unsatisfactory housing options and denying renewed leases, among other discriminatory actions.[25] Racial-ethnic discrimination also happens in housing markets during preliminary phone conversations. Douglas Massey and Garvey Lundy found that "for every call a white male makes to find out about a rental unit in the Philadelphia housing market, a poor black female must make two calls to achieve the same level of access, roughly doubling her time and effort compared with his."[26] This disparity is, in essence, white privilege. Housing authorities harm women of color by acting on racial-ethnic inferences based on their appearance, accent, or language as well as gendered stereotypes about their circumstances and deservingness.

Additionally, the disproportionate effects of carceral systems on people of color seep into the housing market through restrictions based on criminal records, hurting their chances of establishing a home post-incarceration.[27] The Fair Housing Act (FHA) prohibits housing discrimination in sales, renting, and financing based on race, color, religion, sex, disability, family status, or national origin, but having a criminal record is not included as a characteristic protected from discrimination. Still, the Department of Housing and Urban Development (HUD) argues that using criminal records to justify housing restrictions can result in discriminatory effects. By refusing to rent to people with criminal records or to renew their leases, these actions impose excessive burdens on people of color and thus violate the FHA.[28] A criminal record alone does not indicate a risk to property or to the safety of other residents.

Therefore, housing authorities should not use unfounded prejudices to justify restrictions based on criminal history. Instead, HUD argues that housing authorities should consider the nature and severity of convictions as well as the time that has passed since the convictions.[29] The assumption is that these considerations should weaken the discriminatory nature of blanket policies restricting housing from anyone with a criminal record.

Even if reducing housing discrimination against formerly incarcerated people of color is possible, they may still encounter various hurdles after incarceration that limit housing options and complicate living arrangements. Mothers believed housing opportunities for them in New York City were limited, but so was assistance from agencies, housing programs, and counselors to help them secure housing after incarceration. When counselors were accessible during their incarceration and tasked with helping them locate housing (among other things), the mothers considered them unhelpful. The counselors "[weren't] doing crap," Donna surmised two and a half weeks after her release.

> I didn't have a counselor that said, "Okay, you can go here, or you could go here, or we could do this." . . . I just think there needs to be better counselors who can help guide people into that direction.

Donna continued, critiquing the reliance on resource guides:

> Like, they have these *Connections* books.[30] However, you're on your own to write [to] these programs. I think it should be more of places that women can go with their children. . . . You know, although we look through these books and see a lot of resources, [but] when you come home it just don't seem like they're all that they're supposed to be.

Even though the New York Public Library releases the *Connections* reentry resource guide on an annual basis, the demand for housing far exceeds the available resources, especially for housing opportunities that allow mothers to live with their children. This demonstrates the necessity to help mothers obtain housing—efforts that should begin during their incarceration and continue throughout reentry. The mothers believed they were largely left to fend for themselves in figuring out their reentry into the community. The work of critical sociologists supports these findings, arguing that "reentry is not an integral part of correctional programming inside prison and that when women are released to reenter society, they will likely be unprepared or overwhelmed with what needs to happen in order to reenter successfully."[31]

*Maintaining and Enhancing Maternal Relationships
in the Shelter System*

Overall, mothers understood shelters as temporary living arrangements and as the last resort if all other options failed. Yet at least 18 of the 37 formerly incarcerated mothers had spent time in the shelter system or were staying in a shelter at the time of their interviews. The shared experience in shelters demonstrates how difficult it was to find housing in New York City, leaving the shelter system as their only option even though it was in no way a "home."

The New York City Department of Homeless Services (DHS) provides shelters for single adults, for adult families, and for families with children, including pregnant women. The officers at adult family shelters are DHS peace officers, ostensibly trained in basic life support and crisis intervention practices that demand de-escalation skills. While visiting adult family shelters, I received hostility from these officers, who immediately asked me why I was there and then dismissively told me no visitors were allowed. I also felt some resistance from shelter personnel, who seemed uninterested in my presence and dismissed me as quickly as possible. This resistance from staff and security at the adult shelters was a glimpse into the daily treatment mothers may experience. In fact, they described adult family shelters as being "horrific," "filthy," and having personnel who just "didn't care" about the people living there. Interestingly, however, the mothers' experiences in shelters for adult families differed from their experiences in shelters for families with children under 21 and for pregnant women. Parallel with these differing experiences, I also received distinguishable treatment from shelter staff and security depending on whom the shelter served.

I did not receive resistance at a family shelter I visited for women and their children. Instead, staff at this location allowed me to set up a table on the main floor to inform mothers about my interviews. Security was also relatively lax, with no metal detectors or DHS peace officers. Yet these shelters still pose problems for formerly incarcerated mothers. Even though some may allow visitors, this is typically restricted to designated time frames and does not permit overnight stays unless there are exceptions for mothers with joint custody of children. Social workers, visiting nurses, parole officers, and child welfare personnel are allowed into designated rooms, but outside family members (including children) are typically restricted from entering rooms and limited to the main floor or open spaces like multipurpose rooms. These regulations presented a number of problems for mothers living with their children and mothers with children living outside of the shelter.

Bianca, for instance, was living with her teenage daughter in a shelter for formerly incarcerated and "at-risk" mothers and their children. When I arrived at the shelter, she had just finished throwing out the trash and was starting to prepare breakfast. As I sat in her living room, the smell of French toast and sausages began to fill the apartment-style shelter. Though she only lived with her 16-year-old daughter, she believed shelter regulations limited quality time with her 28-year-old daughter, who was pregnant with her first child. "You can't be involved with your family," Bianca explained. Her daughter was unable to visit whenever she wanted and was not able to interact with Bianca comfortably within the shelter. As Bianca explained, "We see each other often. But it's just like it's not the way we want to see one another." Bianca wanted to be able to cook and have dinner with both daughters, to watch TV together with their feet up, and to give her oldest daughter the opportunity to sleep over if she desired. But these things were not allowed. She had to meet her daughter in a multipurpose room located on the main level of the shelter. "Who wants to go sit downstairs in the multi-purpose room for three hours? Sitting there. You can't cook, you can't watch TV, you can't do nothing but sit there. Who wants to do that?"

Living in a shelter was also not conducive to helping Bianca's teenage daughter overcome her suicidal thoughts. As Bianca finished cooking breakfast, she called out to her daughter to pick up her plate. Bianca's daughter wore a rainbow-colored T-shirt with a smiley face on it and, as she walked toward the kitchen, she smiled at me through her glasses. Yet four days earlier she had spent the entire day on suicide watch at Bellevue Hospital. The rules and restrictions of their shelter were taking a toll on Bianca and her daughters. Bianca believed that by leaving the shelter system, she could improve the mental health of her youngest daughter, spend more quality time with her eldest daughter, and be available after the birth of her grandchild.

Though some mothers had hopes of leaving the shelter system to establish a home of their own, other mothers tried to make the best of unfortunate circumstances when leaving a shelter was less practical or more difficult than anticipated. Priscilla, for instance, focused on creating a home environment for her children despite living in a shelter with dreadful and uncomfortable conditions. "They don't make it comfortable for you but ... you're gonna stay there because you don't have a place to go." At the time of her interview, Priscilla was staying at a family shelter with her 17-year-old son, her 9-year-old son, and her husband. Her youngest son appeared to focus on the benefits of having his mother back. "My little one, he's happy; he don't care. He's like, 'Mommy's back.'" Her teenage son, however, openly expressed his dislike of the shelter. "My 17-year-old hates the fact that he's in a shelter 'cause, you know, it's a little room connected to a bathroom. And, he complains constantly about it." Priscilla believed that as a teenager, her son had less tolerance for living in a shelter, especially after he had lived with his father in a "big" and "nicer" two-level house. Her son's distaste for the shelter motivated her to "keep it clean" and "try to make it as homely as [she could]."

Establishing a Home with Dependent Children

As discussed in this chapter, othermothers sometimes provided a more stable home for children when mothers were unable to do so. Given practical concerns about their reentry into the community, some mothers did not pursue caregiving responsibilities, believing it was in their children's best interests to stay with othermothers while their blood mothers adjusted to their post-incarceration circumstances.[32]

Qiana reminisced about reuniting with her son six days after her first incarceration. He was 4 years old at the time. The quick transition to having sole responsibility was overwhelming for her. "I left him when he was one years old. Came home when he was four. So, even though he knew me and I knew him, we really didn't know each other like that because I was gone for so long." She continued, "I was trying to get to know him [and] he was trying to get to know me. He was just all over the place and he wasn't listening and it was just like, it was crazy." In addition to Qiana's struggles with mothering post-incarceration, the requirements of her reentry program and of her parole added extra stress:

> I had the expectations of this [reentry] program . . . doing the interning and all that, and then having stipulations from parole: drug treatment, the whole mental health, anger management, domestic violence. So, it was—I had a lot of expectations on top of taking care of myself and also being a mother. So, it became overwhelming.

Motherhood in general can be stressful, but post-incarceration motherhood means mothering within a state of hypersurveillance and dealing with parole officers who serve as gatekeepers to freedom. Qiana believed she was "so overwhelmed the first time, [that] things really didn't work out." She eventually violated her parole and was reincarcerated.

Approximately two and a half weeks after her last incarceration, Qiana expressed learning to "take things one day at a time" during her reentry and purposefully leaving her son under the care of her aunt and grandmother. The mothers did not view the decision to leave children with othermothers as evidence of ignoring their motherly duties but rather as being good mothers by doing what was best for their children, even if this meant that their children's home was away from them.

"It doesn't matter how much time you do, coming back into society is just an adjustment alone. So let alone having children that depend on you, you have to be considerate of they every needs. It's *hard*," said Madison. Even though she was not completely fond of her own mother, who took over in shared mothering, Madison appreciated that her children stayed with family while she worked to "get [her]self together" for the first five months after her incarceration. "I appreciated having to come home and just worry about myself and get myself together. I got a job and I took care of things that I needed to take care of before I actually received [the children]." While shared mothering helped provide mothers with some sense of stability, living with and caring for their children post-incarceration was still nerve-racking. As Madison explained:

> 'Cause you being a mom, you feel like you're a mom 24/7. You don't have a fucking moment to just be like, "Ahh!" . . . I couldn't even cry. Like, me and my kids lived in the same room together. I couldn't cry without them being like, "What's wrong mommy?" and then upsetting them and have them crying.

Madison believed the time her children spent with their grandmother was essential for some sense of stability for her before taking on additional maternal responsibilities living with them. "I feel like that was really good that I didn't get them as soon as I came home because it is just too much." Even though the formerly incarcerated mothers admitted their desire to "do things quick" and reunite with their children after incarceration, looking back they appreciated the time that shared mothering gave them to somewhat prepare for reunifying with their children.

The mothers generally emphasized the need to "get [themselves] together" and "get established" or "situated" before reuniting with children with whom they maintained communication. The time children live with family should, *in theory*, help mothers get situated within the community and perhaps establish housing where they could live with their children. After all, reentry programs often stress this notion of "self-sufficiency."[33] Yet formerly incarcerated mothers must still navigate their marginalized status, which follows them after incarceration. In reality, they often struggled to find any housing, not only as women of color but also as women of color with criminal records.

I found that the HourChildren program helped many formerly incarcerated mothers overcome housing obstacles as a marginalized group while meeting strict housing requirements for maternal custody. The program prides itself on providing mothers a home where they can live with their children after incarceration. Carolina was one of the mothers living in HourChildren's communal housing, and she highlighted the program's role in preparing her to regain custody:

> [T]he support system is really, really good here and they give you housing so you can be able to reunite with your children again, especially children that are in the foster care system. . . . They give you room, they give you the bed where the agency will prove that the address is good. . . . [When] I do get custody back of them, they'll be able to stay with me because I have two bedrooms: one for me and one for the kids. And it's furnished and everything.

HourChildren provides mothers with sizable accommodations for the entire family, beds for each member, and appropriate sleeping arrangements for kids' ages so families can receive a stamp of approval from the child welfare system. Carolina noted that "HourChildren's mission [is] to reunite incarcerated mothers with their children," suggesting that this program was doing a good job in standing by its mission. In fact, she believed formerly incarcerated mothers with a child welfare case had a "better chance with being with HourChildren than just coming out and going through the regular shelter system."

Understandably, childhood is expected to go hand in hand with dependency, and mothers' involvement (as well as state involvement) is expected to diminish as children get older. Yet restricting research to maternal experiences with children under age 18 limits our understanding of mother-child relationships and of motherwork for children in their young adulthood and beyond. When mothers discussed a "home" in relation to their adult children who were not yet independent, their ideal home had enough space and privacy for both parties to live comfortably together as adults. Onika, for instance, was living in a one-bedroom apartment but wanted a two-bedroom apartment to provide sufficient space for her 20-year-old daughter, who was sleeping in her living room. Like Onika, Francesca wanted a two-bedroom apartment. She believed her studio apartment was "too small" for both her and her 19-year-old son, who was away at college.

When I met Rashida, she was living in a residential drug treatment program but was hoping to find a five-bedroom house for rent. The death of Rashida's 98-year-old father had triggered a downward spiral and drug relapse that had resulted in her last incarceration. "My father, when he died, we lived in the house. I lost everything. . . . House. Car. *Everything. . . .* Money. *Everything.*" Rashida's youngest son went to live with his father, while her daughter found her own apartment with her two children. Even though Rashida believed it was a "good thing" that her daughter was able to get her own place after losing their home, her daughter was forced to settle and did not have the best housing conditions. "I feel like she wouldn't be in that condition if we was all under one roof. . . . I'm not secure with where she's at so I rather keep her with me." Rashida wanted to live with her 18-year-old son, her 22-year-old daughter, and her daughter's two children. "That's what I'm looking for: everybody under one roof." This ideal living arrangement, however, did not include Rashida's eldest child, her 29-year-old son, who had stable housing and good living conditions with "his own family." Since Rashida had three adult children who differed in their independence, she focused her attention on those who were more dependent and needed additional support.

As Rashida's case shows, mothers' efforts to create a home typically excluded their adult children who were self-sufficient. Instead, mothers preferred to find a separate dwelling from these adult children. For instance, Henrietta had three children who were 43, 32, and 25. Even though she had an open relationship with her three children, in which she could visit and stay for as long as she pleased, she did not want to intrude on her children's space by moving into any of their homes. Henrietta opted not to live with her children because they were "grown" and had their own lives to manage without more responsibilities associated with her presence. Despite their adult children's willingness and ability to house them, mothers may not want to intrude in the households of their self-sustaining grown children, especially when they have families of their own. Henrietta was living in a shelter not because it was the most fitting option for her, but because it was the best arrangement for her adult children.

CONCLUSION

Society expects women to be primary caregivers, and while mothers largely accept maternal responsibilities, their ability to meet gendered expectations of motherhood are shaped by social and structural barriers tied to their social position. This chapter demonstrates how standards of maternal fitness are grounded in social constructions of motherhood that impose white middle-class standards of intensive mothering. Mothers of color are harmed by these state-imposed standards and biased evaluations of their maternal fitness that disregard the impact of socioeconomic disparities. Then, when mothers of color do not fit normative ideals, they are under public scrutiny and criticized as visible (m)others by entities like the child welfare system. Language referring to them as "unfit" (m)others is then used to justify additional monitoring and state-imposed requirements to fix them into "fit" mothers, with less attention devoted to the marginalization that shapes mothers' circumstances.

The public assumes noncustodial arrangements mean the women are irresponsible and careless (m)others; I argue, however, that custodial (and living) arrangements are not definitive markers of mother-child relationships or mothering efforts in a racialized and patriarchal society. Patriarchy, as a social system, suggests that men in political power have the moral authority to make life-changing legal decisions about women's bodies. Furthermore, anti-Black racism has historically controlled the reproduction of Black women, through forced sterilizations in the 1900s based on racist eugenics claiming that Black women were "feeble-minded" and supposedly needed to be prevented from passing on undesirable genes to the next generation.[34] Once Black women become mothers and challenge normative white middle-class ideals, their motherhood is "redefined as a privilege that can be revoked."[35] More specifically, the state argues that their children must be "saved" by removing them from the home until mothering behaviors are seemingly corrected. As a proponent of state control, the child welfare system purposefully takes this individualistic approach to highlighting mothers' setbacks and instructing them to take personal responsibility for their circumstances, including their criminalization. As researcher Josephine Savarese argues, "The deficient responses ignore the systemic drivers of child welfare and criminal legal involvement, thereby leaving oppression and historical trauma unchallenged."[36] It is easier and cheaper to try to "fix" mothers of color than to fix broken social and carceral systems.

The racialized attention to children as needing to be "saved" from mothers of color who, according to the state, must be "fixed," has resulted in the overrepresentation of African American and Latinx children in the child welfare system. Once under the watchful eye of the child welfare system, mothers of color must prove their maternal fitness according to agency standards, and they are expected to do so regardless of their marginalization in society. An expectation of maternal fitness is having what society deems as suitable housing, which mothers must demonstrate before they can regain custody of children. Yet as shown in this chapter, the mothers believed they were deprived of viable pathways to find and obtain housing after incarceration. Even if mothers were able to secure housing within their limited housing options, any satisfaction with having a roof over their heads was often met with dissatisfaction and disapproval from the child welfare system. The agency's strict housing requirements were in the name of child safety and to ensure mothers' preparation for custody, but these requirements simultaneously functioned as a form of state control over visible (m)others. Overall, the infantilizing nature of assessing suitable housing and criticizing women's motherwork disempowered them in asserting their maternal fitness and undermined their authority as mothers.

This chapter demonstrates that, as a way to support mothers through carceral hardships and reentry barriers, family and community members accepted some of the childcare responsibilities from blood mothers to share the mothering load as othermothers. With the exception of children's fathers, who were often uninvolved or only slightly involved with their children, family members largely functioned as othermothers before, during, and after incarceration. Shared mothering was intended to help the mothers establish some sense of stability, especially before taking on primary caregiving responsibilities—a challenging goal given their social position as formerly incarcerated African American, Latina, and West Indian mothers. Thus, unless their underage children had been adopted or there was no communication, the mothers considered shared mothering to be temporary support. For some mothers, however, family's temporary caregiving arrangements became more permanent. When this happened involuntarily, mothers like Josefina felt stripped of their custodial rights by punitive systems and cynical family members alike. In other cases, women voluntarily allowed othermothers to assume guardianship. This is consistent with research that shows women may navigate motherhood by accepting their diminished involvement as caretakers.[37] Such distant parenting demonstrates the complexities between motherhood and caregiving, as mothers struggle to overcome reentry hurdles. Unbeknownst to the general public, mothers' decisions (like leaving children under family care) may be in their children's best interests, and yet their actions are still criticized.

In spite of practical factors that impact custody and influence distant parenting, children often gave the mothers a sense of purpose regardless of any physical distance.[38] A range of comprehensive reentry services may support mothers in creating a home not only as a means of navigating motherhood but for some stability and empowerment post-incarceration. For the mothers, a home signified a sense of freedom from state intrusion, freedom to be themselves, and freedom to navigate motherhood post-incarceration beyond subjective social constructions of motherhood. As Beth Richie has stated, "Even if regaining custody is not a desirable option, the availability of services to assist in responding to these issues is critical to successful reintegration."[39] All things considered, formerly incarcerated mothers are best supported when provided with support that evens out an unequal playing field for them as criminalized mothers of color.

CHAPTER 3

Employment and Finances

"I Just Want to Be Able to Provide"

"I made a mistake in my life and I have taken major steps to become a productive member of society. Given the opportunity, I will show and prove to be an asset to your company." This was Marie's response to inquiries from employers about her felony conviction. Seven months after her release, however, Marie was still unemployed.

Approximately three weeks before we spoke, Marie had waited in line for two and one-half hours to attend a public job fair. After leaving her résumé for a retail position, she was called the next evening for an initial interview. As required on the job application, she disclosed her felony conviction. "The application says, 'Have you ever been convicted of a felony?' I checked yes. It's on the first page, like the fourth line down." After the initial interview, she was asked to interview with another manager of the retail chain. Both managers did not directly inquire into her felony conviction during the interviews, but they asked about the large gap in her work history. Interview questions about large gaps in résumés are an indirect way to learn about incarcerations.[1] Her response was, "I took off time; my mother had Alzheimer's." It had been ten years since Marie was a junior accountant for a bank. But, as she expressed to me, "I was not in prison for 10 years. I didn't want to say I was smoking crack and I was in and out of program, jail, and rehab for 10 years." Marie later learned that they wanted to offer her a position at the retail store. "I'd like to offer you this position," she was told by the hiring manager, "but it's contingent on a background check." Some time had passed after the expected start date, and the managers told Marie that they needed to wait for the results of the background check before making their final decision. Marie shared her frustration with me. "And you know what really upset me? All those other people you interviewed, you mean to tell me you're waiting for background checks for them too? No. You're waiting for people that checked off convicted felon." Marie believed the need to disclose her felony conviction on the job application ultimately hurt her visibility as a prospective employee and put her at risk of missing a job opportunity. "If I didn't check off convicted felon, I would've started two weeks ago and then what? I would've gotten fired. So, I'm damned if I do, damned if I don't. . . . You're knocked down before you can even get up."

Other mothers also described being in a bind during the job application process, believing employers "don't give us a chance." Whether employers gained knowledge of their criminal record from job application paperwork or during criminal background checks, the mothers believed that employers' access to this information tainted the nature of their visibility and posed serious challenges in finding work. In fact, excluding 4 mothers with internships, over two-thirds of the mothers I interviewed were unemployed. Some believed questions about previous convictions "shouldn't be on the application at all." These questions forced them to disclose this information to potential employers at the very start of the application process. As a result, the mothers felt "prejudged" before their applications were even considered. As Marie described, she felt "damned" if she truthfully disclosed her criminal record on the application but was also "damned" if she lied about her criminal record, since lying about this on job applications is grounds for dismissal. This was a double-edged sword given that mothers, like Marie, believed they needed to lie to get an opportunity, but feared being penalized for doing so:

> You gotta lie on your application and if they find out you lied, then they wanna fire you anyway. But that's the only way you would have given me a chance. And that's extremely hard. That's the hardest thing.

A point of confusion was the language of the question on job applications and the amount of detail they should give during interviews. Marie explained. "He asked me, 'Is there anything else in the background check?' And I was like, 'No, I don't have any other felonies.'" Marie was honest in responding that she did not have any more felony convictions, other than the one noted on her job application. "It says 'convicted of a *felony*'—that's what the paper asked me and I checked off *yes*." Even though she had "some misdemeanors," Marie explained that the hiring manager "didn't ask me about misdemeanors." This reveals discrepancies between what is asked on the job application paperwork, how questions are posed during job interviews, and the extent of information provided in background checks.

After I finished interviewing mothers in October 2015, new laws in New York City banned employers from investigating job applicants' criminal records before a conditional job offer was made. Even if formerly incarcerated individuals are fortunate enough to receive a conditional job offer, like Marie, they may still be disqualified after the background check, which can be used as sufficient evidence to deny employment. In other words, they can be brought along on a time-consuming interview process and given hope with a conditional offer, to ultimately still be denied a job. Although such policies are intended to help formerly incarcerated individuals, in reality they may only prolong the inevitable denial of hire. Additionally, even though it has been deemed unlawfully discriminatory to deny someone a job in New York City solely based on his or her criminal record, two exceptions exist. This policy does not apply when the job has a direct relationship with the person's past convictions or when there is "an unreasonable risk to property or to the safety of others."[2] Still, the majority of employers remain reluctant to hire an applicant with a criminal record.[3] Criminal records have become extremely accessible with the advance of technology and the release of criminal records on the internet, and this personal information can be framed as an "unreasonable risk" for the workplace, justifying the denial of employment and hindering the hiring process.[4] While "ban the box" prohibitions are a step toward acknowledging discriminatory hiring practices toward individuals with criminal records, this does not undo the harm done or offset employment obstacles.

Marie's narrative demonstrates how individuals, in general, reenter the community with a multitude of obstacles to obtaining work postincarceration. In addition to the issues they face as "offenders," formerly incarcerated women of color encounter unique problems obtaining and maintaining work. Historically, they have been treated as "double minorities" because society marginalizes them as a result of their gender and racial-ethnic background.[5] As Marie explained:

> When you apply for jobs, up front, you already have a strike against you. One, you're a woman, you're a minority. You already know that men make more money in any sector that we compare with them. Two, I'm a *Black* woman. And then, on top of that, I have *compounded* my situation by becoming a felon.

Marie's account demonstrates the interplay of criminal legal involvement, gender disparities, and the collective impact of racial assumptions in barriers to women of color finding work post-incarceration. In this chapter I expand on the obstacles women of color face while looking for work even *without* prior criminal legal involvement, and even more so *with* a criminal record.

Motherhood further complicates matters given that mothers often want and are expected to do motherwork while marginalized based on their gender, racial-ethnic background, and criminal record, and then they are penalized as visible (m)others for challenging middle-class constructions of motherhood during financial distress. This chapter highlights what women consider suitable work for themselves as mothers, exploring their maternal needs in potential jobs after incarceration. I found that most of them understood their decisions about employment and money as the embodiment of motherwork, even when these decisions were made under financial distress and unemployment. The role of motherwork differed, however, when it concerned children whom the mothers did not have contact with or when it concerned adult children who were independent. In addition, their money problems were shaped by a variety of factors that were peripheral to motherhood but relevant to life after incarceration as mothers of African American, Latina, and West Indian background. Specifically, when living in a predominantly African American community, there was a sense of social pressure to spend a lot of money on their children's image so the children could fit in and avoid bullying. The Latina and West Indian mothers encountered setbacks in financial support from family and ethnic communities resulting from cultural beliefs about certain crimes. The West Indian mothers also suggested that their criminalized status as visible (m)others made them vulnerable to exile within West Indian communities that are otherwise supportive. Accordingly, while they tackled shared obstacles as formerly incarcerated mothers of color, this chapter suggests that we should also consider their experiences as an ethnically diverse group.

MARGINALIZED IN THE LABOR MARKET AND WORKPLACE

In general, women of color encounter both gendered and racial inequalities that shape their experiences in the labor market and workplace. Employers' hiring practices and preferences place constraints on women job applicants.[6] Even with the same qualifications as men, women are still less likely to be hired in predominantly male occupations; when hired, they continue to experience gendered disparities in the workplace.[7] Much research documents a "glass ceiling," a metaphor for hidden obstacles that block women from moving up in their career merely because they are women.[8] Scholars have also acknowledged a "glass wall" that restricts women's ability to move from one job position to another of equal or similar rank to gain work experience and to excel.[9] The glass ceiling and glass wall cause women to receive less pay than men, to face gendered barriers in receiving promotions, and to encounter paternalism and harassment that may push them out of male-dominated workplaces.[10]

Yet women are not simply women. Race and ethnicity play a critical role in shaping gender inequalities in the labor market. Historically, women of color were treated as slaves, whose work consisted of reproducing children that would later provide additional labor to slave owners. Currently, women of color are still not viewed or treated as equal to white women. Society continues to regard them as subordinates, and these stereotypical judgments impact employers' evaluations for hires and promotions. Not surprisingly, women of color are less likely to be hired and more likely to be unemployed than white women.[11] Some scholars try to explain these workplace inequalities through human capital explanations, which focus on what potential employees bring (or cannot bring) to the table. In other words, they suggest that women of color are less likely to be hired and more likely to be unemployed due to their own lack of skills and experience for the job. Human capital explanations, however, have limited utility for explaining how women of color are situated within the labor market.[12] Even when women are similar in their human capital, women of color remain marginalized. Relative to whites, they receive lower wages and fewer employment "rewards" for the education, skills, and experience they bring to the workplace.[13] In other words, compared to white women, women of color must break through a thicker glass wall to progress through different departments in a job, and they also encounter a thicker glass ceiling that further blocks their upward mobility.

As Marie described earlier, she believed her marginalized status as a woman and as a person of color was further compounded by having a criminal record. The women I interviewed believed a criminal record—and more specifically, a felony conviction—created a larger disadvantage for women of color in obtaining work than it did for men of color. Kerry-Ann insisted, "Almost every one in three Black males that you meet, you find that they had some bout with the criminal justice system." Her comment speaks to the impact of mass incarceration on Black males, but Kerry-Ann also suggested some public surprise and discord when women are incarcerated. "I find that society accepts [males] more readily than if a female was in there [i.e., incarcerated]." This unequal tolerance of men's incarceration and condemnation of women's incarceration is likely tied to public perception that women of color who become visible as "felons" are doubly deviant because of their crimes and for arguably representing the opposite of true "womanhood": being docile, fragile, and compliant.

Greater stigma against women in the criminal legal system can be especially problematic as they try to find work post-incarceration. Women of color are not only tasked with overcoming both gender and racial disparities in society but, to find work with a criminal record, they must combat gendered stigma about their incarceration and find their way into male-dominated "felony-friendly" jobs that hire people with felony convictions. Makayla was incarcerated for approximately two years on a felony gun charge. At the time of her interview, she was unemployed and surmised:

> I feel like when we are formerly incarcerated—I can't say that for men, but— for women coming home, we will work the hardest. Because we know we already have plus one up on us, that we have a felony.

The women believed that felony convictions posed obstacles in trying to find work but also that as women they had to work harder than men to obtain a job with a felony conviction. The women believed it was slightly easier for men to find work after incarceration because there were more work opportunities that catered to men's interests and physical capabilities than was the case for women. Stocking or warehouse associate, delivery service technician, and construction work have been some common "felony-friendly" jobs in New York City. As Marie argued, men return from prison and are more likely to obtain these jobs involving physical labor because the employers "don't care about the felony." When felony-friendly job opportunities cater to men, this makes it harder for released women to find work as well.

When the women obtained jobs post-incarceration, these jobs typically fell under the general umbrella of low-wage service work. This brings to the forefront the type of jobs held by the 8 mothers who had paid work, including work that was "off the books," in which earnings were not reported or taxed. Among the employed mothers, 4 worked as providers of some sort (e.g., nanny, unlicensed caregiver for the elderly, outreach counselor), 2 worked in cleaning, 1 worked in customer service, and 1—an outlier—worked as a college professor. With the exception of the professor, all of the employed mothers worked in the low-wage sector and in occupations consistent with perceived "women's work": caring for and communicating with others as well as keeping things organized and tidy. I found that after a stint of incarceration, they were personally interested in service work and found value in giving back to help others in need. As Marie explained, "The women, we usually stick close to customer service [or] home health attendant. Being honest: things that are basically dealing with the private sector." According to criminological research, this "giving back" to others is a valuable healing process for "giving up" crime.[14] These low-wage service jobs, however, are also a function of the job opportunities available to them as women of color with criminal records.[15] In fact, these low-wage service jobs were largely the types of jobs present at the job fair that Marie attended. "I don't know why society feels that the felon cannot want more than Burger King or customer service. Why? Because I have a felony, I have to settle?" Marie's narrative shows that despite her work experience as a bank accountant, she felt forced to settle for customer service. And still, her employment status was ultimately contingent on an employer's acceptance of her past criminal history.

Ethnic Companions and Competitors. Researchers have examined an array of post-incarceration employment obstacles for Black women, but perceptions of Black women may differ beyond race and run deeper into their ethnic background. I found that along with their gender and racial background, the women's ethnicity played a role in their employment status and experiences after incarceration. The 21 mothers who identified with an African American background were more likely to be unemployed (67%) than employed or in an internship (33%). Like the African American mothers, the 15 mothers who identified as Latina were also more likely to be unemployed (60%) than employed or in an internship (40%). The 8 mothers who identified as West Indian, however, were equally as likely to be unemployed as they were to be employed or interning, a 50:50 ratio. Put differently, the West Indian mothers were more likely to be employed or interning post-incarceration than those of African American or Latin American background.[16] While it is beyond the scope of this study to determine the reasons for these differences in employment status, the mothers presented some interesting interpretations to explain employment differences, which mostly focused on West Indians and African Americans as being different from one another.

Economists have infamously claimed that differences in labor market and economic outcomes like income must be due to cultural differences, because West Indians had better circumstances than other Black individuals despite having a shared racial identity. These cultural distinctions to explain job market success are extremely problematic given that they reinforce the "dichotomy of ethnic West Indian success and black American failure."[17] Public perceptions of West Indians have referred to them as the "model minority" compared to African Americans, seemingly presenting less of a hiring risk and seemingly transcending African Americans in their work ethic. In fact, published work has referred to this ethnic group as "the other African Americans."[18] Not only do cultural arguments contribute to the exceptionalism of one ethnic group over another, but differences in the labor force are more nuanced than what is suggested by cultural arguments like the model minority hypothesis. More specifically, the extent of progress among underrepresented racial-ethnic groups is shaped by everyday social interactions and systemic conditions. This is evident in employers' fancying West Indians based on controlling images of them as domestic servants, while our hierarchical society has historically limited African American's access to wealth across multiple generations.[19] It is therefore problematic to claim that cultural differences account for employment disparities since this overlooks the impact of discriminatory treatment of ethnic groups.

Employers associate West Indians with a sense of "foreignness": a controlling image of them as more submissive or obedient than controlling images of modern-day African Americans.[20] In this way, hiring decisions are guided by employers' beliefs that West Indian women would bring ease and compliance to the workplace, while African American women would bring problems and disappointment. Relatedly, research also shows that employers believe West Indians have a stronger work ethic concerning flexibility, loyalty, and self-discipline, making them presumably more worthy of being hired.[21] As a white male manager explained in Mary Waters's book *Black Identities*, "If I had one position open and if it was a West Indian versus an American black, I'd go with the West Indian." When Waters probed the white manager for additional information, he explained that West Indians "have a different drive than American blacks," noting their reliability and willingness to do the job.

Other research has also presented personal accounts from West Indians about the disproportionately better treatment they have received from whites compared to the white treatment of African Americans.[22] Thus, it is possible that when white employers are aware of a job applicant's criminal record, these ethnic stereotypes about a model minority may counteract preconceived notions about those in the criminal legal system; this merits further research.

Unfortunately, public perception of West Indians as the model minority and of African Americans as the weaker ethnic group are not only held by white employers. Some conversations during my interviews suggest that West Indians may also share this point of view. Marie was of Haitian background. She spoke about employment and welfare differences between West Indians and African Americans, whom she referred to as Black Americans. In doing so, she also highlighted a clash between the two groups and their perceived work ethics that shaped their employment status:

> A lot of times, like, Americans and Haitians have always clashed because I guess they thought that: "Haitians, oh, they got three or four jobs. They always got three or four jobs." But you know what? They not on welfare. They're not. You seldom find many Haitians or Jamaicans on that stuff, they'll have three or four jobs.

Marie argues that West Indians have multiple jobs and this is the source of conflict between West Indians and African Americans. Holding multiple jobs seemed to be understood as a negative characteristic of "workaholics" who undermine African Americans' chances for getting available work, especially with a criminal record. Even though research shows that West Indians do not earn more than African Americans, hiring preferences from white employers may influence hostility between the groups.[23]

"Haitian people think they better than Black Americans," Marie said, speaking from her own Haitian background. African Americans, she explained, are "seen as the lazy laidback type from the Haitian people." In a tone of disgust, she imitated other Haitians saying *Black Amerikan sa*, which is Haitian Creole for *This/That Black American*—as if they were in a group criticizing someone around them. She elaborated on this sentiment in English: "It's bad, but it's the truth because they feel like, 'Black Americans, they are on welfare, they're in projects. . . . They don't try to get out of the projects. They don't try to do better for themselves.'" In defense of West Indians like herself, she then argued that because they have multiple jobs, they are rarely on welfare. This account, however, assumes that welfare is equivalent to a lack of work ethic, which places full blame on the victims of poverty. According to these narratives, West Indians may seemingly look down on African Americans, believing that they do not take advantage of available opportunities, while African Americans seemingly dislike West Indians for taking their work opportunities by holding multiple jobs. Without a doubt, these narratives are based on broad stereotypes and controlling images of both ethnic groups. Although unity largely helps women of color overcome the social and structural barriers placed in their paths post-incarceration, the mothers' narratives suggest that this collective value is somewhat complex across different ethnic groups.

Preconceptions about ethnic groups may introduce additional obstacles once they are employed and potentially harm relationships between coworkers and administrators in ethnically mixed work environments. Ten and a half years after her release, Kerry-Ann was working at a local college close to home. With an administrative turnover and new African American superiors, she experienced animosity from them because of her West Indian background as a Jamaican woman. Kerry-Ann believed her superiors "hated West Indians" and treated her unfairly because of stereotypes that West Indians take African Americans' jobs:

> *Kerry-Ann:* One of the things when you identify with a West Indian that I found with the former administration: they don't like West Indians.
>
> *JGH:* Why?
>
> *Kerry-Ann:* They just don't. They feel like we come here and take their jobs. . . . But the administration, they hated West Indians. You find that a lot.

As a result of these workplace clashes between ethnic groups, Kerry-Ann described "passing" as African American to advance in a predominantly African American work environment. "I identify with being a West Indian, but I also identify with being a Black American *only* because sometimes I have to do that to get around the system and get in the system." While literature on passing typically discusses those who pass for a more privileged racial group (i.e., as white), Kerry-Ann describes passing for another ethnic group under the same Black racial umbrella. This highlights some of the nuances in ethnic experiences, along with potential steps taken to progress in the labor market and the workplace. While passing as African American may be beneficial within predominantly African American workplaces, this passing can have the opposite impact in white workplaces, since white employers prefer to hire West Indians over African Americans. Still, this ability to "pass" is not always possible for West Indian women, especially those with noticeable accents that can serve as a marker of their West Indian background.

Although the West Indian women alluded to ethnic clashes in the workplace, this dialogue did not surface when speaking with African American women, which leaves their own understanding of ethnic clashes unclear. The African American women may not have described ethnic clashes because they were less likely to focus on ethnic differences and more likely to highlight racial barriers pre- and post-incarceration. Sociologists argue that given everyday realities, African Americans prepare for racial discrimination and are highly cognizant of their racial status, which allows them to recognize how society marginalizes them as Black people.[24] West Indians, on the other hand, may emphasize ethnic experiences and distinctions.[25] Doing so allows them to create a social identity in the American context that recognizes their ethnicity without lumping them into a broad racial group with ethnically diverse others. This is consistent with research showing that West Indians are more likely to highlight ethnic disparities with African Americans than to draw attention to racial differences from whites, while African Americans are more likely to view negative experiences as the direct effects of racial oppression and systemic racism.[26] The African American women may have overlooked ethnic differences with the West Indian population and instead highlighted their shared racial discrimination as formerly incarcerated women of color. This merits further investigation, as it relates to their search for employment post-incarceration and to their interrelationships while employed.

As ethnic groups under the same racial umbrella, West Indians and African Americans are "both each other's closest companions and each other's closest competitors."[27] Together, they share obstacles in obtaining work as formerly incarcerated women of color, yet they are each other's closest competitors in searching for and maintaining work amid the combined obstacles of their gender, racial-ethnic background, and criminal record. Given the diminished work opportunities after incarceration, perceptions of differential treatment may create a divide between the ethnic groups if one group is seemingly allowed to progress while the other is left in the dust. This invites conflict within ethnically mixed work environments. Failure to account for these experiences blurs existing differences in obtaining and maintaining work after incarceration and complicates efforts to create community-based and community-driven coalitions for all ethnic groups.[28]

SEEKING SUITABLE EMPLOYMENT AS MOTHERS

Beyond the sexist and racist glass ceiling and glass wall, a "maternal wall" blocks mothers (and women perceived as mothers) from job opportunities. In fact, law professor Joan Williams argues that "most women never get near [the glass ceiling] because they are stopped long before by the maternal wall."[29] The maternal wall is an unfair disadvantage for mothers in the labor market and in growing in the workplace due to assumptions and treatment of mothers' motherwork. Opposed to fathers, mothers hold a social role as primary caretakers for their children. Yet mothers are penalized as job applicants because motherwork is viewed and treated as a hindrance to being the ideal employee. More specifically, employers view mothers as less reliable and expect women to experience shifts in their job commitment during pregnancies and as they manage maternal duties.[30] Research also shows that the mere display of pregnancy triggers employers' judgment of a woman as showing low work performance and being a financial liability.[31] Employers' view of motherhood as a burden and limitation creates a maternal wall that blocks job opportunities for women perceived as mothers. In fact, mothers are less likely to receive callbacks and recommendations for hire than women without children who share equal work qualifications. These disparities, shaped by the maternal wall, stress the importance of legal protections for mothers and expecting women.

The maternal wall presents a larger barrier when shaped by biased assumptions and stereotypes based on mothers' racial-ethnic background that put mothers of color at a greater disadvantage. White employers may perceive women of color as being single mothers during the hiring process and subsequently act on these perceptions by underestimating their competence to do a job and filtering them out of potential work opportunities.[32] Even though research shows that women of color are more likely than white women to be single mothers, negative perceptions of single motherhood are based on the faulty logic that single motherhood is equivalent to incompetency in the workplace. In this way, women of color run across a thicker maternal wall than white women do, one that includes racialized assumptions of single motherhood that are used against them to justify their disqualification for work and to block potential work opportunities. This faulty logic is an even greater maternal wall when the women are, in fact, single mothers coupled with having a criminal record.

A maternal wall introduces unique obstacles compared to gender or race alone; combined with a criminal record, mothers of color are exposed to animosity about their previous crimes, social fears that they will commit another crime, and employers' doubts about their competency as criminalized (m)others. Kerry-Ann described a magnifying effect of being stigmatized across multiple aspects:

> I worked twice as hard before, now I have to work four times as hard because I had an *extra* stigma attached to me. It wasn't just: you're Black, you're a woman. Now, it's you're single, you had children out of wedlock, and you have a criminal conviction. It quadruples it.

Kerry-Ann's account demonstrates how formerly incarcerated mothers of color are exposed to judgment based on the intersection of their race, gender, criminal charges, and maternal circumstances. In the battle for work after incarceration, the general public remains on the offense, demonstrating animosity, fear, and doubt to justify the denial of work opportunities, while mothers of color remain on the defense, forced to combat society's preconceptions about their character as visible criminalized (m)others that are constantly used against them. "I find like I'm *always* on the defensive," Kerry-Ann explained, "and always having to work." Kerry-Ann's situation illustrates how mothers of color not only must work to overcome barriers that are tied to their status with having a criminal record but also must work to overcome the racist and sexist maternal wall and glass ceiling.

Maternal Needs in Post-Incarceration Employment

As discussed in chapter 1, formerly incarcerated mothers often feel the need to make up for lost time, to gain positionality in their children's lives after losing place, and to do motherwork through troubled relationships post-incarceration. Chapter 2 highlighted how their motherwork after incarceration often consisted of them navigating the interference of the child welfare system and going through the necessary requirements to gain custody of children. I found that the mothers, as a result of these challenges, sought employment that was specifically conducive to their mothering role and their maternal circumstances after incarceration.

The following section tells the stories of Tia and Ana as they discuss common maternal needs when seeking suitable employment upon their release. Specifically, they highlight the importance of pay and potential work schedules as mothers as well as employers' recognition and acceptance of their motherwork. Their narratives illustrate how work-family conflict remains an institutional problem affecting formerly incarcerated mothers in their search for suitable employment, yet these mothers made efforts to do motherwork even under financial distress and unemployment.

Tia spent eight months incarcerated at Rikers Island on drug possession charges. Two months after her release, she was still unemployed and found herself on welfare for the first time in her life. Before her incarceration, Tia had worked as a driver for a private bus company and had a commercial driver's license (CDL), which is required to drive large vehicles like buses. However, Tia explained, "When I came out, my license got suspended because of the court fees. So, they suspended my license for six months." To reinstate her CDL, she needed to pay associated fees including termination fees. Put simply, she needed money for everyday expenses, but before she could earn income using her work experience, she needed money to cover her pending fees: a double-edged sword of needing money to earn money. Such indebtedness to a predatory carceral system of fines and fees, combined with mounting day-to-day expenses, reproduces poverty and social inequality among formerly incarcerated individuals.[33] Still unemployed, Tia hoped she could pay all of her court fees and termination fees, then reapply as a driver at her previous job because it was felony friendly.

And yet Tia did not believe this felony-friendly job was suitable for her as a mother with an infant. Tia was pregnant with her fourth child during her incarceration. When I met her two months after her release, her baby was 3 months old and they were living together in a supportive housing unit for formerly incarcerated mothers and their children. The pay she received from her previous job was equated to not receiving any income at all: "They not even paying you." She continued, elaborating that "they pay you like $25 for a trip. . . . Then, they draw it back out in taxes. . . . When you give daycare $100, what's in it for me?" Low-paying, felony-friendly jobs are a common issue after incarceration. Low pay is not sufficient to cover day-to-day expenses, lingering court fees, or other miscellaneous charges, not to mention childcare costs. Tia described needing to take childcare expenses into consideration when looking for jobs. The hourly pay of any potential job needed to be sufficient to cover childcare costs so Tia could, in turn, go to work and earn income for everyday expenses and carceral debt. Yet like many other mothers, Tia found herself hindered by the high costs of living in New York City and the low pay of potential job opportunities for people with criminal records. She wondered, "I don't know how they expect you to live." Her reality was that low pay did not correspond well with having children, especially a newborn.[34]

Potential work schedules were also important in seeking suitable employment as formerly incarcerated mothers. At Tia's job pre-incarceration, she was tasked with driving as early as 4:00 a.m. and ending as late as 11:00 p.m. "When I was there I used to work, work, work. . . . I put in so much hours." In conjunction with getting small paychecks after long hours, these long hours would pose an issue with childcare for the baby she lived with. "You're not even gonna get a good schedule to drop your kids to daycare and pick dem up back [sic]," Tia explained. "The schedule is crazy." Instead, Tia preferred to work as a driver for a school bus since this would only require her to work during the day and on weekdays. She believed this work schedule would be more accommodating for daycare drop-off and pickup for her 3-month-old baby and would also be conducive to maintaining a relationship with her oldest three children, whom she did not have custody of or live with. Tia's brother had legal guardianship of her 2-year-old and 15-year-old sons, while her 11-year-old daughter lived with the girl's father. Though Tia lived with her baby in the Astoria neighborhood of Queens, these three children were spread out between the Canarsie and East New York neighborhoods of Brooklyn. Getting all four children in one place was her greatest challenge as a mother after her release, but this was extremely important for her to do on the weekends. Despite living apart from three of her kids, Tia believed the weekends spent together were the most pleasing moments for her as a mother after incarceration. As she expressed, "That's all that I make matter." Working on the weekdays and having all weekends off would make it possible for her eldest three children to continue visiting or staying with her on weekend visits.

The low pay and unaccommodating work schedule were problematic for her as a mother, but Tia considered applying for her previous job because it was felony friendly. Unfortunately, felony-friendly jobs may intensify women's financial problems after incarceration because low pay does not align well with outstanding fees or caregiving obligations. Furthermore, work schedules may either complicate or complement mothers' efforts to visit their children, to have their children visit them, or to arrange supervised visits in a mutual location. Work schedules thus serve as a double-edged sword in mothers' attempts to make up for lost time or to regain positionality in their children's lives, as discussed in chapter 1. All things considered, the mothers believed that suitable employment helped them do motherwork not only when they lived with underage children, but also when they had nonresidential or noncustodial arrangements after incarceration. Yet given that employment is often a condition of parole and some income is vital to survival, formerly incarcerated mothers like Tia may feel forced to apply for and potentially accept felony-friendly jobs that will hinder their motherwork.

Ana, on the other hand, had worked as an accountant and worked part-time as an event planner before her last incarceration. When I met her about fourteen months after her release, her goal and ideal work situation was to start a "family company" in event planning. She smiled as she thought about what it would be like to own an event planning business with her three children, who were then 12, 13, and 21. She described the eldest, her daughter, bringing her creativity to the company, one son managing the events, and the other son driving the company truck. When asked what had motivated her to have this goal over the years, she responded: "Having my family together. . . . I can still be a mom but work; and I can see my family grow." For Ana, a family company was an ideal way to accomplish work-family balance. She understood, however, that it would be some time before she could potentially start an event planning company with her children. Her reality was that she needed a job as soon as possible. In fact, when I first met Ana, she was at a reentry program for formerly incarcerated mothers and was doing a job search using one of the program computers. In looking for work, she stressed the importance of a "good" and "stable" salary to provide for her children. "That's always my concern, always providing. That's always on top of my head. I need to be able to provide for them." This reiterates maternal interests in job opportunities that allowed them to financially care for their children.

In the absence of a family company that Ana envisioned as a work-family balance, the minimum criterion she looked for in job opportunities after her release was that employers understood family was her priority as a mother. "I *am* a mother. Something goes down or goes wrong, I have to be a mom first." Ana's statement demonstrates how mothering responsibilities may take precedence in the search for post-incarceration employment and may hold more weight in a balance between work and motherwork. Prioritizing motherhood, however, can conflict with ideals of a favorable employee as someone who is willing to make sacrifices for the job; given the maternal wall, if women "observe the norm of parental care, they are condemned as bad workers."[35] Ana's basic job criterion of respecting her motherhood as a priority may be hard to put across without her being dismissed as a burden.

To complicate matters further, potential work conditions may also hurt efforts to put motherwork first after incarceration. Many positions, particularly in the low-wage sector, do not offer sick leave or paid vacation days and do not allow mothers to use work phones for personal use.[36] Felony-friendly jobs may also have work schedules that extend into the evenings or weekends, interfering with work-family balance, or entail work schedules that are not flexible when children are sick or school is closed. These work conditions present a maternal wall in the workplace against which mothers are evaluated negatively as bad workers because of gendered barriers attached to the maternal role. Although mothers in the criminal legal system are typically excluded from literature about the maternal wall, the narratives from Tia and Ana suggest that they too are affected by the gendered nature of work-family conflict. Scholars typically write about work-family conflict to highlight problems in balancing family with work outside of the home. The mothers' narratives suggest that work-family conflict remains an institutional problem that affects formerly incarcerated mothers as they search for suitable employment and as they are actively working post-release.

Motherwork during Unemployment

Of the 37 mothers I interviewed, over two-thirds were unemployed at the time of their interview.[37] A bout of unemployment typically did not pause everyday necessities or obligations while searching for a suitable job. In fact, mothers described doing motherwork even within the financial constraints of being jobless. Makayla and Ana believed that being unemployed gave them the opportunity to do motherwork after spending time away from their children during incarceration, framing their unemployment in terms of what it means to be good mothers.

The week before her interview, Makayla left her job at a local supermarket where she had worked for the two years since her release. She had been exposed to sexually inappropriate suggestions by her employer, and when she had resisted his advances, he had retaliated by sending her home or mandating overtime when she needed to take care of motherly duties. She also described work conditions in which she had to work late and return home to her son feeling exhausted and stressed:

> That's not healthy for me and I have to go home and be a mother to my kid. I cannot be stressed by this job that you ain't paying me nothing, to go home and then I'm mad from what you're doing and I gotta go home and then my son does something, I'm screaming at him. But it's all gonna [stem] from what you are doing at work.

Instead of dealing with this unhealthy work environment that trickled into her home, Makayla preferred to focus on her motherwork while unemployed. "I rather stay home and be poor and raise my son and find a way how we gonna eat and stuff." Having recently quit her job, Makayla noted that because she was unemployed, she was able to spend more time with her only child, who lived with her in transitional housing provided by a reentry program. She had more time to "help him out with his school," to "discuss more" with him, to be "more relaxed" at the end of her day, and to create "positive memories." This time spent with her son was something particularly special and important for her as a mother after spending two years incarcerated. This was also the essence of what Makayla considered being a "good" mother, highlighting the importance of "attention with your kid" and "doing things with your kid" even when you do not have "everything or anything."

Even though Ana was looking for work when I met her, she valued the time spent with her three children while she was unemployed. Ana was first incarcerated at 19 years old under the Rockefeller Drug Laws. She thought she had completed her parole until she learned during a traffic stop that she had a 12-year-old arrest warrant for a parole violation, failure to report. Almost two decades later, she was reincarcerated for approximately five months because of this technical parole violation. During the eighteen years between her first and second incarcerations, Ana was working two jobs as a single parent and found herself postponing quality time with her children to work. "I used to love working, but I took it for granted. I just was like, 'Okay, we'll do this [family activity] next week.'" The priority she gave to work, however, shifted after her incarceration:

> I realize that you can't always wait for next week. You take that moment and that moment could be your last. You know, if your kids wanna go out hiking with you, go out, change your plans. Spend as much time as you can with them. Work, it will be there.

The time lost during her incarceration made her realize that spending time with her three children was more valuable than the time spent at work. Even though she was actively looking for a job that was suitable for her as a mother, she made it clear that motherhood came first and that she would take advantage of the time with her children, believing the system could "uplift" her life at any moment and change everything "from one day to the next."

When faced with unemployment, both Ana and Makayla saw these circumstances through a positive lens by focusing on the maternal value in spending time with their children. Their narratives demonstrate how mothers can do motherwork during unemployment according to their understanding of what mothering entails, such as spending time together, communicating with each other, being relaxed in each other's company, and helping with homework. This was motherwork they were able to do while limited by the financial constraints of unemployment. It is important to note, however, that both Ana and Makayla lived in transitional housing. This helped simplify their mothering experiences during unemployment since transitional housing offsets living costs and helps them avoid the New York City shelter system. Ana and Makayla were also 2 of the 7 mothers who lived with underage children while they were unemployed, which means their children were easily accessible for the mothers to do motherwork. Still, their narratives demonstrate how mothers may highlight their motherwork during unemployment and emphasize their motherwork as a form of resiliency through post-incarceration barriers that leave them jobless. Such self-verification likely gives mothers a sense of control and meaning within unsatisfactory financial situations.

POST-INCARCERATION MOTHERING THROUGH FINANCIAL PROBLEMS

While the previous narratives focused on doing motherwork during unemployment, the current section highlights how the formerly incarcerated mothers did motherwork through a range of financial problems, whether they were unemployed or working for little pay. Financial distress was a common theme throughout my interviews with formerly incarcerated mothers. This is consistent with research showing that formerly incarcerated individuals are often poverty-stricken or burdened by financial problems and frequently report difficulties paying court fines, supervision fees, and child support, in addition to meeting household or familial expectations.[38] I argue that these hurdles are greater for mothers because of social expectations to be primary caregivers for children. Not only do women need money to support themselves post-incarceration but, often hoping and expected to support their children, they may also seek out funds to perform motherwork. About a quarter of the mothers I interviewed considered unemployment and insufficient finances the greatest challenges they had faced as mothers since their release. In addition to the systemic hurdles that imposed indebtedness, limited their job opportunities, and restricted them to the low-wage sector, the mothers' narratives also suggest that their money problems were shaped by the role of motherhood in their lives as well as the support-strain nexus of community and family relationships. The following discussion highlights how mothering through financial obstacles post-incarceration varied based on the age and dependence of their children, their contact with children, and cultural beliefs that shaped the family's financial help, as well as the influence of community support and communal strains.

Underage Children

The women understood motherwork as being grounded in their ability to provide for their children. The mothers with underage children were most likely to emphasize the financial demand of motherwork and financial strains from doing motherwork. When they had both underage children and adult children, their discussions of money problems and the financial demands of motherwork focused on the underage children. They described needing enough money to care for these children whether this was for leisure items, necessities like food and clothing, or bills such as for daycare and their children's cell phone charges. The previous narratives by Tia and Ana illustrated this financial demand as they stressed the importance of take-home pay as mothers. Despite their desire to do motherwork, having limited funds complicated mothers' efforts to care for children after incarceration.

For instance, Latoya was released at the beginning of August, right before the school year begins in New York City. She was eligible for Supplemental Security Income (SSI) because of a history of disabilities, but she had to wait approximately one month before receiving those funds after her incarceration. "The most challenging moment was when school was starting," she said. At the time of her release, her kids were about 10 and 14 years old, and they needed school supplies and school uniforms. Latoya recalled thinking to herself, "I don't have any money for the uniforms. What am I gonna do?" Previously convicted of identity theft, she pondered her previous crimes as a potential solution to pay for school uniforms after her release. "I said the old me would just go do something, and then I would have all the money I want." She didn't return to crime, however, believing "a closed mouth can't get fed, and I needed to ask someone where I was living." She was released to a women's shelter for formerly incarcerated and "at-risk" women and their children, run by the Women's Prison Association in New York City. Reluctantly, Latoya asked them for help paying for school uniforms. "I never asked anybody for anything my whole life, so that was a challenge to be able to say that [I] need something." To her surprise, they covered the cost of her children's uniforms. Latoya's narrative demonstrates how limited funds may complicate efforts to attend to children's needs and can potentially push mothers into crime as a solution to these money problems. Luckily for Latoya, she had access to a not-for-profit organization that was able to assist her financially. Even though this may be an isolated case, it shows the importance of community-based programs that recognize the gendered responsibility of childcare and that help women navigate motherhood post-incarceration.

The financial demands and strains of motherwork were not limited to mothers with custody or those who lived with their underage children. Odessa's 15-year-old son was under the full custody of his father, and Odessa owed the state $20,000 in child support that had accrued over the years. The high amount of unpaid child support hindered Odessa's ability to move forward and get a job to support herself. Her ideal job was to work with mentally impaired children at a local New York City organization. She had a personal interest in mental health issues and was hoping to study them further in school. The unpaid child support, however, led to the suspension of her driver's license, which she needed for the dream job she was trying to land. Annoyed, she described being indebted to the state and shared the impact of this debt on getting her ideal job. "I owe $20,000 in child support; I can't drive, I can't find a job driving because I can't get my fucking license." Without her driver's license for the job, she described what seemed like her only option: "I'm gonna take whatever job is hiring a three-time felon." So instead of following her interests in helping mentally ill children, she found herself settling for a low-pay job cleaning a fast-food restaurant during the overnight shift. The impact of Odessa's child support debt reiterates how carceral indebtedness places constraints on formerly incarcerated mothers and reproduces social inequality.

Odessa believed that her child support debt was not a representation of how much she did as a mother. "I owe $20,000 in child support like I don't take care of my son, when I clearly take care of him." Even though Odessa had child support debt, she did not believe her son's father was adequately caring for their son. Their son relied on her for money and would contact her about several things he wanted and needed. Odessa paid for cell phone bills and bought things like school clothes that he needed. She also made an effort to take her son out to eat and provide him with the material things he wanted. "He want a guitar. He wants to play the guitar. . . . I'm not even sure if he's gonna play it but if that's what he wants, I'm gonna buy it." Given that her son lived with his father and was under the full custody of his father, Odessa wondered, "Why can't he ask his father?" Odessa's situation suggests that some underage children may still rely on their mothers and seek their support even when they are in another person's custody. In fact, this is consistent with research showing that when adolescent children live with single fathers, these fathers are not more involved than nonresidential mothers.[39] This may be because mothers still "do gender" in traditional ways and may work harder than fathers to compensate for nonresidential or noncustodial arrangements. "I don't mind taking care of my kid," she said as she discussed things that she had purchased for him and tried to do with him. Yet she believed that her son's father was teaching him the "wrong values" because he "only call when he want something." Chapter 1 discussed how some mothers tried to make up for the time lost during incarceration by trying to "do everything" for their children and trying to "buy them everything." In cases like Odessa's, mothers' actions were driven not only by their personal desires to support their children, but also by expectations placed on them by their underage children. Odessa's account, however, suggests that formerly incarcerated mothers may toe the line between being needed and being exploited, as they search in empty wallets to make up for lost time. She explained to me, "I'm tired of telling him: 'My name is not ATM. I'm fucking 'mommy.' I'm your mother and you're gonna treat me like your mother, not the fucking Bank of America.'" Though she shared that she didn't mind caring for her son, Odessa felt like she was being used financially, without the emotional attachment she expected as a mother. This reiterates the problems and uncertainties with trying to make up for lost time, but also shows the added stress on mothers as they try to cover expenses for underage children when they have financial constraints post-incarceration.

Adult Children

Without a doubt, criminologists tend to focus on underage children instead of adult children when writing about incarcerated or formerly incarcerated mothers. The general assumption is that the need to support children and do motherwork is minimized when women's children become adults. Although I found that this was largely true compared to mothering underage children, adult children were still important for motherwork as mothers discussed the role of motherhood in their financial decisions and the negative impact of money problems on doing motherwork post-incarceration, though with two noteworthy caveats. First, mothers directed our conversations to their adult children when these children were in financial need or still relatively dependent on their mothers. Second, mothers highlighted their adult children when they believed these children could benefit from role models of how to navigate financial problems.

Rashida had a 22-year-old daughter and two sons, who were 18 and 29 years old. Although her children were adults, Rashida was one of the mothers who considered finances to be her greatest challenge as a mother since her release. Her youngest two needed financial help. "My son, he wants things and I think he deserves it. Not only *deserves* it, but *earned* it." The mothers often believed their children merited particular attention and assistance, especially after experiencing their mother's incarceration. "My daughter was struggling with where she lives at right now," Rashida explained, "the apartment, there were a lot of difficulties with it." Her daughter's housing conditions took an emotional toll on Rashida since she blamed herself for her daughter's problems. She believed that with a better financial situation, her daughter would be living with her and could have avoided these housing problems. Rashida, however, was not in a financial position to help her children, a troubling reality. "Right now, with my finances, I won't be able to help *any*body and that bothers me *a lot*."

Onika also had three children, a 22-year-old son and two daughters, who were 20 and 25 years old. She was released from incarceration four years before I met her. "I came out and they had expectations of me to do this, do that." Given her absence, Onika felt it necessary to meet her children's expectations when she was released. She recalled, "I used to be like, 'Okay, I feel bad for saying no because I wasn't there.'" Even though she originally felt bad saying "no," her financial problems and an inability to say "yes" led her to feel guilty as a mother. For instance, Onika's youngest daughter was raised by her father and was about 16 years old when Onika was released from her last incarceration. Eventually, when her daughter was about 18 years old, she was kicked out of her father's home for fighting with his girlfriend. She then moved into Onika's one-bedroom apartment and was sleeping in the living room. Onika's daughter would compare the material things her friends had to what Onika couldn't do or provide for her, making statements such as, "Oh, when I was living with dad, he did this. My friends have this!" Statements like this originally made Onika feel guilty for being unable to give her daughter what she wanted. "That's what we do: we allow our kids to make us feel guilty."

However, this feeling of guilt faded over time. Onika described being stretched thin financially, saying, "She come to me like I'm the bank." This comparison is similar to the one made by Odessa, who told her son that her name is not ATM and she is not the Bank of America. But unlike Odessa, who had a 15-year-old son, mothers of adult children generally expected these children to be more independent. "My daughter don't wash dishes or nothing in my house. She don't do absolutely [any]thing." In response to her daughter's requests for money, Onika began replying with, "Alright, get a job!" Onika believed that if her daughter wanted something, her daughter should "go get it" and needed to learn how to "earn it" because Onika had needed to earn things herself when she was young. Onika believed that some mothers, including herself, "absolutely" tried to make up for the time lost during incarceration. Yet Onika's efforts to make up for lost time subsided over time while her children grew older and presumably should have been more independent.

Some mothers of adult children dealt with scarce funds by focusing on themselves as role models for their children to avoid crime. Emma described "finding employment" as the greatest challenge she had faced as a mother since her release, noting, "It's a barrier because a lot of times they want background checks." Emma's daughters, who lived together outside of the city, were 28 and 30 years old. They were both aware of Emma's challenges in finding employment and gave her advice to keep her "chin up and don't give up." Though her children were adults and relatively self-sufficient, Emma still interpreted her unemployment and money problems through the lens of motherhood. Specifically, she performed motherwork by serving as a role model to them. "I can be an example to just don't give up. No matter how many opportunities close. . . . I'm still gonna be a powerful example for my children." Emma noted that being a mother motivated her not to succumb to the label that society had attached to her as a robber. "You don't have to be what people say even if you're not. 'Oh you say I'm a robber, so I'ma rob.' I'm not gonna be that. I'm not gonna be what people say I am." Despite feeling weighed down by tons of money problems, being a positive role model to her daughters encouraged her to avoid crime to meet her financial needs. This demonstrates how the presence of adult children and associated motherwork can prevent mothers from committing money crimes to deal with the money problems they face post-incarceration.

However, when their children were much older and had families of their own, motherwork for these children was less evident when mothers were discussing their financial problems and decision-making about work. For example, Henrietta was 62 years old and had three children, who were 25, 32, and 43 years old. Of her three adult children, her eldest child and middle child both had their own families, with two to three children each. Like most of the mothers I interviewed, Henrietta had an interest in finding work, but her interests were not shaped by maternal responsibilities. Instead, she wanted to find a job as a way to "keep going" and remain active. "I'm at a point in *my* life where my kids are grown," she explained, "I've seen them grow up. They [are] having their own kids." Since her children were adults and creating families of their own, Henrietta described having fewer maternal responsibilities and being motivated to work because of her free time to do so. "I got a lot of time on my hands. . . . I'm driving myself crazy not doing anything." Unlike mothers of underage or dependent adult children, Henrietta's decision-making to find work was not motivated by an interest or demand to do motherwork.

In other cases where mothers had adult children, their children were not mentioned at all concerning money problems or work decisions. Lucinda, for instance, was 59 years old. Her children were 25, 29, and 35 years old, and she had a 10-year-old grandson from her middle child. Lucinda was unemployed at the time of her interview, but because she received Supplemental Security Income (SSI), she was reluctant to work and risk losing her SSI benefits. "I can't risk being cut off at this time because of a job. . . . They say you can work a certain amount of hours, but some people have problems with that too." Lucinda may have been comfortable with unemployment and remaining on SSI benefits simply because her children were older and self-sufficient. In fact, at no point during our discussions did Lucinda mention her children as a financial burden or driving force to earn more income. In general, the narratives of Henrietta and Lucinda suggest that at this stage of independence, mothering adult children is a minor aspect in mothers' everyday tasks and decision-making about work post-incarceration.

Disconnected Children

Throughout my interviews, I found that when mothers did not have contact with at least one of their children, these children were excluded from mothers' decisions about work and money. Of the 37 formerly incarcerated mothers, 2 women did not have contact with their only child: Jesenia and Laura. When I met Jesenia, she was looking for work. She explained that she was looking for "anything and everything" that was available to "save up." Laura, however, was employed as a peer educator at a local New York City hospital. When she discussed her job, she focused on the pleasure she felt in "caring for people" as a peer educator. Even though she was not content with her low income, her interest in better pay was not associated with maternal responsibilities. She was motivated to receive pay that was comparable to her income before incarceration. Both women made no mention of their disconnected children or motherwork as things motivating them to find work or to search for better pay. Instead, they directed our conversations to focus on their individual interests in earning money.

During discussions of financial problems and work-related decisions, mothers with multiple children skirted around talking about disconnected children with whom they did not have contact and instead directed my attention to other children. For instance, like many of the other mothers, Emily noted: "When I came out, I wanted to get a job and take care of my kid." Here, she referred to only one child even though she had three children at the time of her release. It was apparent that her attention was focused on obtaining a job to support the one child who lived with her prior to her incarceration, which was also the only child she had contact with. She believed that taking care of a child gave mothers a sense of "purpose" in life, so it was unsurprising that she focused on the only child she had contact with, as a way to fulfill this purpose post-incarceration. Unfortunately, however, her desire to care for her son never came to fruition. "I didn't get a job. I have a B-felony, so it was hard for me to get a job. It still is." Seven years after her release, her son was 24 years old and living with his wife and newborn baby. With her son now having a family of his own, Emily internalized her motivation to get a job. "Right now, I just want a job so bad. I mean, I wouldn't care if I was making minimum wage. Just a job." Emily's narrative demonstrates how mothers may focus on children they have with contact with but, as discussed earlier, once a child reaches an assumed point of self-sufficiency, mothering this child is only a minor incentive in their search for work. Mothers' decisions about work become internalized and more likely driven by individual interests.

Josefina had five children. She did not have contact with her youngest two sons (who were 10 and 15 years old), she lived separately from her daughters (who were 22 and 26 years old), and she lived with her 20-year-old son. Even though Josefina was 1 of the 8 mothers who were employed at the time of their interviews, she described finances as "the only big challenge." In addition to working at a balloon company, she was also working off the books to supplement her income because, as she explained, "I have to worry about my son." Yet she did not mention her other children as being incentives to earn more money or to work a second job. Josefina's focus on her 20-year-old son who lived with her illustrates the role of motherwork in work-related or money-related decisions when mothers have adult children who are still dependent. Her focus also suggests that motherwork has a weakened influence on these matters when mothers have more independent adult children or do not have contact with other children.

Cultural Beliefs and Financial Help

Of the 37 mothers I interviewed, the West Indian and Latina mothers were more likely than the African American mothers to describe their previous involvement in crime as a justified way to meet monetary demands at the time. For instance, Kerry-Ann was a West Indian mother who sold drugs after her brother's arrest to pay for his lawyers, address his immigration hold, and financially support the family in his absence. The family's sole provider, Odessa was a West Indian and Latina mother who was incarcerated for possession of stolen property, which was a way to "get some money because [she] was taking care of the household." Still, the West Indian and Latina mothers were expected to adhere to the cultural values of family and society in their home countries or be subject to little or no support from family. They described a cultural stigma in which family members and other people from their family's native country looked down upon those who did not legitimately earn their income. Once visible for committing a crime as an illegitimate way of gaining money, they understood that their family members and ethnic communities would be reluctant to offer support after cultural values had seemingly been ignored. In this way, the mothers' experiences were shaped by cultural ideals and beliefs attached to their perceived worthiness for support as criminalized women.

Josefina was a Latina mother who had been out on bail for ten weeks when I met her. She was in Rikers Island for about three months before her family bailed her out. Even though it is common for Latinxs to *send* money to family members living in their native country, Josefina's mother *borrowed* the bail money from family in the Dominican Republic. Instead of telling their family the truth about why Josefina was in jail, Josefina's mother lied about the criminal charges she was facing. "She told my aunt that I had a fight and cut a girl—that's why I was in jail." The truth, however, was that Josefina was being charged with identity theft after she was found with another person's credit card. "I said, 'Ma, why would you lie? You put me like I'm violent!'" Josefina was concerned that she was falsely presented as a violent person facing assault charges, but her mother assured her that this was the best approach to actually receive financial help from family members. Often facing their own money problems, family members may be more willing to give bail money if they believe the actions were justified or, at least, understandable. Interestingly, however, a fight that resulted in harm was considered more worthy to ask for bail money than the nonviolent act of identity theft. In lying about her charges, Josefina's mother tried to protect Josefina from the judgment she would have received if their family thought she was trying to steal another person's finances for her own benefit. "They'll look at me different," Josefina explained. To complicate matters further, the bail money she received from family members added to her debt, even outside of the United States. "I'm struggling because I'm paying a debt in the Dominican Republic—the bail money." Although Josefina was working at the time of her interview, she was struggling to pay the debt, which was accruing interest, and it was getting harder and harder to get out of her transnational indebtedness.

Marie was a West Indian mother incarcerated for burglary. She believed that burglary was a better moneymaker than sex work because it was quicker and came with less emotional baggage. Her Haitian mother, however, disagreed. Marie depicted a conversation she had with her mother about the burglary charge that had led to her incarceration:

I said, "You know what, mom? I rather be a thief than a whore."
[She said]: "Oh really? Well, I rather you be a whore than a thief."
[I said]: "*Oh, really?*"
She's like: "Yes! Because in my country a whore has more respect than a thief."

Mimicking a tone of disgust, Marie imitated her mother: "They would cut you. . . . You see what they say: 'Oh *vole* (Haitian Creole for *thief*).'" Marie explained to me why she believed Haitians responded this way. "A thief is seen as somebody who cannot be trusted, cannot [be] let in your house. Like, you have no respect." Even though she too was deemed a "thief," Marie reiterated: "In Haiti, that's a really *bad* thing to be known as." Arthur Fournier and Daniel Herlihy have found that "in Haitian culture the worst thing you could possibly be is a thief, a *vole*."[40] They found that it was more socially acceptable for the women to engage in sex work during periods of extreme poverty, possibly because this was seen as *work* and a way of earning income. Perceptions of commercial sex as being work have been widely discussed within the sociology of sexualities, criminology, and labor studies. Marie's account contributes to this literature as she suggests that more cultural respect is available for women who worked for their money as sex workers than for women who took money that was not earned.

Marie's experience as a West Indian woman was similar to Josefina's experience as a Latina woman in that their crimes put them at risk of extra judgment from family and society in their affiliated countries. Crimes like identity theft and burglary were socially unacceptable, more so than other crimes that occurred at the spur of the moment (like assault) or an alternative form of work (like sex work). Research suggests that when West Indians and Latinxs do not seemingly work for their money, they contradict cultural values of being hard workers and working as an honorable way of earning income.[41] For instance, research shows that West Indians who did not earn their money legally were viewed by their community as "exceptions," contradicting the nature of the larger ethnic group as good law-abiding people.[42] These narratives draw attention to cultural beliefs and the role of these beliefs as family members offer or withhold support to visible (m)others in the criminal legal system.

In describing the negative impact of their charges on getting help, both Marie and Josefina referred to family members in their home countries. While the response to their crimes was generally disapproving of women who unlawfully obtained funds, family responses may have differed within the American context. For instance, both of Kerry-Ann's parents are Jamaican, but her mother lived in the United States while her father remained in Jamaica and has never lived in the United States. After her interview, Kerry-Ann noted that her father was the most disappointed by her drug charges, but her mother's side of the family, who were living in the United States, were okay with drug dealing and, in fact, saw it as a justified way to support the family. While it would be premature and debatable to attribute these differences in familial responses merely to location, they do introduce some interesting nuances worthy of further research regarding time spent in the United States, assimilation, and acceptable survival mechanisms in different cultural contexts. Class-based differences may also shape differences in familial responses. Kerry-Ann noted during her interview that her father was "pretty accomplished in Jamaica," often sending her money to cover expenses when she was younger. Her mother's side of the family was not as fortunate, however, and her father's side "always looked down on [her] mother." Kerry-Ann believed the class-based differences between the two sides shaped their responses to her drug charges, despite the shared West Indian background. Further knowledge of family members' assimilation and socioeconomic circumstances might provide a better understanding of their willingness (or lack thereof) to help those involved in the criminal legal system.

Community Support and Communal Strains

In my previous work, I have discussed the collective value of mothers joining forces with other formerly incarcerated women of color to share knowledge of available resources and empower each other to collectively survive punitive carceral systems.[43] Establishing a village to support one another is important not only as a group sharing experiences of oppression in the criminal legal system, but as an underrepresented group marginalized across both gender and racial-ethnic background. A valuable way for women of color to build social networks and to locate jobs is within ethnic enclaves, which are concentrated areas of an ethnic group that are typically recognizable by cultural markers and businesses that cater to this group. For instance, the Flatbush neighborhood of Brooklyn is an ethnic enclave for West Indians in New York City. While walking through Flatbush, I can smell curry spices coming from restaurants, hear the sound of soca music as I walk by stores, and see numerous West Indian flags both inside and outside of local businesses. Upon entering local family health centers, I have also observed workers translating in Creole. When individuals speak little English, ethnic enclaves may allow them to speak with others in their native language or have access to (in)formal translators to overcome language barriers.[44] Ethnic enclaves also provide social capital as residents share valuable information with each other about jobs, housing, social services, and more. This community support and the social networks established between residents are fundamental aspects of ethnic enclaves.[45]

However, informal conversations with West Indian community members hinted at a communal disdain for visible (m)others in the criminal legal system. One woman at a West Indian association noted that it would be difficult for me to reach West Indian mothers who are or have been involved in the criminal legal system because they are "so down low." This notion was repeated by a man leading a nonprofit organization who believed West Indian families had a "high level of intolerance" regarding incarceration, which keeps them "as hush-hush as possible." One colleague of Jamaican background warned me that this was a "hard target group . . . especially coming from a culture where the incarcerated are damn near outcasted." While ethnic enclaves may be beneficial in building community relationships and overcoming systematic oppression, these accounts suggest that they may simultaneously "outcast" subgroups of individuals like those in the criminal legal system. This suggests a heightened stigma in certain communities, such as West Indian ethnic enclaves, which has serious implications for the potential reach of community-based programs. Specifically, it sparks concerns about the presence of reentry programs in these areas and, if available, the possibility that West Indian women and mothers may be discouraged from seeking assistance due to the stigma of incarceration.

In addition, formerly incarcerated mothers of color must battle strains found within their communities. Upon release from incarceration, people often return to their previous communities, which can have friends and associates that may not have their best interests at heart. Surroundings packed with negative influences likely serve as an additional strain as mothers try to find work and earn legitimate money. Other community characteristics may also jeopardize their efforts, much like when mothers are released to poor and high-crime areas, neighborhoods with a large number of parolees (whom they are forbidden to interact with), or an environment overwhelmed by substance use (which can trigger a relapse).[46] While these communal strains are widely discussed in criminal justice research and surfaced in my conversations with the formerly incarcerated mothers, one mother also discussed how neighborhoods can impose social pressures or protections that shape how much money should be devoted to their children's appearance. Makayla grew up in Harlem, a predominantly African American community. As a child, her mother never bought her "up-to-date fashion" and as a result, her peers bullied her about her appearance. Consequently, Makayla learned how to physically fight back against the verbal abuse, and she sold drugs to maintain a better appearance, saying "name brand is the thing to be." Her childhood experiences in Harlem, where she used to sell drugs, shaped her focus on her son's appearance and attire.

Since Makayla had sold drugs at a young age to support herself, she was concerned that her 11-year-old son would take the same route she had of going "to the street" and selling drugs if she was unable to financially support him post-incarceration. "I sold drugs to get my own stuff. . . . If I can't do it for him, this might be where he might go." She continued,

> My biggest fear is that he will go to jail. . . . I just want to be able to provide for him. I wanna be able to keep him happy. I just want him to be a happy person 'cause I was a miserable kid. So, I want him to be like: no worries, no stress, no worry about people talking about him.

Still, Makayla believed finding a job was the greatest challenge she faced as a mother after her incarceration. Even though she could not always buy him name brand clothing, she made sure that her son always wore name brand sneakers to prevent the verbal abuse and fights she faced when she was his age and living in Harlem. "His sneakers have to be something [name brand] because these are the issues I had to deal with as a kid: always punching somebody in the mouth." In this way, Makayla tried to compensate for her unemployment and money problems through her son's appearance with up-to-date fashion and with name brand attire. The assumption was that as long as her son looked the part, this would prevent him from feeling pressured to sell drugs.

Makayla also suggested that the strain of money problems differed based on the neighborhood where children lived and the largest ethnic group in that neighborhood. Makayla believed that the ethnic demographic of her current neighborhood protected her son from the type of bullying she had experienced as a kid. She and her son lived in a predominantly Latinx area of Astoria. "We're in between two of the biggest projects, but there are a lot of Hispanics and they're not really into that." "Into what?" I asked. Makayla clarified that based on her experience living in this ethnic enclave, she believed the residents were not as critical about dressing "fancy, fresh, fly." Chuckling, she explained, "It's not much that I have to compete with in this neighborhood." This differed from her childhood experience since her peers had judged each other based on their appearance: "They are talking about you and your mother and everybody else. Here, they're not like that. It's different." Compared to Harlem, she felt less pressure in Astoria to buy expensive, name brand clothes. High poverty rates in Astoria can account for some of this difference, potentially shaping reduced community pressure to have a "flashy" wardrobe if people in the area were also struggling financially. Yet Makayla did not mention socioeconomic status as a determining factor for community lack of interest in designer clothing. Instead, she attributed differences in self-representation between Harlem and Astoria to the main ethnic group living in these areas. This raises the question of whether Makayla's actions were shaped by stereotypes of Latinxs in her new neighborhood post-incarceration.

Still, Makayla's account alludes to communal differences in social pressures as mothers try to provide for their children post-incarceration. Specifically, certain communities may introduce additional pressures that are linked to social interests and children's risk for being bullied. Not only are children susceptible to bullying when they have an incarcerated or formerly incarcerated parent, but they may also be exposed to bullying because of markers of a lower social-economic status like clothing, which is relatively common among families in the criminal legal system.[47] Writers Paula Fried and SuEllen Fried argue that "students who cannot afford the clothing status symbols are raw bait for teasing."[48] They also note the reality that children may resort to crime because of financial pressures to "fit in" with their classmates fashion-wise. As Makayla's account shows, mothers may feel compelled to spend money on designer clothing and shoes for their children as a form of self-representation, as a symbol of worth, and as a means of keeping their children content. These social pressures about finances can be detrimental for mothers after incarceration. In the face of systemic barriers to finding work with criminal records, combined with maternal needs and obstacles in finding suitable work as mothers, these extra social pressures add to the long list of financial problems in reentering the community post-incarceration.

CONCLUSION

Research has exposed how the labor market and workplace marginalize Black women, including those with children. I argue that the presence of a criminal record exacerbates the unequal playing field for African American, Latina, and West Indian mothers as they search for work after incarceration and try to overcome money problems during their reentry into the community. The mothers in this study believed that others, especially employers, viewed them negatively as formerly incarcerated individuals and, more specifically, as formerly incarcerated women who seemingly contradicted social norms of womanhood and motherhood. They described a need to work harder than men and than women without children because of society's multifaceted judgments of their character and the unique obstacles they faced as criminalized (m)others. Even the felony-friendly jobs were not as welcoming to them as mothers who were often trying to make up for lost time with their children. The imposed work conditions of these felony-friendly jobs typically consisted of low pay and problematic work schedules, which often did not work well with the mothers' circumstances and complicated their motherwork. Therefore, mothers hoped to find work that was not only accepting of their criminal record but also accommodating for motherwork: a combination of work conditions that is not the norm.

This chapter not only demonstrates the role that motherhood may have in women's post-incarceration employment and finances, but it also highlights how these reentry experiences are further shaped by children's age and dependence, the degree of contact with children, and sociocultural factors tied to mothers' racial-ethnic background. It was common for the mothers to be unemployed, or if employed, to receive low pay. This was complicated by their indebtedness for things like child support and court fees, plus trying to manage maternal expectations and expenses for things like children's clothing. Mothers' narratives addressed how financial problems affected their lives after incarceration and, more specifically, how financial problems affected their motherwork. Even though they do not *want* to jeopardize their freedom, as discussed in chapter 1, returning to crime remained a tempting risk to fulfill maternal roles and do motherwork. Latoya, for instance, considered her previous crime of identity theft an easy solution to her money problems to pay for school uniforms. In the absence of the not-for-profit organization that was able to help her financially, we have no idea what she would have done to provide for her dependent children. This is a testament to women's efforts to balance motherwork along with tackling issues in finding work and overcoming money problems post-incarceration.

I also found meaningful differences in the role of motherwork within their work decisions and in their financial problems. The two mothers who did not have contact with their only child shared interests in finding work and earning money that were not associated with or motivated by maternal responsibilities. Nevertheless, mothers more commonly had contact with at least one of their children and directed their attention to these children in their lives. As one might expect, underage children were typically at the center of mothers' attention, seeing as the children generally relied on adults and the mothers believed these underage children benefited the most from mothers' progress. Some mothers also discussed adult children within the context of their post-incarceration finances and employment when they were still in need of mothers' support and the mothers were driven to be role models for them. On the other hand, when their adult children were more self-sufficient, it was rare for the mothers to discuss motherwork for these children within their plans and decisions about work. Even though these children typically had families of their own, and the women's motherwork often shifted to grandchildren, as discussed in chapter 1, their grandchildren were not considered financial burdens or motivating factors in their decisions about work. All in all, when mothers were disconnected from their only child and when they had older independent children, their discussions about work and finances did not revolve around doing motherwork for these children; they instead emphasized the individual need for resources to tackle the constraints of carceral indebtedness and to overcome obstacles finding work as formerly incarcerated women.

Despite being surrounded by the negative consequences of punitive carceral systems, the mothers remained resilient. Unemployment is an unfortunate and yet intentional consequence of incarcerating people of color, but I found that some mothers, like Ana and Makayla, framed their unemployment as an opportunity to spend quality time with their children. By focusing on the maternal value of quality time, which was broadly defined, they fought against common rhetoric of them as uninvolved or bad (m)others and instead highlighted how they did motherwork even while unemployed. Despite their financial obstacles, these mothers demonstrated endurance that was nourished by their maternal desires and their interpretations of their financial situations. Even though their money problems were an awful reality after incarceration, these women did not let their circumstances define who they were as mothers.

This chapter also reveals how African American, Latina, and West Indian mothers saw the role of sociocultural ideals and treatment in their labor market and workplace experiences as well as the impact on support they received from family and could potentially receive within ethnic enclaves. These nuances in their experiences are peripheral to motherhood yet still influential in their lives as formerly incarcerated mothers. For one thing, I found that their experiences differed according to social perceptions of different ethnic groups. They discussed stereotypes of West Indians' and African Americans' work ethics that can shape the hiring process and introduce a tense workplace dynamic between both groups. Although the mothers focused on comparisons between West Indians and African Americans, research shows similar dialogue comparing the work ethics of Latinxs and African Americans.[49] While these stereotypes about work ethic are often used to distinguish between ethnic groups that fall under the same racial umbrella, this promotes the "othering" of the so-called weakest group. Consequently, African American mothers may be at a greater disadvantage in finding work after incarceration because of these stereotypes, partially explaining employers' role in why the African American mothers were most likely unemployed compared to Latina and West Indian mothers.

I also found that the mothers' financial circumstances were shaped by treatment from family members and ethnic communities. Research shows that ethnic enclaves are largely protective of underrepresented groups like West Indians and Latinxs, yet ethnic enclaves can still introduce problems for mothers in the criminal legal system.[50] A backlash effect appears for mothers seemingly contradicting notions of being hard workers, shaming and ostracizing those who commit crimes, especially crimes that entail some financial gain without legitimately working for it. As the mothers highlighted, family and communal discontent with these crimes can affect the financial help they receive from loved ones or could receive from ethnic communities. Denying them help can be detrimental given that it is nearly impossible to navigate the various stages of the criminal legal system without some support, such as help with bail money and with childcare expenses after their release. Community-based efforts should capitalize on the protective features of ethnic enclaves that provide empowerment and social capital, while guarding against the vulnerabilities that cultural beliefs and treatment may impose on mothers in the criminal legal system.

While this study cannot and does not allege cultural differences between the three ethnic groups in their criminal activity, it does assert differences in perceived opportunities, monetary aid, and emotional support the mothers received from others. The mothers' narratives illustrate how social networks, financial resources, and emotional support post-incarceration can be influenced by nuances in how they are treated within larger racial classifications. Their accounts draw attention to issues with homogenizing ethnic narratives of reentry under large racial umbrellas that do not capture the variation in experiences. Future research should not be constrained by overarching racial categories or by emphasizing African Americans to generalize all ethnic groups under a Black racial umbrella. Instead, scholars should further explore ethnic nuances in access to job opportunities and in financial support and burdens before, during, and after incarceration.

CHAPTER 4

Life in Recovery

"There's No Turning Back"

It was just straight crack, with no nothing else besides that glass. Yea. That was the worst thing. That was really the downfall. That really was. So, yea. But it's okay 'cause I had to be somewhere in order to get where I am right now. And that's just how I look at it. Right now, I'm at a place, it's not a *perfect* place . . . but I know I'm going to be alright 'cause I'ma stay positive.

—Vera, formerly incarcerated mother of two

The morning I met Vera, she was walking from the Mott Haven area of the South Bronx to my neighborhood, Harlem. This was approximately a 45-minute walk that required her to cross a bridge over the Harlem River. The walk across the bridge, however, was not motivated by an interest in a morning stroll but instead by necessity. She had recently lost her job and was facing financial difficulties. Unable to pay the rent, she was considering going into a shelter with her 22-year-old son and her significant other. Together with her significant other, Vera walked to Harlem to get their affairs in order because they anticipated significant changes in their living conditions. Despite the difficulties she was facing after incarceration, Vera remained optimistic. She believed this did not compare to the hardships she had encountered when she was using drugs.

Vera was 45 years old and had used drugs for about thirty years of her life. As a child, her family used to throw parties that included alcohol. After the parties ended for the night, Vera was often responsible for clearing the tables. Here and there, Vera would take little sips of alcohol, which was openly available. One day she found a bottle of Jamaican rum and fell "in love" with alcohol consumption. At 11 years old, she found herself exposed to alcohol use as her "first" and "main controlling substance." Her alcohol use then progressed to smoking weed, which she referred to as the "funny cigarettes." Vera would smoke the funny cigarettes recreationally, usually on the weekends. From smoking funny cigarettes, Vera then transitioned to smoking the "funny joints." This was weed mixed with crack cocaine. She did the funny joints for about eighteen years and was still able to manage everyday life, like "keep a job" and care for her daughter and son. However, this all changed when she "graduated" to using crack cocaine in her thirties. She described crack cocaine as the cause of her downfall: "Once we went from the 'funny joint,' we went down."

Once she began using crack cocaine, Vera found herself in trouble with the law on numerous occasions. She went from "having a recreational habit that turned into not being recreational some years later." As she explained:

I've used for about thirty years. So, I went from being recreational and on weekends, to abusing. . . . I had a [criminal] history but all the history dealt with the simple fact that I was addicted to drugs. So, then, eventually I had to do time.

Like many women in the criminal legal system, her criminal record emerged from the physical need to continue her substance use and the financial need to do so.[1] In fact, 26 of the 37 mothers I interviewed had histories of misusing drugs, alcohol, or—as one described—money.[2] Cocaine was the most common source of substance use; 15 mothers had histories of cocaine use, including both powder and crack cocaine. Other common, sometimes coexisting, substances were heroin, alcohol, and other drugs like methamphetamine and prescription painkillers. Of the 26 mothers with substance use histories, all but 5 described their use as the underlying cause of nonviolent offenses that resulted in their incarcerations. This is consistent with research that shows women are often under the influence of drugs and/or alcohol when a nonviolent offense is committed—often drug possession and other minor offenses (like prostitution) to financially support the substance use.[3] As Vera described, "It was just about survival, and I had to survive." Although Vera understood her actions as a means of survival, her visibility in society was as an "offender," and the legal response to her survival was to incarcerate her and to continue state surveillance via parole. When Vera's son was approximately 18 years old and her daughter was about 21 years old, Vera was in jail for eight months before placement in a residential drug treatment program, where she stayed for about three years before her release on parole.

Women typically begin substance use well before entering motherhood, and it often continues after they become mothers, so even mothers cannot evade the grasp of drugs or alcohol as pathways into the criminal legal system.[4] Reports by the Bureau of Justice Statistics indicate that 70% of the mothers in state prison with underage children have histories of using alcohol or drugs.[5] This high percentage of substance use is no surprise given that the criminal legal system is punitive toward women and mothers battling substance use. More specifically, once they become visible to the general public for their drug or alcohol use, these mothers are treated as incompetent (m)others, with an assumption that their incarceration results in little social cost to their children; they are then incarcerated under the faulty presumption that confinement will initiate recovery and present more benefits to the public.[6]

Despite common arguments during the war on drugs that incarceration prompts recovery, the mothers' transition to recovery was not a direct result of the correctional setting or a presumed lack of access to drugs. As some mothers explained, "You can still be able to do drugs in prison." The mothers described changes in how they viewed their actions and their impact on their children, motivating them to seek sobriety as they navigated motherhood. For instance, Vera believed the greatest challenge she had faced as a mother was "using" and "slacking." The mother she believed she was supposed to be was not the mother she was. Sighing, she explained: "Even though I still did [things for my children], I wasn't on it the way I would've been on it if I had not been using."

Despite her history of substance use, Vera was proud to be clean at the time of her interview. In fact, the birth of her granddaughter was a major source of motivation to remain drug free:

> My daughter had just had my granddaughter and the only thing that hurt me: not the fact that I got caught, not the fact that I had to do time, but [it] was not seeing my granddaughter grow up. So, I wanted to get back home as soon as possible.

When I spoke with Vera, she was thrilled with being in recovery for approximately four years and having an established relationship with her granddaughter as "Gammy." Over the years, Vera cautioned her children that there is no manual to motherhood. She described loving the way her 22-year-old son and 25-year-old daughter viewed her as a mother, commending her for remaining drug free after so many years using controlled substances:

Once I learned how to live life again—again—sober, there's no turning back. There's no turning back. No. There's no question or a doubt. I love this life. I love where I am. I love the way the kids look at me. I love the way when I'm giving them praise and I'm happy and proud of them, they like: 'Lady! What about you?!' And I cry.

These were the most rewarding moments for her as a formerly incarcerated mother: changing her life around and hearing her children tell her that they were proud of her recovery.

Like Vera, other mothers' experiences reentering the community post-incarceration were largely dependent on their ability to navigate recovery. But life in recovery was extremely complicated for the formerly incarcerated mothers of color because several factors could shape their recovery. As described in this chapter, these factors include, but are not limited to, the age of their children, the degree of contact with children, the phase of their recovery, and social interactions with family and intimate partners, as well as social forces like societal perceptions of substance use, state surveillance and control, and judgment of and hostility against them as visible (m)others within reentry and treatment programs.

Overall, carceral and societal threats to their maternal role complicate mothers' recovery efforts post-incarceration. Women of color must navigate motherhood under social scrutiny as visible (m)others in punitive carceral systems. I found that while their navigation of motherhood often encouraged them to seek sobriety, it simultaneously introduced unique obstacles in recovery efforts. In this chapter I examine problems the mothers experienced in their mothering relationships, in coping with stressors after incarceration, and in preventing a generational cycle of substance use and incarceration in their children. These factors often increased their anxiety about recovery and about meeting maternal expectations. Furthermore, even though social support networks are intended to encourage sobriety and to support the reentry process, I highlight some of the complexities that exist within these social support networks. For instance, reentry and treatment programs are not judgment free. Cultural norms may also expose some ethnic groups to a heightened sense of stigmatization and exclusion as visible (m)others, limiting the family support they receive and complicating their recovery. This chapter reviews and analyzes the influence of individual actors and program interactions on mothers' reentry when they had histories of substance use. In sum, I offer a close look at the role of motherhood in women's recovery efforts after incarceration and explore how, combined with common obstacles after their release, managing recovery is unique and multifaceted for formerly incarcerated mothers of color.

THE BEGINNINGS OF RECOVERY

Like Vera, mothers worked toward their recovery to remain available to children or grandchildren. Mothers generally had a common interest in righting their wrongs by chipping away at the negative effects of their substance use and incarcerations. They hoped to improve maternal relationships and sought to gain or enhance some sense of trust through their sobriety. These efforts meant working to avoid a relapse.

Carolina's light pink shirt made her lips stand out, not because they matched in color, but because her lips were somewhat of a light purple tint from years of drug use. "I did drugs for many years and to support myself I would sell drugs and I went through the criminal system and I've done a lot of years in prison." Carolina described being in and out of the criminal legal system prior to motherhood when she had "nothing to worry about." As she explained, "I didn't have any responsibility like as far as children; it was only me and it was all I knew." Carolina believed the effects of her drug use and the associated incarceration were "totally different" once she was a mother. When she was released from prison prior to motherhood, she described having less of a "drive." "I wasn't gonna come home and get a job; I'll come home, meet a man, make sure the man was a drug dealer who would support me, and there goes my cycle. I knew this already." Once she became a mother, Carolina was driven to make changes in her life upon her release:

> Now, I have things to worry about because I have these two children. . . . [W]ith this last incarceration, leaving the kids behind is like totally different, you know. It's like I could say today, "I don't ever want to go back to prison"—which I never said that before. I never said, "I won't ever use drugs." I see that now so it's, it's different. It's very different.

After her release, she returned to the community but did not have custody of her two underage children, who were placed in foster care—an outcome that forced her to try to undue the harm caused by incarceration. This demonstrates how the women's substance use was associated with subsequent incarceration that would impose structural limitations on mothering (like custodial separation).

As chapter 2 described, the criminal legal system and child welfare system overlap substantially. Mothers are often stripped of parental custody during their incarceration or preceding their incarceration for reasons such as poverty and substance use that were associated with their offense.[7] By seeking recovery, mothers managed stigmatized labels as criminalized (m)others by presenting themselves as worthy of parental custody. Carolina personally agreed with social constructions of motherhood that it was her obligation as a mother to have parental custody. As a result, she was motivated to go into recovery and remain sober to regain custody and to prevent "leaving the kids behind" again. She believed the main thing helping her along in her recovery was the understanding that "I know if I pick up that drug, I'm gonna go back to selling and I'll go right back to jail."

Like Carolina, Qiana's substance use began prior to motherhood, and she was working on her recovery to protect her child from additional harm. Qiana had been using substances since she was 11 years old. At the age of 19, Qiana learned that her son's father had been intimate with her friend. Under the influence of drugs, she committed what she calls a crime of passion: Qiana set her friend's home on fire "to make a statement." Her son was 1 year old at the time. Qiana was convicted of and incarcerated for arson. Her incarceration lasted two years and five months, after which she was released on five years of parole. However, after violating parole for a technical violation one year after her release, she found herself incarcerated again for another year. She was in the criminal legal system for a crime of passion committed under the influence, yet Qiana noted that she still had access to drugs while incarcerated. Such widespread presence of drugs in prisons and jails suggests that correctional settings alone do not prevent substance use or encourage recovery. The following narratives illustrate common motivations the mothers had for beginning their recovery.

I met Qiana two and one-half weeks after her release from prison for her technical parole violation. By the time of her interview, Qiana had come to a new understanding of the detrimental effects of her previous actions on her developing 6-year-old son. This was an understanding she did not have when her son was only 1:

> It's affecting him and I hate to say it: after I got locked up for this violation, that's when I noticed it was affecting him. . . . I think the first time I became incarcerated, like me being away from him mattered but not as much because he didn't know. So, it really, in a way, didn't affect me but now—due to the

fact he's older and he knows—me using is not an option because knowing the decisions that I've made under the influence are detrimental.

Qiana's account illustrates her motivation to maintain sobriety as a means of protecting her son. This was particularly true when the mothers had underage children who they thought needed additional protection from the harms of substance use and incarceration. Underage children were more likely to be dependent, and as they aged, they grew more aware of their mothers' presence (or the lack thereof) and of their mothers' substance use. Once her underage son became more aware of her absence, "thinking of [her]self as a mother and ready to be a mother" was particularly instrumental in Qiana's recovery. She believed drug use was "not an issue" any longer given her newfound understanding of how a potential relapse could affect her, affect her relationship with her son, and lead to overall negative outcomes of "using again."

In these circumstances, when children were aware of their mothers' actions, mothers appeared to experience more internal conflicts about the negative impacts of their use and incarcerations. This internal conflict in their mothering motivated them to maintain sobriety, which they believed would ultimately help them avoid reincarceration. In other words, the mothers' recovery was not a result of their incarceration, but rather a function of improving mother-child relationships and circumstances by offsetting previous harms to their children and preventing additional harm from potential relapses.

According to the mothers, recovery would allow them to meet their children's needs and to mend the negative effects of previously broken promises. When I met Karen, she had been released on bail for charges of possession of a controlled substance. She had a history of using crack cocaine, but she was proud that she had remained clean for approximately three and one-half months. Karen also admitted to previously breaking numerous promises to her son and daughter when using drugs. Her son had made comments to her such as, "Ma, I love you but this is it," demonstrating an emotional connection but suggesting that he was tired of her drug use. She described how using crack cocaine interfered with her ability to attend her daughter's events: "I made a lot of promises that I broke. Like, times where I knew she was having something coming up, and I got high and couldn't do it." Karen described her previous relationship with her daughter as being "shaky" while using, but she was motivated to "keep doing the right *things*" with hopes that their mother-daughter relationship would "get better with time." The accounts from Carolina, Qiana, and Karen demonstrate how the mothers sought recovery to remain available for their children, to build their trust, and to enhance mother-child relationships, consistent with social perceptions of "good" mothering, though with unique barriers and limited resources within the criminal legal system.

Along with developing or improving mother-child relationships, the mothers also tackled the stigmatized behaviors directly. Carolina's, Qiana's, and Karen's accounts demonstrate how recovery efforts were not only shaped by interests to offset previous harms to their children, but also to avoid the negative effects of potential relapses. One common sentiment among the mothers was, as Priscilla shared, "If I don't work on my sobriety, I will relapse and if I relapse, everything will go to hell, like, my kids, everything—everything goes." Since potential relapses led to more problems like unfavorable circumstances for their children and undesirable conditions in mother-child relationships, the mothers directed their attention to making constructive changes in their recovery. Social constructions of motherhood dictate that motherhood is supposed to be child-centered, but as a means of navigating motherhood, these women needed to be self-centered in maintaining their sobriety. As Jesenia explained, mothers understood that "the more you benefit yourself, the more you're gonna be able to benefit your child." The women expressed some consistencies with social constructions of motherhood, but they also reframed some notions of good mothering according to their circumstances. This reframing of motherhood also occurs among other women, such as employed mothers who may spend substantial amounts of time away from their children, or transnational mothers who may live and work in a different country from their children.[8] In this way, formerly incarcerated mothers share similarities with noncriminalized mothers in how they navigate motherhood within complicated circumstances, but they remain unique in that they are hypervisible as criminalized (m)others of color within various interlocking oppressions of race, class, and gender.

NAVIGATING MOTHERHOOD AND MANAGING RECOVERY AS (M)OTHERS

While motherhood often encouraged the women to maintain sobriety, the combination of post-incarceration obstacles and maternal complications introduced additional hurdles for them. Mothers, especially mothers of color, become visible to public scrutiny and are susceptible to social isolation as visible (m)others when they confl7ict with normative family units. Mainstream society perceives women of color as deviating from norms of motherhood and as having spoiled identities as bad (m)others who give birth to alleged "crack babies." Social and political responses restrict their access to support, which essentially penalizes them and exposes them to state surveillance that fuels their prosecution as "criminals." As law professor Dorothy Roberts argues, "They are punished because the combination of their poverty, race, and drug addiction is seen to make them unworthy of procreating."[9] Yet society depicts white mothers using drugs as innocent victims who are worthy of assistance. As a result, white mothers are more likely to receive community supervision and diversionary treatment programs than incarceration, while the opposite is true in communities of color.[10] Images of white mothers present them as misguided and in need of support, while criminalization is understood as the best response when the perceived demographic of drug use is mothers of color.

This gendered and racialized oppression not only shapes their mass incarceration, but it also presents significant obstacles in mothering post-incarceration and also in managing their recovery as mothers of color. For some mothers, navigating motherhood while managing recovery was able to "ground them," but for others "it may spiral 'em out of control." The following elaborates on mothers' experiences navigating motherhood while working on recovery as visible (m)others.

Coping with Stresses of Reentry While Navigating
Maternal Contact and Accountability

Research generally accepts that drug and alcohol use function as coping mechanisms, and life's stresses may be common triggers for relapse. Mothers' ability to manage recovery was dependent on coping with both the ordinary and extraordinary stresses of reentry, such as meeting parole requirements, obtaining employment, finding suitable housing, and regaining custody of children, to name a few. As part of the recovery process, the mothers learned that instead of "stashing" or "medicating" their emotions as they had previously done, they needed to deal with their emotions without using drugs or alcohol. These efforts can be particularly difficult for them as women of color for two overlapping reasons: first, their marginalization across both gender and racial-ethnic background, and second, state surveillance and control over their actions as criminalized (m)others.

Not only do mothers of color face systematic oppression along racial and gender lines in parole supervision, the child welfare system, housing, and employment, but they are also tasked with overcoming their criminalization while balancing social and familial expectations of them as mothers. In general, the mothers stressed that it was "hard" to be in recovery given that, as Wyndolyn explained, "You're up against so many angles even with children, family members, society—period. You up against a lot." As expressed by Onika, who lived with her 20-year-old daughter, "Sometimes it's hard being in recovery and being a mother." She elaborated, explaining that mothers in recovery "have to deal with the struggles of life, period. Then, now, we're dealing with the reality of: we have to sit down and take time for somebody else [i.e., our children] when we just trying to get our own life in order." These accounts demonstrate the interlocking barriers that mothers of color face postincarceration as criminalized (m)others while simultaneously trying to manage their recovery and "do" motherhood.

Their recovery was also difficult in the early stages when learning how to cope with these life stresses. When asked how she would describe her experience as a mother in recovery, Emily said: "In the beginning, it's hard 'cause every little thing triggers you." Women deemed the early stages of recovery the most vulnerable times for potential relapse, when they were still establishing alternative coping mechanisms. When I met Priscilla, she was living in a shelter with her husband as well as her 9-year-old and 17-year-old sons. She admitted that, as a mother in recovery, she found it challenging to learn how to cope with her emotions, particularly when frustrated with her underage children, who required more attention:

> My experience as a mother in recovery, I can say that . . . it's been challenging because I have to learn to deal with emotions and not use. I have to learn how to cope; so, I learned to do coping mechanisms with my emotions like if I get frustrated with my own children, you know. Anger, I have to learn not to display. And, it's not easy.

Even though it was "not easy" for her, she described eventually learning coping mechanisms for her emotions and learning how to control her anger and conceal her frustration from her children. Priscilla's account highlights that recovery is not an isolated effort for these mothers. Instead, maintaining their sobriety required them to not only learn positive coping mechanisms to tackle structural obstacles, as noted by Onika, but also to navigate the realities of motherhood.

Though mothers in general faced great difficulty in the beginning of their recovery, the degree of maternal contact was also a crucial factor in understanding their experiences. For instance, residing with children may lead to more interactions and more expectations of maternal responsibilities. Onika noted earlier the expectations of taking time for her adult daughter who lived with her, while Priscilla described the frustration that can arise when taking care of underage children. Though these are common experiences of motherhood among women, they also introduced stressors as the women tried to maintain their recovery.

Maternal relationships influenced recovery efforts even when the mothers had diminished contact with children who did not live with them. For instance, Odessa was overwhelmed with difficulties at the time of her interview. Despite her desire and attempts to make some improvements in her circumstances post-incarceration, she felt as though she had no control over numerous aspects of her life. She had recently moved in with a cousin after her ex-boyfriend cheated on her with her friend. She was overwhelmed with a debt of $20,000 in child support, which had resulted in her driver's license being suspended and prevented her from obtaining her dream job. In addition to this, Odessa did not live with her 15-year-old son, and she demonstrated extreme anger at her son's father for the physical and emotional distance in the mother-child relationship. This limited relationship with her son further contributed to her indifference about meeting parole requirements:

> It's like I don't really wanna go to jail, but it's almost like I really don't care. I kind of feel like that sometimes. . . . I don't really care about anything. Like, sometimes I feel empty. Like it doesn't matter. Like nothing matters.

When asked what could help her, Odessa responded that it would be "nice" to be connected with her only child. She believed that the weak relationship with her son contributed to her feelings of being "disconnected" and withdrawn in other aspects of her life post-incarceration, tempting her to relapse. Odessa's narrative demonstrates how the combination of post-incarceration circumstances and maternal relationships can complicate recovery efforts, even when mothers had diminished contact with their children.

The stresses of motherhood were particularly difficult for these mothers of color in recovery because they were tasked with maintaining sobriety while simultaneously meeting maternal expectations and addressing conflicts in meeting their own maternal goals. When mothers had contact with their children, they likely encountered familial expectations to uphold maternal responsibilities. However, if they did not meet these maternal expectations, they were often viewed as letting others down or letting themselves down. These challenges in recovery were shared by both those mothers with residential children, such as Onika and Priscilla, and those with more strained yet persistent child relationships, like Odessa. In a way, having this contact with their children gave mothers some insight into what their maternal relationships could potentially become. Yet they were still overwhelmed with parenting stress associated with motherhood and burdened by practical setbacks imposed upon them as criminalized (m)others, such as parole stipulations, lack of housing, and unemployment. Although motherhood often motivates women's recovery efforts, navigating these challenges of post-incarceration motherhood can present stressors in managing sobriety.

Acknowledgment and Reinforcement in Maternal Recovery

Although the women noted that being a mother in recovery was "not easy," they sometimes received minor acknowledgments of their progress from their children, even during the difficult times. For some mothers, a small gesture of affection from their children was enough positive reinforcement for their recovery efforts. As visible (m)others, they were publicly stigmatized for their substance use as a coping mechanism, yet small gestures of affection and positive reinforcement from children reinforced their identities as mothers and further encouraged their recovery through life's stresses. As Priscilla explained: "It's not easy but when I feel [my 9-year-old's] little hands wrap around my stomach and be like, 'Mommy, I love you,' it's like *all* worth it." Given her long and difficult journey in recovery, she believed she "couldn't ask for nothing better" than the love her children showed her. For Priscilla, this demonstrated progress in her recovery but also in her relationships with her children.

Emily had previously used heroin. She was motivated to stay clean to grant her son's wish for her to remain drug free and to gain his trust that she would maintain her sobriety. "I kept saying: 'If I do this, I'm gonna mess up everything, you know, my son's trust.' That's all he kept saying: 'Please, mommy, don't do that no more. Please, I don't want to see you like that no more.' And I always thought about that." When I met Emily in 2015, she proudly shared with me, "I haven't done heroin since 2006." She had been in recovery for approximately nine years. Emily expressed that even though the recovery process was difficult, "it felt good" to be in recovery because she no longer needed to worry about her son seeing her sick from withdrawal. Instead, she was able to focus on rebuilding a relationship with her son after her incarceration. Though she was still working to build her son's trust, they did "talk a lot," and she was happy that her son felt comfortable enough to "give [her] his kid for *days* at a time" and let her be involved in her grandson's life.

Mothers also received praise from their children when they recognized the progress made in mothers' recovery. This chapter began with the story of Vera, a 45-year-old mother who had used drugs for about thirty years, during which she had a son and a daughter. She noted that her adult children were there through the whole process of transitioning from substance use to a state of recovery. She pointed out that over time she was "looking better and healthier and happier." This progress in her recovery was something that her 22-year-old son and 25-year-old daughter both noticed and appreciated. "Once they found out that I did something about my addiction, they were happy." Vera also believed they viewed her differently and more positively as a result of seeing her recovery progress. This allowed for open invitations for visits and social calls. "We're really still tight," Vera said, sharing experiences when she and her children visited each other and spent time together as a family. This had a positive effect on her, as she was pleased with how far she had come after using drugs for approximately three decades.

Positive actions and remarks from children can encourage mothers' recovery efforts by reinforcing their maternal identities. This is especially the case because formerly incarcerated mothers must sometimes prove themselves to their children and to broader society through their recovery progress. To them, positive reinforcements indicated that they were making improvements toward meeting social expectations as well as their own personal ideals of mothering. As Marcia summarized, "The kids wanna see their mothers doing best. So, when the kid is proud of their mother getting their life together, that makes the mother achieve more." Marcia argued that because of the obstacles in their lives, sometimes women in recovery "end up becoming the best moms." She also noted that she knew numerous women in recovery who had "become the best moms," playing "major roles" in the lives of their children—including herself. Unfortunately for these mothers, this positive involvement in their children's lives is not the common illustration that is portrayed and shared in public dialogues about mothers in recovery.

Educating Children and Preventing a Generational Cycle

Much research focuses on the negative effects of substance use and incarceration on children, which often comes intertwined with mom shaming and mother blaming that treats the mothers as social scapegoats. Contrary to common depictions of mothers as perpetuating a generational cycle and encouraging their children to engage in drug or alcohol use, about a quarter of the mothers I interviewed with a history of drug or alcohol use described trying to prevent their children from embarking on the same path. Whether children were fully aware of their mothers' actions or merely felt their impact (e.g., through their mothers' absence), the mothers made efforts to educate their children about the harms of substance use. This undertaking was an attempt to prevent a generational cycle of substance use and offending that might lead their children to incarceration.

Mothers with younger children were more likely to describe their efforts and dilemmas to answer their children's questions about drugs. These mothers were also more likely to educate their children about the harms of drugs by explaining their previous impact on their own lives. Carolina explained that her biggest concerns were the questions her 7-year-old daughter was asking her regarding drugs:

> Carolina: She has asked me, "What are drugs?" And she's coming up with questions I don't have the answers to, you know. And I'm like, "Well, that's something you can't do." You know, that's all I can say. . . . And then, I lit up a cigarette and she's like, "You're doing drugs." And I'm like, wow.
>
> JGH: What do you think made her ask that question?
>
> Carolina: I don't know and that's something I was talking to my therapist about. Like, where did she come up with that and why [is] she asking me? Did she hear this conversation from "mommy doing drugs" somewhere else and she came to me with the question? I'm wondering where that question came from for a 7-year-old. She's doing homework and she just popped out with that question.

Carolina noted that she "absolutely" spoke with her therapist about her daughter's inquiries, believing her daughter would ask about drugs again:

> Carolina: What [the therapist] told me was like, "Well, you tell her: 'There's two kinds of drugs: there's good drugs and there's bad drugs.

The good drugs is your medicine for when you have a cold (and this and that). And the bad drugs—.'" She said to tell her: "It's something that mommy did and mommy made a mistake and now mommy knows it's wrong. And that's what led mommy to leave you, but mommy is working on that problem." That's what the therapist told me to tell her. So, I don't know when she asks if I'm sick—I don't know—but that's what the therapist said I should say. But, she said not to ignore the question because it's not good.

JGH: How do you feel about what the therapist suggested on how to respond? Do you agree with it?

Carolina: Half and half. I'm just—I don't know. Like, I don't want to tell my daughter: "Mommy did drugs." I'm a little ashamed, you know what I mean? Buuut, see, I shouldn't lie to her either. Like, that's what caused the separation: "Mommy made [a] bad decision and this is what happens when you do drugs."

Carolina admitted that she did not know how her daughter would respond upon her explaining her previous drug use. Yet as she worked to regain custody of her two children, Carolina wanted them to go to therapy together, where they could consider the questions with the therapist's help.

Jesenia explained that her substance use was an attempt to get through her emotions, with a history of trauma, familial neglect, and both physical and emotional abuse from intimate partners.

I was using any drug that I could get a hold of: crack, [powder] cocaine, alcohol, weed, spice . . . Oxycontin, Percocet, Xanax, Vicodin. . . . At one time, I was popping valiums just to try to calm me down to bring me down from the crack high."

Although her substance use originally functioned as a coping mechanism for "getting through [her] emotions," she later learned that she "was just stashing them under" instead of dealing with her emotions head on. At the time of her interview, Jesenia was in a treatment program and was thirty-two days in recovery. When asked about the greatest challenge she had faced as a mother since her release one year and four months earlier, Jesenia responded:

The greatest challenge for me was actually communicating with my child and actually being able to explain to him that: "What mommy did wasn't right, and that mommy's sick, and mommy's trying to get better, and: you don't do this, you don't smoke this, you don't drink this because this, this, and this is gonna happen."

Jesenia found it difficult to explain her battles with substance use but used this opportunity to educate her son about the dangers of drug and alcohol use. She found these conversations even more difficult given that her son was still exposed to his father's drug use while in the custody of his paternal grandmother:

> He's having difficulty understanding that [my drug use wasn't right] because his father is doing just that. So, it's like: "Mommy, why can't you do it and you not with me? And daddy can do it and he's with me?" I said, "'Cause daddy does it when nobody's looking and that's not right. That's not a good thing. But you don't tell him that because you're his son. You just understand that daddy's ill and has issues, and daddy doesn't know how to get through that whereas mommy's getting the treatment that she needs."

Even though Jesenia found this communication with her only son to be the greatest challenge she faced in reentry, she also found consolation in his comforting response: "'Okay, so I'm gonna see you soon. And don't worry mommy. God got you. I be right here. I'm not going nowhere.'" Her son's response remained reassuring for her even though Jesenia had had no communication with him in the four months leading up to her interview.

Although formerly incarcerated mothers in recovery tried to prevent generational cycles, they were not always successful, and their older children did not always respond to their efforts with kindness. For instance, Priscilla's second son, a teenager, had started drinking and smoking weed. She confronted her son about his alcohol use as he entered their home smelling of alcohol, proclaiming that she would not let him enter their home drunk. Even though Priscilla did not want her son going down the destructive path she had previously taken, she found it challenging to educate him while she was in recovery. Specifically, when Priscilla tried to prevent her child from alcohol misuse and a possible downward spiral, her son responded that her previous drug use was comparatively worse than his alcohol use. Priscilla shared her reaction to her son's insult: "I left it alone. I went into a corner, you know, I went to my own room and I cried my eyes out because . . . the truth hurts." Other mothers I spoke with also experienced such conflicts in enacting maternal roles when their children followed their footsteps into substance use. The dismay at their children's drug or alcohol use, however, was not associated with their own relapse; while it was tied to feelings of defeat and disappointment, their children's substance use still motivated mothers to "refuse to lose [children] to the street."

Unfortunately, despite their efforts to prevent a generational cycle of substance use and incarceration, mothers still endure society's mother blaming when children find themselves on this journey. Compared to fathers, peers, and other social-structural circumstances, mothers are typically scrutinized and the first to blame when their children behave in ways that are "unacceptable" according to social standards. Societal expectations of women to serve as primary caregivers lead mothers to remain the most convenient scapegoat when their children engage in any wrongdoing. Even health providers are perpetrators of mother blaming, placing full responsibility on women's failures as visible (m)others.[11] Yet the mothers' narratives demonstrate that their children's actions were not a direct result of their actions as mothers, given their attempts to educate and prevent them from making the same mistakes.

Mothers described feeling proud when their efforts to prevent a generational cycle led to their children not following in their footsteps of substance use or incarceration. Bernadette had six children between the ages of 26 and 44. She described being "very grateful" that none of her children followed her path into cocaine use: "Nobody followed my path, and that's a blessing. None of them use drugs. . . . I'm the only one that did that." Karen, like Bernadette, also had previously used cocaine. As a mother of two, she explained,

> My kids don't drink, they don't smoke, they don't do nothing. So, if that's what's keeping them from not using—seeing me—I would do it all over again 'cause my kids are good. They [are] good young adults. I'm proud of them.

Karen attributed her children's aversion to drugs and alcohol to her own history with substance use, believing that something positive may have come from a negative experience. Latoya shared this same sentiment. She had an 18-year-old son and a 14-year-old daughter, and she had a history of "money addiction" that ultimately led to her incarceration. Latoya said:

> I don't ever have to worry about [my children] breaking the law to get nice things 'cause they know what the price is. They know what the price is, and they're not willing to pay that price. Nothing is that important to them.

Like Karen, Latoya believed her children's knowledge of her actions and their negative consequences ultimately shaped their aversion to crime.

When the mothers' children had not fallen victim to the same problems, this appeared to boost their self-esteem as mothers. Knowing that their previous substance use did not lead to a generational cycle allowed the women to believe they must have done something right as mothers because their children were, in essence, okay and on the right path. This was somewhat of a protective factor of their mothering and maternal identities. Surrounded by a society that criminalized and penalized them, they still held onto and highlighted particular aspects of motherhood to symbolize good mothering on their part. In the same vein, setbacks in trying to prevent a generational cycle of substance use may also have had a detrimental impact on the mothers. Signs that their children were falling into their past behaviors induced disappointment with themselves, as seen with Priscilla. This demonstrates how their children's actions while navigating motherhood could also be a source of stress in recovery efforts and also highlights the importance of having positive social support networks during difficult times and circumstances, which is the focus of the remainder of this chapter.

SOCIAL RESPONSIBILITY IN RECOVERY

Despite the mothers' efforts to maintain sobriety while navigating motherhood, social interactions outside mother-child relationships still shaped their recovery efforts. Initial steps into recovery entailed the mothers seeking external assistance; entering treatment programs; and accepting the support of others when it was available, particularly that of intimate partners, family members, and counselors. In my previous work, I found that positive influences may help formerly incarcerated women cope with negative feelings, drug or alcohol temptations, and social situations.[12] Some formerly incarcerated mothers I spoke with, however, did not have much access to a positive support network in their recovery efforts. Some found that the individuals who provided positive support at the time of their interview had been negative influences in the past or were subject to their own array of obstacles in reentry or recovery. While a positive network may be helpful in recovering from substance use post-incarceration, it can be difficult to find, create, or maintain, and this network may also come with its own history of difficulties.

While third parties may provide formerly incarcerated mothers with resources and empowerment, they can also be detrimental as enablers, as penalizing agents of cultural transgressions, as perpetrators of "defensive othering," and as enforcers of state control. Even though public dialogue focuses on recovery as a change in *individual* choices, social circumstances and interactions bear some responsibility for both the progress and the setbacks mothers experience in their sobriety. For instance, the mothers shared common threats to their recovery, which appeared through intimate partners, family members, or society at large, and even within the presumed safe space of reentry and treatment programs. The following sections elaborate on these complexities of social support networks as both positive and negative influences on formerly incarcerated mothers in recovery.

Intimate Partners

One aspect of social support is intimate partners, who may or may not have had past histories of substance use. Research shows that when women are battling substance use, intimate partners can be useful in providing emotional support like companionship and a "sympathetic ear" as well as tangible support like food, shelter, and childcare help.[13] Bernadette received both emotional and tangible support from her previous partner. When I met her, Bernadette was 63 years old. Even though she and her husband had separated by the time I met her, they had known each other for about 32 years. In fact, she was already in the grip of her drug use before they met. When asked by his mother-in-law (Bernadette's mother) why he married Bernadette despite her drug use, he responded, "I saw something in her." Laughing, Bernadette shared, "I don't know what he saw, but I was glad he seen it." Bernadette believed that his mere presence was beneficial in helping her in the beginning stages of recovery: "It wasn't like when I leave the program or something: 'Where am I going now? What I'ma do now?' I would've ended up back on drugs." Bernadette was able to avoid relapsing because he provided her with stability, the emotional and tangible support she needed to stay afloat during recovery:

> I had a roof over my head; I wasn't in the street, I was able to take a bath and change clothes. So, I'm very *thankful* that he was there for me. . . . He helped me just being there. You know, you have somebody to come home to. . . . I just didn't want to use drugs while I was with him. I didn't want to use drugs anymore; he took me away from that. I tells him today that he's the cause of me not using drugs.

She appeared especially appreciative of his help and involvement in her life given that he himself was not involved in drug use. "He stood by me till I did [stop using]. And most men would've never did that. . . . I'm thankful for that." In all, Bernadette believed that her husband's positive and supportive company, as someone who was not engaged in drug use, contributed to her sobriety.

Other women found a positive support network in intimate partners who, like them, were also in recovery. Onika was expecting to marry her fiancé the month after her interview. She had known her fiancé for nearly two decades. They initially met while using drugs together. Within the last two decades of knowing each other, he had been in recovery for seventeen years and Onika had been in recovery for five years. She described her fiancé as her "best friend," a positive influence on her, and her "rock." Onika found the beginning of her recovery to be "difficult" and found herself "struggling." She shared with me: "In the beginning, it was difficult; sometimes I be arguing with my daughter and she make me feel like I want to drink." In the face of potential triggers while navigating motherhood, however, Onika was able to control her temptations by talking through them with her fiancé. This shows the positive influence her fiancé had in helping her maintain her sobriety and also suggests that his own recovery was helpful in talking through the difficult times.

When I met Jesenia, she also had a fiancé in recovery. Her fiancé was thirty-two years older than Jesenia, and he was approaching twenty-two years of recovery. With only thirty-two days in recovery herself, at the age of 26, Jesenia believed her fiancé was instrumental in her recovery efforts. He introduced her to Narcotics Anonymous and to "working the 12 steps." Furthermore, in working toward sobriety, individuals may find that their substance use may diminish but resurface as a new coping mechanism to fulfill a lost need. For instance, individuals may remain clean from serious drug use, but nicotine or alcohol use may develop as a replacement. In Jesenia's case, she "went from drug addiction to shopaholic [i.e., a shopping addiction]." She credited her fiancé with helping her tackle this replacement: "He's trying to teach me little by little how to manage money." Intimate partners in recovery were able to provide the women with unique support since they had personally been through the same experiences, were likely to understand obstacles from the women's point of view, and were sometimes able to talk them through difficult moments and make suggestions about how to maintain their sobriety.

While some mothers I interviewed discussed intimate partners as a positive support system, discussions of negative experiences with intimate partners far outnumbered the positive ones. Though partners may be helpful in recovery efforts, this was not the case when partners placed them in situations that tested their sobriety and triggered previous relapses, or when the partners were actively involved in substance use and enabled the women's use. In one instance, a woman learned that her husband had had a baby by another woman during her five-year incarceration. She originally tried to make things work with her husband after her release from prison. However, they eventually separated, and she relapsed: "I tried to raise the little girl like she was mine—I couldn't do it. . . . And when I moved out, I left him and I relapsed." Unhealthy intimate relationships were clearly linked to emotional turmoil and relapse.

In addition to the potential stress and triggers women may encounter in their relationships with intimate partners, research shows that intimate partners are one of women's main enablers.[14] Individuals can function as enablers in a number of ways, such as giving them substances or the money to purchase substances, providing them with the space to use, or using with them. Together with intimate partners introducing them to the source of their substance use, the women implied that previous partners were their enablers when actively using and also when trying to maintain their sobriety. A few months before her interview, Paloma had relapsed. Even though she did not provide details about her relapse, Paloma blamed it on the father of her 3-year-old son, whom she met in a drug treatment program: "That's why me and my baby's father not together no more because he's a bad influence on me." Another mother, Priscilla, was more vocal about her ex-partner's role as an enabler. She had previously relapsed and was unable to receive the help she needed from her previous partner, who was "getting high" at the time. After she was able to maintain abstinence, Priscilla realized that her previous partner was not "healthy" for her and if they stayed together, she would eventually relapse again. "It took me to really detox . . . to really see that I didn't wanna be with her no more, that she was not healthy for me [and] that if I stood around her too much, I would get high again." This was enough for Priscilla to distance from her partner to protect her own recovery efforts. Like Priscilla, most women saw a need to disassociate themselves from previous partners who were not in recovery and who posed a serious threat to their own recovery.

Some individuals may not just be unsupportive of the women during difficult times but may also try to take advantage by entering into their lives only for sexual interests. Lucinda described a common scenario in which individuals take advantage of women in the early stages of recovery:

13th-step. That's they job: to go there and prey on the weak women who five-days clean. You know, watch who raise they hand: "How you doin'? My name is Tyrone. You wanna go for some coffee?" All the time, they tryna have sex with 'em; they 13th-steppin' hard as can be. You know, this poor woman just came out of rehab—a program—[and] don't have nowhere to stay. So, the first thing she think: Mr. Wonderful is here and he's gonna sweep her off her feet and take her to la la land. And she goes for it. Next thing you know, she back out there using. "What happened to you?" "Girl, that nigga 13th-step me." And then you all messed up again; you gotta go back into detox. It's a game! They got some people that just prey on women like that, you know?

Though individuals may take advantage of women in various social situations, "13th-stepping" typically refers to women in recovery who are in programs such as Alcoholics Anonymous or Narcotics Anonymous. Lucinda believed some people considered it a "job" to prey on the women who seemed the most vulnerable in these programs. Formerly incarcerated mothers return to a society where others may initiate intimate relationships with dishonest and manipulative intentions, complicating the role of reentry and treatment programs as a safe space for women in recovery.

The Family

Much like intimate partners, family also functioned as both a positive and negative support network. Jesenia's father, for example, had previously served as her enabler, encouraging her drug use since he also had a history of substance use. At one point, Jesenia lived with him for two weeks while trying to remain abstinent, but she ran into issues with her father because of "his attitudes and his alcoholism." She learned that it was not in her best interest to live with another individual suffering from alcoholism, even though it happened to be her father. Notably, Jesenia believed her father still played the most vital role in helping her raise her son:

My father being able to tell me that: "You know what? You're human, you make mistakes but bottom line is that you're getting better. And I just want you to keep going." That's huge for me, especially considering that he's still active [in his alcohol use]. Like, he was my enabler at one point and now he's like my encouragement. . . . He's like: "[S]eriously, you're doing good and I don't want you to mess up and I don't want to be the reason you fall short.'"

It appears as though her father viewed himself as a potential risk to her sobriety, based on his statement that he did not want to be the reason she fell short in her recovery. Yet despite his previous role as her enabler, Jesenia still believed her father was the most helpful person in raising her son because he encouraged her to push forward in recovery to develop her maternal relationship. This demonstrates some of the complexities that even family members may present. They sometimes enabled the women's substance use and were detrimental influences in their recovery, yet they were also beneficial players in certain aspects of the women's recovery.

Research shows that because of the difficulties with navigating motherhood, some mothers find it better to have family members care for their children during and after incarceration—that is, until they are relatively situated in terms of housing, employment, and finances, among other things.[15] Consistent with this research, and as discussed in chapter 2, I found that family networks played a crucial role in shared mothering. Moreover, this shared mothering was particularly prevalent when the mothers had a history of substance use. Family members served as the children's caregivers when mothers were overpowered by drugs and alcohol and when the mothers were in recovery but were still establishing a foundation for themselves and their children. In general, many family members joined forces as a collective to try to avoid state intervention and the intrusion of strangers outside of their immediate community.

Onika's parents were "there" for her in that they raised her two oldest children. "I never really lived with my kids," Onika shared. Still, her parents allowed her to keep "parenting from a distance" by giving her the freedom to remain in contact with her children. "I would call once or twice a week. But, a lot of times, I called and didn't say nothing; I just wanted to hear my mother's voice or the background with the kids." While such positive family support was crucial during previous substance use and during present recovery efforts, this familial support did not come without its own adjustments to the women's actions and to the potential increase in shared mothering. Onika explained how her parents—especially her mother—remained helpful in her life, but some changes occurred in their relationship:

> My mother never, never turned her back on me; in spite of whatever I was doing, my mother was there. But, she was [there] from a distance because she couldn't take seeing me messed up. But, she was there—her and my dad.

Onika described her mother as being there, but being there "from a distance." During her interview, she gave some insight into *how* this distance surfaced. "I had to remove myself from her 'cause I couldn't keep seeing the pain." In this way, Onika described precipitating some of the distance as a way to protect her mother. Her mother also appeared to be distant to protect herself and Onika's children, whom she was raising. "She seen me outside in the street and I'm looking all messed up and she's going like this"—Onika demonstrates waving "no" with her hand—"like 'Don't approach me.'" While Onika distanced herself to protect her mother, her mother also did not want her approaching the house when she was under the influence. As Onika explained, "I always been close to my mom. It's just the drugs that had a strain" on the relationship. Some family members remained accessible and were willing to help the mothers during times of need, but the nature of the familial relationships had sometimes altered.

Karen also described shared mothering among her family members. Her children were at one time under the care of Karen's mother, until Karen's cousin ultimately adopted them. Karen believed her family members were "all right" toward her during and after her incarceration. She later elaborated on why, pointing out that her family understood drugs had been a long-standing sickness she faced: "This is like a history; it's like they dealt with it, they didn't scream on me or nothing like that. It's a *disease*. Addiction is a disease." Her family's view of her drug use as a disease appears to have shaped a supportive approach to her recovery efforts after her incarceration, in which Karen believed "everything is good. . . . We move forward. We don't stay stuck [in the past]."

At times, families were hesitant to believe the women had really changed or were even capable of such recovery. This contributed to family members providing relatively less support. For instance, Laura's family was "skeptical" that she would ever get better from her alcohol use because, as she described, she was in "such bad shape for so long." In other words, family's perceptions of the women's substance use shaped their level of assistance in the women's recovery. On the one hand, family members who believed substance use was a disease appeared to be supportive. This disease narrative did not blame the mothers and may have validated mothers' feelings and promoted their self-worth. On the other hand, family members who believed there were little chances of recovery were less likely to aid in the women's recovery, and this further limited the women's access to support. This was particularly evident when family viewed substance use as a cultural transgression, and family members served as penalizing agents of these transgressions by denying mothers their familial support, as discussed next.

"It's a Culture Thing." Common generalizations in existing literature discuss Black ethnic groups and their experiences under a "Black" racial umbrella. This treats the experiences of ethnic groups as joint and shared in all areas, rendering ethnic nuances invisible. While I found no apparent disparities in pathways into substance use between the African American, Latina, and West Indian mothers, I found that they might experience cultural distinctions in their family's response to substance use and assistance with recovery. African American mothers were most likely to have histories of substance use and to believe it contributed to later offending, yet they did not discuss culture or ethnic background as shaping their experiences. My conversations with West Indian mothers raised two interesting points, one concerning their personal experiences with substance use from a cultural perspective, and the other concerning their family's acceptance and assistance when they or other kin were battling substance use.

The West Indian mothers I spoke with were least likely to describe histories of substance use compared to the Latina and African American mothers. Likewise, the West Indian mothers were also less likely to describe substance use as a contributing factor in more serious offending behaviors. These disparities are consistent with other research that comparatively examines drug use among the West Indian population and other ethnic groups.[16] On the one hand, West Indian women may encounter fewer social-structural risks, which can protect them from using drugs or alcohol as a coping mechanism. On the other hand, West Indian mothers may have also been less likely to volunteer for an interview if they had a history of substance use given its stigma in this ethnic community. Scholars have found that the West Indian population may be especially susceptible to a "sanctioning network," stigmatizing and ostracizing those who do not conform to cultural ideals.[17] Drug use is seen as contradicting cultural ideologies, particularly when displayed by West Indian women and mothers, since cultural perceptions and expectations dictate that women and mothers should be good, trustworthy, responsible, and easy to control.[18] So it is possible that fear of further stigmatization discouraged more West Indian mothers from contacting me for an interview.

Of the West Indian mothers who volunteered their time to speak with me, their interviews suggest that they perceived my presence and conversation as being nonjudgmental, given their openness to discussing battles with substance use and sharing family conflicts from a cultural perspective. Marie, for instance, believed her family's West Indian background played a prominent role in her battles through substance use and incarceration because they misunderstood substance use and offending behaviors as a whole:

> I think culture plays a very big part in . . . a lot of things that *I* went through too because my family couldn't understand them. They couldn't understand prison, they didn't understand drug addiction. . . . And I said, "Ma, drug addict[ion] has no prejudice, just like prison has no prejudice."

Like Marie, West Indian mothers described a family disconnect with understanding substance use: a disconnect grounded in cultural ideology and a limited cultural understanding of what they were going through. In their work on drug and alcohol use among the Haitian community, Eustache Jean-Louis and his colleagues found that this population did not typically perceive substance use as an emotional or medical issue.[19] Instead, they often considered it the result of a jinx or curse placed on the individual, which was sufficient for exclusion. In addition, Jean-Louis and his colleagues found that the Haitian community in their study described family members as being unfamiliar with recovery, leading to further misunderstanding in familial relationships. Marie believed that this limited understanding of substance use weakened the support she received from family, hurting efforts at recovery for herself and for other West Indians in similar situations.

Compared to the narratives of family disappointment discussed among the African American and Latina mothers, the West Indian mothers were more likely to center their experiences on a cultural perspective of disappointment and subsequent indifference from family about their whereabouts. As Marie noted, "West Indians carry a lot of pride." The West Indian mothers suggested that this pride is harmed when there is drug use in the family, which contributes to family shame and abandonment. Kerry-Ann described a familial pride, sharing that her family in Jamaica included a nurse, a banker, and an engineer, who were "elitist." Although she did not have a history with drugs or alcohol herself, Kerry-Ann noted that her family had "discarded" her uncle, who had a history of drug use. Her father, for example, had severed communication with his own brother. Interestingly, she laughed in a distant manner as she derogatorily referred to her uncle as "a crackhead," in diminished concern for his well-being. Her choice of words and her laughter while talking about her uncle demonstrate her own personal disconnect from him due to his substance use. Although Kerry-Ann was incarcerated for selling drugs, her account suggests that substance use was relatively more dishonoring to her family.

Compared to the African American and Latina mothers, the West Indian mothers were most likely to describe such ostracization because their substance use was seen as a violation of group norms. As a result, their family members functioned as penalizing agents of this cultural transgression by withholding their emotional support and tangible assistance. Considering the importance of family members in shared mothering, disengaged family can have serious implications for formerly incarcerated mothers battling substance use. For instance, weakened family acceptance and assistance may worsen West Indian women's financial condition during times of need, discourage their efforts to seek emotional guidance, and limit shared mothering when they are seeking employment or attending to other post-incarceration responsibilities.

Social Perceptions of Substance Use and Motherhood

Once they become visible to society as having "spoiled identities" in which they are called "addicts" or bad (m)others, it becomes challenging for mothers of color to disassociate from these imposed labels. Instead of being seen as people who could use support through unfortunate circumstances, the public sees them as flawed *individuals*. Even as they made progress in their recovery and in maternal relationships, this progress was often not sufficient to alter the image that society had of them as visible (m)others. Direct attacks on their maternal identities were less common when the women were in recovery compared to when they were actively using, but they still encountered undesirable judgments and personal attacks on their character that conflicted with how the mothers viewed themselves.

Priscilla, for instance, had a history of using crack cocaine, heroin, and methamphetamine. She believed that society automatically stigmatized individuals because of a problem they were battling and ultimately treated them, including herself, as "bad" people. Even though she was fifteen months clean at the time of her interview, Priscilla believed society continued to stigmatize her because of a label imposed on her, even though she did not view herself in the same way:

> The stigma is: once an addict, always an addict. Some people admire the courage of someone in the process of recovery in life. And some people don't; some people look at that person as a junkie even though they go to meetings."

Like Priscilla, other mothers were exposed to negative commentary and treatment based on social perceptions that "once an addict, always an addict." Marie described how this stigma was exposed through the biased questions she was asked by the welfare office. When attempting to apply for welfare, the welfare office representative asked her, "What's your drug of choice?" Marie perceived this question as having an underlying assumption that she was *still* engaged in drug use although she had been clean for two years. She described her response to me. "I said, 'Excuse you? What *was* my drug of choice?'" In her response, she corrected the welfare office representative and provided her with a form of questioning that was more suitable for her current situation. This correction was an active way for Marie to alter and improve the nature of her visibility from someone who was actively using drugs (as implied by the representative's wording) to someone who was in recovery and whose drug use was behind her. The distinction between "What is your drug of choice?" and "What was your drug of choice?" may appear minute to the general public, but correcting this is a protective response to present herself through a more positive lens within a context of stigma and state disempowerment.

Still, mothers commonly described feelings of worthlessness as they dealt with public criticism and navigated complex circumstances tied to their previous substance use. They made statements such as, "I felt worthless about myself and I felt that I wasn't a good mother." When I met Priscilla, she had three sons, who were 25, 17, and 9 years old. As Priscilla explained: "I felt that I lost half of my kids' life.... It brings your self-esteem down for you as a woman." According to the mothers' narratives, however, these feelings of worthlessness changed once they were able to disregard societal perceptions of them.

> *JGH:* What is something that you would say to society?
>
> *Priscilla:* That I'm not a bad mother.... That I'm a person that suffers from addiction.... And I will forever be in the process of recovery in my life.... And that there are many people out there who are being

stigmatized, and it doesn't have to be addiction or drugs. It could be mental health issues, you know. It could be mothers suffering from mental health issues. It could be so many other different things that society automatically stigmatizes you and you're not good because you have this problem.

Despite the nature of visibility to the general public that focused on her substance use history, Priscilla began to believe in herself, with the help of others. She believed "there's hope with help," noting the role of a positive support network in helping her gain self-confidence in maintaining her sobriety:

I started going to meetings, and networking and meeting other recovery addicts, and seeing that I'm not alone and I can't do this alone. Having a good network behind my back and the staff of [drug treatment program], I just started feeling, I guess.

As Priscilla described, she began "feeling" again once she realized that she was not alone with her maternal obstacles in recovery post-incarceration. Priscilla's narrative demonstrates how having a positive support network can be instrumental in helping the women build their self-confidence, further encouraging recovery efforts.

Reentry and Treatment Programs

The mothers I interviewed often discussed the impact of reentry programs and treatment programs on their recovery journey. The purpose of reentry programs is to help individuals transition from prison or jail and reenter the community. Some reentry programs are offered within correctional facilities to prepare individuals for their forthcoming release, but others are offered after incarceration to support individuals through the various obstacles they may encounter post-incarceration. Due to the criminalization of substance use that fuels incarceration, reentry programs often include a treatment component for people in recovery or seeking recovery. In addition to these reentry programs that are intended to broadly help those in the criminal legal system reenter the community, treatment programs are intended to assist individuals with histories of substance use. Treatment programs can be open to the general public seeking recovery support or can be catered specifically to those with some involvement in carceral systems, often collaborating with judges and parole or probation officers interested in progress reports about substance use.

Both reentry and treatment programs had some benefits for the formerly incarcerated mothers. For instance, mothers described the positive impact of treatment programs on their recovery, which was true whether such programs were inpatient programs, in which the mothers lived in residential programs, or outpatient programs, in which mothers lived elsewhere and traveled to the program location. This was also true whether the women voluntarily enrolled in treatment programs or were mandated to participate in treatment programs as a condition of their parole. These programs provided the women with a space to discuss their obstacles, to listen to others with similar experiences, and to see the visual proof that it was possible to make progress in their recovery despite past and potential hurdles. As Marie explained:

> It's the networking with people who have been where I've been. The NA [Narcotics Anonymous] meetings that I don't have to go to, but I choose to go to. That I have a commitment in and they teach me to have a commitment and hearing the people share that have been through what I've been through. People that's been through where I've been through and have gone far. . . . Who have said that their lives are amazing now. And even so, their lives are still bad some days but it's better than that [drug] life.

Seeing that progress *is* possible often gave the women hope in their own recovery and facilitated the development of self-confidence:

> I started loving myself and realizing that—you know what?—I'm not this bad person that society says I am. And I can change this around if I don't like the situation I'm in. *I* am in control and I can change this around.

Women also described program workers' interest in "trying to understand, why do we use?" as another helpful aspect of treatment programs. Jesenia explained that she previously held a mindset that was "all about staying clean," but this changed once she joined a program: "I'm learning that the program isn't just about staying clean; it's about coping mechanisms and learning how to live life on daily terms and learning what the responsibility entails in doing that."

In a way, reentry programs and treatment programs boosted the mothers' self-confidence and protected them from some of the negative social perceptions. However, as I describe in the following sections, this protection was still limited because the stigma about them as visible (m)others persisted within these programmatic spaces.

Treatment Programs as Enforcers of State Control. Even though social and political interest in treatment programs has grown, such programs may function as enforcers of state control. In some jurisdictions, individuals battling substance use can be diverted to a specialized court program called Drug Court that functions as an alternative to incarceration if the person completes drug treatment and other designated requirements. If incarcerated, individuals are often required to attend drug treatment programs post-incarceration as a condition of their community-based parole supervision. Given the overlap with the criminal legal system, these treatment programs report progress to Drug Court judges and parole officers, and determinations of poor progress could result in (re)incarceration. Yet the systemic understanding of "progress" is shaped by a stigmatizing ideology about substance use that individualizes blame; progress is often defined as the complete removal of any and all substance use, in which a relapse signifies a lack of personal control or individual change. This largely ignores the social circumstances (like trauma) and structural circumstances (like restricted services for invisible mothers of color) that influence substance use and trigger relapse. To complicate matters further, program practices that individualize blame are often intentionally demeaning and punitive toward criminalized (m)others of color, hindering the completion of treatment programs and then reincarcerating the women for not meeting parole requirements. In this way, treatment programs function as enforcers of state control by, one, partnering with parole officers to regulate mothers' whereabouts and, two, extending their punishment due to punitive program policies and program assessments of progress and setbacks that are tied to stigmatizing ideologies of substance use.[20]

Some mothers associated being ready for recovery with "admitting that I had a problem," critiquing themselves and accepting the need for individual change as the initial steps to recovery. Unfortunately, however, they likely learned this way of understanding within the country's punitive carceral systems, which forces mothers to condemn themselves to receive treatment assistance.[21] Sociologists have found that judges delivered "tough love" as they seemingly provided defendants with an opportunity for treatment instead of incarceration, all the while threatening them with incarceration if they failed the standards of treatment programs.[22] Stacy Lee Burns and Mark Peyrot found that Drug Court judges required defendants to describe themselves as "addicts"; otherwise, the judges believed they were in denial, were not taking ownership of their actions, and were less worthy of receiving treatment. This illustrates how the carceral system individualizes substance use and encourages individuals to take full personal responsibility for falling victim to the grasp of controlled substances.[23] A rhetoric of personal responsibility is used to justify why the women are the problem and not the social-structural circumstances that led to their substance use.[24]

By expecting and often requiring women to take full personal responsibility, treatment programs are seemingly arguing that they can "fix" visible (m)others with substance use histories. This notion of "fixing" individuals fuels collaborations between punitive carceral systems and treatment programs, further expanding a coordination of state control. Criminal justice personnel and social service providers expect women to describe themselves as "broken" and in need of "fixing," which demonstrates the politics of therapeutic language and a linguistic script that clients must follow when trying to portray themselves as sober.[25] Criminologist Erin Kerrison argues that within prison-based therapeutic communities (TCs), the "failure to master these linguistic performances can result in the denial of material and symbolic resources, thus participants learn how to use TC language to present themselves in ways that support existing institutionalized hierarchies, even if that surrender spells their self-denigration."[26] As seen with the mother who described herself as a "money addict," learned self-denigration was also evident among the women I interviewed. This understanding of a money addict is the epitome of institutional language that encourages the mothers to accept personal responsibility in a denigrating way while diminishing the reality that their actions were often survival mechanisms against the systematic oppression they faced as women of color.

Ultimately, the coordination of state control and the scripts of "broken" selves imposed on these women may cause more harm than good, as this approach perpetuates the disempowerment that women of color experience as a marginalized group. These definitions of substance use are embedded in racialized and sexist narratives. Throughout this book, I have highlighted how, as a marginalized group, women of color encounter oppression across various aspects of social-structural systems like custody, housing, and employment. This systematic dismissal of social-structural factors has serious social implications in how narratives about substance use pertain to women of color. Put simply, society does not view or treat women of color as victims of systematic oppression; instead, their visibility in society is a function of their being seen as incarcerable subjects. Once visible, women of color are especially vulnerable to criminalization and to state-imposed control within punitive carceral systems.[27] This visibility of women of color battling substance use differs compared to more privileged groups, particularly white women, who are viewed and treated as innocent victims of their circumstances. White women are viewed through a lens of victimization and necessary assistance that is not afforded to women of color.

Furthermore, the nature of their visibility and the individualizing of substance use have serious practical implications for how treatment programs function and respond to mothers of color. Qiana was in a reentry program for the second time, after initially relapsing during her first time in the program. She described some issues with program practices that complicated women's participation. For instance, treatment programs concentrate on the surveillance of their program participants, arguing that this is to protect the women. Qiana countered that this surveillance from her program was the equivalent of having "a fine microscope" constantly focused on her merely because of her past. Such a microscope is simply another way to scrutinize and control marginalized populations beyond prison walls. As the women have highlighted, the program staff did not "really trust them or believe in them due to the past." Instead, Qiana argued that program staff members focused on making constant remarks about the women's need for abstinence. "That's actually annoying to hear everybody [say]: 'straight and narrow.' Okay, I understand. I know that I have to do that. I don't need constant reminders every day because that gets annoying." As described throughout this book, formerly incarcerated women of color may encounter a wide array of obstacles after their release in meeting the expectations of family, the criminal legal system, and broader society. Combined with the post-incarceration obstacles women typically face, the fine microscope of treatment programs and the hypersurveillance of what women *shouldn't* do may create additional tensions. Qiana cautioned against the constant reminders from program personnel of their recovery obligations and the program's emphasis on negative consequences from potential setbacks. As she explained:

> Hearing that repetitive[ly], for one, it could go in either a positive way or a negative. Most cases—not gonna lie—it turns out negative. When . . . somebody constantly feels like they're being watched and that they're not doing what they have to do or that they don't feel like they're good enough, that's when that person goes downhill.

Qiana's account demonstrates how treatment programs have become complicit as a manifestation of state control and hypersurveillance. Such repetition from program staff to remain on the "straight and narrow" translates to enduring doubt of their abilities and systemic disempowerment, even within programs that are supposed to help them.

If programs are genuinely invested in helping women of color in recovery, they must have a clear understanding of who the women are and who they want to be. At the time that I met Rashida, she was in recovery from heroin and was interning at a local counseling center in Queens to help other formerly incarcerated women in their recovery. Her internship experience at the counseling center provided some unique insight into program downfalls. "What are they offering in the program?" Rashida asked. "If they're just going there to keep clean, then no. That's not a good thing." As she explained, "It's not one of these 1, 2, 3 things. It's not about statistics. It's not about your fiscal year. It's not about that; it's about the people." She argued that some program personnel emphasized the mere functioning of the program, upholding a more distanced approach rather than getting to know the women personally and providing each of them with individual assistance specific to their needs:

> If you're taking away the way they used to living, what are they gonna do when they return? You gotta give them options: "You can go to this now." "You can go for that now." "What do you choose to do?" "What was your desire?" "What is your dream?"

Being in recovery herself and also in a position to help other women, Rashida believed the most important components of treatment programs were inquiring about the women's own dreams and personal desires and providing them with practical suggestions based on this knowledge. The problem is that treatment programs often have limited ability or interest to provide program participants with needed personalized attention and assistance. The default approach then becomes one that is detached from the women's realities, which is ultimately less helpful for the women.

Mothers argued that instead of the hypersurveillance of telling them what they *shouldn't* do and the generic demands for them to make progress, treatment programs should devote more attention to providing constructive suggestions about what they *can* do in the midst of their circumstances. Rather than denigrating the women and perpetuating a system of penal control, treatment programs would be more effective as a source of empowerment that recognizes their strengths and provides positive reassurance about the women's abilities to remain in recovery. Qiana's treatment program lacked this type of empowerment.

Fortunately, for her, she was able to receive constructive suggestions and empowerment from family members:

> My family is the type of people that like: 'Listen, okay, yeah you messed up, but these are the other areas that you're good in. So use *that* to overcome *that* negative.' You know so that's the difference between my family and here [at this program].

Qiana criticized her program in that it did not provide her with the strengths-based approach she found helpful to remain in recovery.

Though she was fortunate enough to receive this empowerment from her family members, many other women seek the support of treatment programs for this very empowerment. Qiana believed successful programs were those that took this approach in attempting to understand the underlying issues women faced and working with them to "find other ways" and show constructive alternatives to drug or alcohol use. As Qiana argued:

> If I'm doing something good, at least once in a while like: "Listen, you're doing a good job." I'm not saying all the time but just to let me know that I'm doing what I have to do and it's being *noticed*, and not just the negative 'cause I think people focus on the negative more than they do the positive.

Qiana's account is consistent with research that shows a strengths-based approach that provides empowerment is especially beneficial for marginalized groups.[28] More emphasis on empowering formerly incarcerated women of color, specifically acknowledging their strengths in enduring a system of oppression and providing them with positive reinforcements when they make progress in their recovery, would be a productive step forward.

Additionally, mothers believed that programs varied based on whether the program personnel had personal experiences with substance use and were able to relate to their maternal experiences post-incarceration. They believed the most beneficial programs employed women who personally understood their past struggles, current realities, and goals of sobriety. In the absence of personal or vicarious experiences with substance use and maternal incarceration among program personnel, programs may contribute to mothers' othering and run the risk of exposing them to additional stressors in their recovery. In fact, research shows that a lack of compassion makes for a "bad" counselor, and having "bad" counselors can weaken women's investment in treatment programs and may push them to leave.[29]

Hostility within Treatment Programs. Even within treatment programs designed to assist formerly incarcerated women in their recovery, state help remains embedded within a culture of policing and stigmatizing mothers who have histories of substance use. Unfortunately, the environment and structure of treatment programs exposed the mothers to hostility from other program participants who echoed the individualizing of blame that is forced upon them by the carceral state.

When a woman enrolls in a drug treatment program, the question arises: "Is she gonna make it?" As Carolina described, these questions come from the women who have managed some time in recovery:

> Everybody comes—mostly everybody—from prison with a history of this and a history of drugs or whatever. Some make it, some don't. . . . The ones that's made it will be like: "Will this one make it or she won't make it?"

Jesenia shared that she went into a drug treatment program to "learn how to stay abstinent," but she was overwhelmed by verbal "attacks" from other women who had been in recovery longer. Although she was making progress by avoiding drug use, other program participants criticized her drinking with remarks like "you're not working the steps." She explained:

> I lost the hope because I was getting judged by certain people—not everyone, but certain people with substantial clean time. . . . I was like, "You know what? If you gonna attack me, I'm better off in the street. I didn't come here to be attacked."

This account is consistent with research demonstrating that the criticism of women battling substance use comes not only come from broader society, but also from others with substance use histories and those with more time in recovery.[30]

The judgmental treatment Jesenia and Carolina received from others with more clean time is an example of "defensive othering": the symbolic degradation of another group. Since one's sense of self is defined in relation to other groups, defensive othering is a common way to form one's own identity.[31] This may be especially true for criminalized (m)others since defensive othering allows them to say defensively that *other* mothers are worse than they are. I argue that this defensive othering in treatment programs is a protective response to the culture and structure of these programs. Treatment programs operate within the carceral state and, as previously discussed, carceral systems individualize substance use as a sign of "brokenness" in response to which program personnel engage in hypersurveillance as a corrective measure to supposedly "fix" them. This individualizing of blame within treatment programs encourages participants to police and judge those in early recovery, shifting the gaze of state control toward others while protecting their own image. Yet the culture of hypersurveillance in treatment programs may encourage participants to form their identity at the expense of other criminalized (m)others, undermining solidarity among them. In fact, these hostile program interactions previously caused Jesenia to have "lost the hope" in her recovery. She argued that others' doubt about their recovery often contributed to feelings of worthlessness and low self-esteem. Jesenia shared that the more judgment is directed at mothers, "the more they're gonna feed into it, the more they're gonna feel worthless, the more they're gonna feel like why should they even bother if you gonna judge her anyways." Unfortunately, the program conditions that foster defensive othering may not only injure the self-confidence that helps mothers manage recovery, but may also impact their reentry into the community more broadly.

Hostility within Reentry Programs. Similar to treatment programs, reentry programs might also expose formerly incarcerated mothers to hostility and defensive othering within networks of other criminalized groups. Of the 11 mothers I interviewed *without* some history of substance use, some said little about those battling drugs or alcohol, while others openly expressed their beliefs and their agitation with this group.

For instance, in speaking about her upcoming release from parole supervision, Ana shared that she was continuing to follow parole conditions like reporting to her parole officer. Yet she added that "some people have a problem reporting [to parole]," highlighting those battling substance use. Ana distinguished herself, noting that because she did not do drugs she "don't have to worry" and "don't even have a problem" with reporting to parole. This comment came with the assumption that those with histories of substance use inevitably *do* have such problems and concerns with reporting to parole. Other mothers, however, were more critical. "I never done drugs or alcohol," Francesca proclaimed. "I can't understand these fuckers," she said, laughing. "Believe me, I learned *one* thing: drug addicts and alcoholics, they *always* go back. They can't help it. They just go back. . . . They'll sell their mothers. They'll sell their own asses. They sell their kids." Francesca believed that "there's no recovery," which coincides with some public rhetoric about drug and alcohol use.[32] Francesca took these assumptions a bit further than common public rhetoric, arguing that because there was "no recovery," these mothers had a "death wish."

> If you have a motivation to go try to kill yourself; instead of killing yourself softly, just take yourself out of your Goddamn misery. . . . Why torture and torment other people around you, and torment yourself? You're killing yourself slowly. So, since you're on a death wish, might as well do it all together. Overdose and get it over with. That's my sentiment towards drug addicts and alcoholics.

Francesca showed no sympathy toward those battling drug or alcohol use, believing they were on a suicide mission. I found that mothers like Ana and Francesca tried to deflect the stigma they faced as formerly incarcerated mothers by describing themselves as different from and better than other released mothers who battled with substance use. In doing so, they were engaging in defensive othering, singling out other women with similar experiences of incarceration by disparaging them for their substance use. This is consistent with research demonstrating that criminalized women use defensive othering narratives to disassociate themselves from being labeled as "addicts" and to differentiate themselves from generic stigmatization as bad (m)others.[33]

The prevalence of defensive othering encouraged me to consider my positionality in these conversations. Did they feel the need to disassociate from (m)others battling substance use in order to protect their own identity in my presence? I examined statements of defensive othering to understand the conversational context. For instance, it appears as though Ana's defensive othering was not an act of protecting her identity in my presence but was grounded in her criticism of parole surveillance. She believed her parole supervision was excessive: "I don't feel I should have to be supervised. I just don't feel it. I feel it's absurd." Yet she believed it was excessive and absurd *because* she "don't do anything illegal" and "don't do drugs." Her comments and criticisms of parole came with underlying assumptions about who deserved parole supervision and who had issues with reporting to parole that were ultimately critical of individuals with drug use histories. Additionally, it appears that Francesca's defensive othering was grounded in her perceived learned knowledge within carceral systems. Although I asked Francesca about public perceptions of mothering among criminalized mothers, her response focused on what she personally had "learned" about people during and after incarceration. She presented herself as an outside expert on women battling substance use, but in doing so, her statements were bluntly critical. As we sat across from each other in her home, it was clear throughout her interview that Francesca felt comfortable sharing her personal opinions with me as she gave long and detailed responses to my inquiries, filled with jokes and cursing. Thus, I do not believe my positionality as a researcher influenced her defensive othering to protect her identity in my presence, given that straightforward comments and frank criticisms were consistent throughout our conversation.

Unfortunately, such negative perceptions and hostility may complicate relationships between participants in reentry programs and among formerly incarcerated mothers. At the time of Valerie's interview, she was homeless and waiting at an intake center for placement in a New York City shelter. She had no history of substance use and wholeheartedly believed this hurt her opportunities in receiving housing placement:

> I don't sell drugs, I don't use drugs so I wanna get an apartment, but I can't. . . . It's *sad*, 'cause I even went somewhere and asked the lady can they help me get an apartment, and she said, "Oh no. You didn't have a dirty urine, so we can't help you." So I said, "If I had a dirty urine, you'd help me?"

Valerie then imitated the housing representative responding to her with an annoyed voice, "She said, 'Miss, I don't make the rules, I just work here!'" At the time of her interview, Valerie believed she was at a disadvantage to receive housing placement because she was "not messed up on drugs or [had] no dirty urine." It is true that some supportive housing agreements in New York City have targeted populations such as young adults at risk for homelessness after foster care; homeless adults with mental illnesses or battling substance use; and families that are chronically homeless or at risk of homelessness with a household head suffering from mental illness, substance use, or with HIV/AIDS.[34] These target populations are typically identified to address chronic homelessness and to ensure these groups receive supportive services in specialized housing units. But as someone who did not have a history of use or mental illness, Valerie viewed target populations as an unfair disadvantage for her that seemingly downgraded the impact of her housing obstacles on her children's well-being: "So, they try to say that my kids aren't important because I don't do drugs?" Interestingly, this narrative suggests a sense of deservingness in which some may believe they are more deserving of reentry services because they are not associated with drugs or alcohol. Despite the women having some shared reentry experiences as mothers in the criminal legal system, the fight for limited reentry services may contribute to defensive othering to highlight one's own deservingness for help over that of other visible (m)others, as shown with Valerie.

Although doubts from other formerly incarcerated mothers may mimic those of the larger public, these mothers are rarely discussed as perpetrators of defensive othering toward those with substance use histories. Furthermore, defensive othering is rarely examined within the social and structural context of treatment and reentry programs that individualize blame for substance use and that may encourage defensive othering. It is important to understand these perceptions given that defensive othering may be subtly or overtly apparent to mothers in recovery, complicating their interactions and undermining the potential benefits of reentry programs.

CONCLUSION

In general, formerly incarcerated mothers share similar experiences not only as women with children, but also as visible (m)others in the criminal legal system. This chapter has emphasized the maternal experiences of those in recovery and examined how histories of substance use complicated how they were viewed and treated by others.

As a means of navigating motherhood post-incarceration, the mothers felt encouraged to seek recovery. This was true for mothers both after one stint of incarceration as well as after multiple cycles of incarceration. Though some mothers worked to recover maternal roles that were perceived as lost and others worked to enhance weakened maternal roles, the mothers shared the motivation to offset negative effects of drug or alcohol use and to prevent further harm to their children from a potential relapse. However, this chapter has demonstrated that it was often difficult for these mothers to enact their social role as caretakers and to fulfill their personal desires to rebuild and maintain mother-child relationships while in recovery. They experienced tensions in meeting the expectations of family, of parole supervision, and of broader society while simultaneously trying to cope with these stressors without relapsing. Furthermore, these efforts were sometimes more stressful for mothers in the early phases of their recovery, mothers with at least some contact with their children, mothers with greater maternal accountability, and mothers of West Indian background who seemingly committed cultural transgressions.

While bouts of incarceration may generally elicit societal and familial stigma against criminalized women, previous substance use subjected these women to further criminalization, more criticism of their maternal identity as visible (m)others, skepticism about their progress, and additional isolation from assistance. The mothers encountered stigma from society not only as visible (m)others in the criminal legal system, but also as visible (m)others with histories of drug or alcohol use. Yet judgment and stigma came not only from those outside the criminal legal system. In fact, mothers experienced hostility and defensive othering within reentry programs from those without substance use histories and within treatment programs from those with more clean time. Labels like "addicts" or "bad (m)others" imposed on the women influenced the treatment they received, even when in recovery, and at times prompted additional obstacles to their recovery and their reentry into the community post-incarceration.

Bearing in mind the interplay of gender and racial-ethnic nuances, social service providers should not ignore the intersectional experiences of women of color. Nuances existed in familial responses to the women's past use. West Indian mothers, in particular, expressed a cultural disadvantage in receiving help from family because of cultural meanings and misunderstandings about substance use and perceptions of cultural transgressions. Although I cannot argue that familial lack of support contributed to more serious offending when alcohol or drugs were involved, the women's narratives demonstrate how this weakened support from family complicates their recovery. The nature of their visibility, as seemingly tarnishing family pride and social status, may deter these women from seeking help with their substance use. Work by Eustache Jean-Louis and his colleagues illustrates the benefits of programs that understand the culturally specific obstacles faced by West Indians battling substance use. Even though their study emphasizes the experiences of Haitians, it highlights the role of cultural perceptions in family members' understanding and treatment of those with substance use histories. As the authors argue, "Many treatment programs lack an understanding of and sensitivity to ethnic cultures. This understanding and sensitivity is necessary to be effective."[35] Developing an adequate understanding of these social circumstances and cultural experiences should be a goal in current and future efforts to aid formerly incarcerated women and mothers of West Indian background.

Understanding this overlap between post-incarceration motherhood, recovery, and reentry is also crucial for individuals tasked with helping this population. Obstacles in navigating motherhood and managing recovery can have serious implications for gender-responsive programs grounded in the realities of women's experiences. On the one hand, we see that motherhood often encouraged mothers' sobriety to offset the negative effects of substance use on their children. Since motherhood often shaped their plans and actions, reentry and treatment programs should not overlook the role of motherhood for formerly incarcerated mothers in recovery. On the other hand, however, navigating motherhood while managing sobriety also introduced additional stressors that further demanded the presence of positive social support networks. Consistent with existing reentry research on formerly incarcerated women, the mothers believed the presence of a positive support network after incarceration was instrumental in balancing life in recovery and reentry after incarceration. They described how positive social interactions with others facilitated their self-confidence and encouraged recovery efforts. As I have highlighted, however, the women's social networks had both costs and benefits. While this chapter displayed the benefit of programs in demonstrating to mothers that they were not alone and recovery was possible, these programs must also safeguard against further condemnation from other program participants and belittling from program personnel, as this conduct may offset the potential benefits of reentry and treatment programs. Ultimately, I urge programs to incorporate the information in this chapter into anti-carceral approaches that support and empower formerly incarcerated mothers within this overlap of reentry, recovery, and navigation of motherhood as a marginalized group.

Conclusion

"Within this country where racial difference creates a constant, if un-spoken, distortion of vision," argues feminist activist Audre Lorde, women of color "have on the one hand always been highly visible, and so, on the other hand, have been rendered invisible through the de-personalization of racism."[1] *Invisible Mothers*, as a form of matricen-tric (i.e., mother-centered) feminism, analyzes the paradox of mothers' invisibility as mothers of color and their visibility as (m)others for supposedly mothering in ways "other than" what is normatively ex-pected or accepted. More specifically, mothers of color are invisible to the public eye as targets of racialized oppression in which they are systematically restricted from resources and stripped of equal oppor-tunities given to white mothers to do motherwork. *Invisible Mothers* demonstrates how African American, West Indian, and Latina mothers become visible if and when they pursue unconventional ways to do motherwork with restricted resources, then are demeaned as visible (m)others for challenging white middle-class norms of motherhood. In an effort to adjust the blurred lens and challenge the distorted vi-sion of them as (m)others, this book shares personal narratives from formerly incarcerated mothers of color. In doing so, *Invisible Mothers* demonstrates the complexities of motherhood for African American, West Indian, and Latina mothers within punitive carceral systems and portrays them as visible human beings who deserve to be heard, rather than spoken about and condemned.

On the one hand, *Invisible Mothers* supports existing research showing that motherhood is a motivation for women post-incarceration.[2] On the other hand, the book also demonstrates how carceral systems can have a detrimental impact on mothers as they struggle with the socio-structural and psychological toll of systemic oppression and penal control, while navigating motherhood as criminalized (m)others. This conclusion reviews how our carceral state of disempowerment, hyper-surveillance, and criminalization denies the maternity of mothers of color and overlooks their motherwork. It discusses how suppressing the dissonance between their maternal hopes and their practical reentry barriers allowed these mothers to lean into their motherwork as a form of resiliency after incarceration. I also present areas for future research and suggest steps forward, using anti-oppressive efforts to minimize the carceral grasp and its punitive impact on mothers of color.

THE RESILIENCY OF MOTHERWORK
THROUGH DISSONANCE

Even though a maternal role often empowers mothers during and after incarceration, *Invisible Mothers* reveals how mothers' social position within a carceral state is often tied to complicated circumstances and state-imposed obstacles in navigating motherhood. This book synthesizes the added strain that mothers of color encounter from parole stipulations, custody requirements, limited housing, and restricted employment opportunities. It also demonstrates how stigma attached to criminalized (m)others can influence complicated treatment from their own family members, local communities, and program personnel and clients. The formerly incarcerated mothers described their motherwork as trial and error through these complicated circumstances. They at times simultaneously met their ideals of motherhood while also contradicting them in practice, which was typically due to a combination of social treatment, structural obstacles, and individual efforts as marginalized and limited agents. Despite this dissonance between their maternal hopes and their practical experiences,[3] the formerly incarcerated mothers engaged in protective functions to reduce dissonance and remain resilient in their motherwork. They accomplished this through three mechanisms. First, mothers fought for their maternal interests as they dealt with state control (like parole) and navigated state interventions (like child welfare services). Second, mothers reframed social constructions of motherhood to fit their circumstances and disassociate themselves from imposed labels of being bad (m)others. Third, mothers trivialized the extent of maternal disengagement and reaffirmed their maternal identities and their motherwork by highlighting positive maternal relationships. The following subsections examine the dissonance mothers experienced in a carceral state and how they made efforts to reduce this dissonance.

Dissonance and the Carceral State

Invisible Mothers displays how the carceral state complicates the post-incarceration experiences of mothers of color by imposing various burdens on their personal lives and maternal relationships during reentry. One challenge is that these women are forced to mother through the hypersurveillance of parole and of law enforcement in their communities. The carceral state also imposes unequal burdens on mothers of color through state demands to adhere to white, middle-class social constructions of motherhood, especially as a prerequisite for regaining custodial rights post-incarceration. Upon their return to the community, the women are stigmatized as (m)others for seemingly contradicting maternal expectations because of their previous incarceration, especially when they have been criminalized as a result of substance use. These social and structural circumstances create a dissonance between what the mothers strive for after incarceration and what they are able to do as criminalized (m)others within a carceral state of disempowerment, hypersurveillance, and criminalization.

Mothering in a State of Disempowerment. "An important feature of the law," argues professor Keesha Middlemass, "is how it establishes who matters and who does not while simultaneously empowering some while making 'others' invisible."[4] Mothers of color have historically been restricted from equal opportunities compared to their white and male counterparts and are systematically deprived of power within various social institutions.[5] As shown throughout *Invisible Mothers*, this disempowerment of mothers of color is intertwined with their (in)visibility. Mothers of color are treated as invisible mothers who do not matter and who are not valued as a social group in a stratified society. As a result, they are left systematically disempowered with structural obstacles in their everyday lives and in performing social expectations of motherhood. They only become visible (m)others when they reframe social constructions of motherhood to fit their circumstances, and then they are criminalized and punished for how they overcome their disempowerment. This demonstrates a nexus in mothers of color being treated as both invisible mothers and visible (m)others.

Invisible Mothers highlights how child welfare policies can misconstrue living in poverty as signs of neglect, deeming poor mothers of color unfit parents as a result of their underprivilege and disempowerment. This determination from the child welfare system apparently demands state intervention to remove children from mothers' custody instead of empowering the mothers by providing them with the tangible resources to meet family needs.[6] After losing custody, mothers of color remained penalized in trying to regain custody rights when their motherwork did not coincide with preconceived notions of maternal fitness. Even though mothers prided themselves on the emotional care work they dedicated to their children and the effort they devoted to improving maternal relationships, this motherwork was still insufficient to demonstrate maternal fitness to child welfare services. As discussed in chapter 2, the mothers often found themselves facing an uphill battle to be deemed fit amid the multiple strict requirements to gain custody of underage children. When mothers had no contact with underage children, they believed it was because of the disempowerment by child welfare services and the actions of temporary caregivers, who could facilitate or hinder mothers' communication with their children. To complicate matters further, mothers expressed frustration with program personnel and parole officers who exploited their custodial status to constantly hold threats over the women's heads if they did not meet technical parole standards or program expectations. This is an attack on the very maternal relationships that can be a source of empowerment and motivation to persevere after incarceration.

Mothering in a State of Hypersurveillance. In a way, law enforcement personnel—whether local police officers, correctional officers, parole officers, or federal officers—function as gatekeepers to freedom, particularly for people of color.[7] Chapter 1 demonstrates how parole officers function as gatekeepers to "earning" freedom post-incarceration. More specifically, it highlights various parole stipulations that the mothers were required to follow but that were difficult to accomplish given the wide reach of punitive carceral systems in communities of color. The mothers considered parole supervision to be unpredictable, time-consuming, and composed of stipulations like curfews that not only complicated their reentry but also complicated their efforts to retain or improve mother-child relationships. To them, parole supervision operated as social-structural oppression that imposed additional burdens post-incarceration more than it facilitated reentry into the community. In fact, the mothers equated their parole supervision to a "surveillance state," with modern-day lynchings designed to lead to their demise. Hypersurveillance of mothers under parole and within carceral systems more broadly is tied to their hypervisibility for having a criminal record, which follows them well after incarceration. The mothers were forced to overcome the obstacles of parole to fight for their maternal interests and essentially earn their freedom as mothers in this community-based form of penal control.

Mothering in a State of Criminalization. Motherhood in general is not free of difficulties and parenting stress, but the literature has focused on the parenting stress among single mothers, first-time mothers, teenage or older mothers, and disabled mothers or mothers with ill or disabled children, as well as working mothers in a variety of professional fields.[8] Like these mothers, mothers in carceral systems also deal with the stresses of motherhood, but in the process they must face the policies that criminalized them and must also tackle their marginalization for having a criminal record.

In the same way that systematic disempowerment and state hypersurveillance are tied to their invisibility as mothers and visibility as (m)others, mothers of color are subject to criminalization, especially when they have a history of substance use. Possessing their drug of choice and dealing with the influence of substance use on other nonviolent behaviors render them "incarcerable subjects" who are supposedly deserving of penal control, ensnaring them into carceral systems. In addition to facing common parenting stresses of motherhood, mothers of color who are battling substance use must deal with the gendered and racialized marginalization pushing them into and holding them under the grasp of the criminal legal system, while also trying to navigate recovery and motherhood in a state of criminalization.

As shown in chapter 4, recovery efforts were driven by the women's desires to establish or mend mother-child relationships and to prevent potential relapses that could lead to more unfavorable circumstances in their reentry and for their children. Even though maternal roles inspired mothers to maintain sobriety, especially when they had contact with children, social-structural reentry barriers put them at greater risk of emotional turmoil and endangered recovery efforts that triggered relapses as a coping mechanism. Positive toxicology tests could extend their time under parole supervision or land them back under incarceration. In this way, substance use is used as a proxy for treating them as disposable, incarcerable subjects.

Remaining clean from drugs or alcohol was a distinctive and critical endeavor post-incarceration, in which progress and setbacks in sobriety were affected by other individuals and carceral systems. Formerly incarcerated mothers of color remain a marginalized group within the carceral systems imposed upon them, forcing them to navigate interlocking oppressions that may infiltrate third-party support. Chapter 4 demonstrates that even treatment and reentry programs are not judgment free. In treatment programs, mothers' recovery efforts and potential progress were questioned by treatment personnel and by other women with more time sober. In reentry programs, the mothers were vulnerable to criticism via stigmatized labels as "addicts" or bad (m)others, as uttered by other program participants. The formerly incarcerated mothers without histories of substance use engaged in defensive othering to argue that *other* mothers battling drugs and alcoholism were different from them and worse off than they were. Though both groups are criminalized (m)others of color who are subject to interlocking oppressions, this defensive othering among them is a survival mechanism to deflect stigma away from themselves and to present themselves as deserving of public sympathy, second chances, and structural opportunities in a state of criminalization.

Reducing Dissonance between Maternal Hopes and Realities

When a mother lives apart from her children and does not have contact with them or custodial rights, she is publicly criticized as someone who is "unbecoming" a mother due to a shrinking maternal status. The concept of unbecoming a mother entails "moving from an authentic state of mother to a delegitimated category of bad mother or nonmother."[9] This process of seemingly unbecoming a mother—in the public eye—is shaped by the stigma against mothers and ostracizing of mothers who somehow contradict or diverge from social constructions of motherhood. *Invisible Mothers* highlights how some mothers purposefully disassociated themselves from narratives of unbecoming a mother and becoming a bad (m)other. The mothers I interviewed accomplished this in three main ways: by reframing social constructions of motherhood, through self-affirmations highlighting positive maternal relationships, and by trivializing the extent of maternal disengagement by omitting or diverting attention away from maternal disengagement.

Reframing Constructions of Motherhood. Like most women, the formerly incarcerated mothers considered good mothering "being there" for their children. This notion of being there, however, was not restricted to a constant *physical* presence or interaction, as is socially expected of mothers. With complicated relationships and nonresidential and noncustodial arrangements, a constant physical presence was not always possible for mothers after incarceration. Reframing social constructions of motherhood was a protective response to tackle sources of stigma that relied on continuous *physical* interaction. Chapter 1 demonstrates that they viewed themselves as being there for their children through an *emotional* connection of unconditional love and a *communicative* relationship wherein they could talk and listen to their children. The mothers emphasized meanings of motherhood that best fit their individual circumstances and their social position as criminalized (m)others, highlighting practical actions they could perform. This allowed them to latch onto positive representations of good mothering behaviors. It functioned as a form of resilience to combat remarks that they were bad (m)others.

Reframing social constructions of motherhood functioned as a way to construct their maternal role and protect their overall maternal image, particularly in the face of various reentry barriers. White middle-class notions of intensive mothering emphasize financially expensive approaches to motherhood, but the mothers I interviewed reframed these social constructions to best fit their financial and employment reentry barriers as mothers of color, as discussed in chapter 3.[10] Though employment and income are necessities for survival, their definitions of motherhood focused on maternal behaviors that were not dependent on finances, like communicating with their children and spending quality time together. The mothers' narratives in chapter 1 show that it was important for them to make up for lost time and to gain positionality in their children's lives post-incarceration, recognizing over time that this was something money could not provide. As shown in chapter 3, two mothers reframed their unemployment through a positive lens by focusing on the maternal value of quality time with children. Though financial obligations and employment barriers were extremely stressful for the mothers during reentry, reinterpreting the impact of their circumstances was a form of resiliency in reducing dissonance by leaning on their motherwork to support children in nonfinancial ways.

Mothers battling drugs and alcohol may be among the most stigmatized group of (m)others. Indisputably, substance use alone is deemed socially sufficient to impose a stigmatized identity as a bad (m)other. The mothers' narratives in chapter 4 demonstrate that the alleged "bad" mothering behaviors tied to previous drug or alcohol use were not indicative of their overall character. They understood the unfortunate situations surrounding their substance use as previous mistakes that were temporary in nature, rather than as a component of their personal character. They viewed and presented themselves as being overall good mothers. Very rarely did the women view themselves as having been bad (m)others, but when they did, they considered this a phase in their lives that was in the past. This reveals the dynamic and subjective concept of good and bad mothering and also demonstrates mothers' efforts to maintain control over their image and public narratives about them as mothers.

Self-Affirmations and Trivializing Disengagement. Invisible Mothers demonstrates how formerly incarcerated mothers made efforts to reduce dissonance through self-affirmations highlighting positive maternal relationships and trivializing the extent of maternal disengagement by omitting or diverting attention away from maternal disengagement. These protective functions were especially prevalent among the 9 mothers who did not have contact with a child (2 without communication with their only child and 7 without communication with at least one of their multiple children).

Chapter 3 demonstrates that when mothers were disconnected from their only child, these children were often missing from the mothers' narratives about searching for work or their interest in better pay. This demonstrates the value of understanding things that are left unsaid. Communicating with at least one child post-incarceration, regardless of whether they lived together or separately, shaped mothers' reentry concerns and motivated reentry efforts that were grounded in mother-child relationships. When they did not have contact with their only child, they seemed to have less opportunity to hold onto their maternal role as a motivating factor through reentry. Instead of presenting motherwork as a key motivation to find work or as a consideration for suitable employment, the mothers' reentry efforts were largely motivated by the goal of making individual progress. Focusing their reentry efforts on personal endeavors and self-development presented mothers with hope that exceeded current possibilities tied to their maternal role due to the lack of communication.[11] Chapter 1 shows that despite their current lack of communication, they understood their personal endeavors as potentially benefiting their children in the future, showing hope that relationships with these disconnected children could eventually improve.

When mothers maintained some form of communication with at least one of their multiple children, they diverted attention away from any maternal disengagement and instead directed our discussions toward examples in which they met their maternal ideals of good mothering. For instance, chapter 1 shows that mothers sought to compensate for rocky relationships with children by trying to meet personal ideals with subsequent children or grandchildren. Having multiple children or grandchildren allowed the mothers to focus their motherwork on them as second chances at motherhood. Even though these efforts did not directly address problems with their other children or completely resolve dissonance, they served as a protective method to highlight more positive representations of their mothering and reinforce their sense of self as mothers.

The mothers' understanding of motherhood was consistent with research examining how incarcerated women negotiate the mother role and construct their maternal identities from behind prison walls.[12] This research has shown that given their circumstances under penal control, incarcerated mothers define motherhood as meaningful behaviors they can perform within the restricted and controlled parameters of correctional facilities like providing children their love, emotional support, and guidance.[13] *Invisible Mothers* extends this discussion beyond prison walls and back into the community, where mothers of color continue to negotiate the mother role. As with the incarcerated mothers, motherwork that the mothers of color engaged in post-incarceration allowed them to hold onto their maternal role.[14] They confronted stigmatized labels by building on and emphasizing maternal actions and circumstances that are socially supported. All things considered, mothers of color engaged in protective functions to find meaning in their motherwork and remain resilient, despite the dissonance between their maternal hopes and the maternal behaviors they could perform post-incarceration. They fought for their maternal interests in a state of disempowerment, hypersurveillance, and criminalization while reframing social constructions of motherhood, trivializing the extent of maternal disengagement, and reaffirming their sense of self as mothers. These efforts embodied the concept of *recovering mothering*: "the identified phenomena of engaging in regaining, not just the physical custody or physical motherhood of their children, but rather the psychological sense of self that is intricately linked to their role and performance as mothers."[15] By holding onto reframed notions of motherhood and combatting controlling images of them as unfit or bad (m)others, the formerly incarcerated mothers of color were able to portray themselves as *being* good mothers and *doing* a good job as mothers.

MOVING FORWARD: FROM PROGRAM NUMBERS TO VISIBLE MOTHERS

Invisible Mothers highlights how even programs can be counterproductive when they treat formerly incarcerated mothers as merely numbers in program evaluation reports, instead of as the visible mothers they identify with and try to reinforce through motherwork. Reentry programs are expected to prepare and support individuals through reentering the community after incarceration, while treatment programs are supposed to encourage and assist people with recovery. Many of these programs claim to be gender responsive by supposedly addressing the unique obstacles and needs of women in punitive carceral systems. However, *Invisible Mothers* displays how the nexus of carceral and welfare systems treats these women as the problem, justifying the regulation of their identities and whereabouts.[16] More specifically, carceral systems regulate women's mothering quite rigidly in ways that seep into reentry and treatment programs, punishing mothers of color according to normative constructions of motherhood. This book's critique of systemic pathologizing of mothers of color is not to argue that harm to children should be overlooked, but to highlight that our norms and social expectations for mothering should be broadened. Instead of treating them as detached program numbers (or invisible mothers) and punitively regulating their mothering as (m)others, reentry programs should support them as visible mothers through validation and empowerment using anti-oppressive efforts to address systemic barriers stacked against them.

To Be Heard and Understood

To be visible as mothers means more than simply being seen by the naked eye; formerly incarcerated mothers of color must be heard and understood, which—as shown throughout *Invisible Mothers*—is often not the case. The following illustrates how they remain unheard and misunderstood by the general public surrounding them, within programs designated for them, and by policymakers making decisions that affect them. The following also suggests ways to move forward in rendering formerly incarcerated mothers of color the visible mothers they are.

The mothers believed the potential benefits of reentry and treatment programs were diminished when the staff facilitating components of these programs (like parenting classes) were personally or emotionally withdrawn from the women's circumstances. Some mothers believed it was a hindrance when program personnel had never personally experienced maternal incarceration or other common hardships, like substance use while mothering. Programs should be careful to avoid hiring staff who display judgmental communication and privileged ignorance of the women's life stories. Otherwise, a hierarchical undertone may counteract the potential benefits and impose another form of state control that merely demeans them as incompetent mothers.[17] Commonality can help minimize hierarchical undertones while mothers seek support through parenting within carceral systems. The mothers believed they received better support when the women leading program efforts "understood more what [they] go through as parents," as Carolina noted. Chapter 4 shows that the women found it meaningful and therapeutic to have an open space in which to meet other mothers who were previously incarcerated and/or had also experienced substance use. Despite cases of defensive othering from other formerly incarcerated women, this is consistent with research showing that commonality in group settings can boost attachment and belonging and lead to validation of participants' experiences.[18]

Generally, research demonstrates the importance of social support networks that validate mothers' feelings and experiences.[19] I argue that this validation should be in tune with the intersectional experiences of mothers of color and also responsive to their multiple marginality, systematic disempowerment, and criminalization. Once society perceives criminalized mothers of color as having "spoiled identities" as (m)others, it can be difficult to disassociate from these negative labels imposed upon them by society.[20] The impact of this stigma can be reduced when program personnel have personal knowledge of the mothers' experiences and can validate them.[21] Even when reentry experiences cannot be validated by program staff who are personally disconnected from the reentry process, staff can still validate mothers' feelings through understanding their personal hopes, plans, and reentry obstacles and through positive reinforcements of progress under a carceral state.

It is imperative that program staff be sensitive to mothers' circumstances, such as their residential standing, custodial arrangements, and degree of contact with children. This information should not be used to further disempower them; instead, it can be a valuable asset to empower formerly incarcerated mothers with customized support strategies that acknowledge their everyday truths, embrace their maternal interests, and recognize their strengths. This includes understanding that "good" mother-child relationships can come in diverse forms, not simply traditional custodial or residential arrangements that adhere to notions of intensive mothering. For instance, mothers should not be criticized for opting to leave their children with othermothers who are willing and able to care for their children during times of need.[22] This shared mothering is especially vital for mothers of color since it applies the collective value of family and community bonds to protect children from structural oppression.

Scaling versus Breaking Down Maternal Walls

While a social support network can help mothers scale or overcome maternal walls that perpetuate intersectional disparities for formerly incarcerated mothers of color, it is not enough to simply help these mothers deal with oppression without trying to dismantle the systemic oppression itself. Social support efforts must be paired with strategies to break down maternal walls altogether. Policy makers have substantial power to curtail legalized state violence toward mothers of color who face multiple marginalities due to their criminal record, racial-ethnic background, gender, and maternal role. Yet colorblind and gender-neutral policies do not address the historical legacy of patriarchy and anti-Black sentiments in social and penal institutions.

We have a responsibility to promote social equity for the marginalized women and mothers in our patriarchal and racist society who are pushed into carceral systems. As shown in chapter 1, penal control extends beyond correctional facilities and into parole supervision, which the mothers equated with modern-day slavery because of the restricted freedom to live their daily lives and do motherwork without invisible shackles. Even though community-based social service providers are supposedly tasked with providing reentry support, research shows that in practice they are deputized "as stewards who track, document, manage, and report on criminalized women to their respective probation or parole officers."[23] Such community-based practices that are embedded within carceral systems merely aggravate social inequities, reinforce punitive responses, and fuel penal and state control, demonstrating the reality that "community-based" does not necessarily mean "community-driven."[24] Reform efforts should be driven by those criminalized and directly affected by the criminal legal system, who can advocate for liberatory practices in their communities. Reinvesting in community-driven efforts is a step in promoting anti-carceral efforts, positioning communities of color to mobilize against systemic disempowerment and carceral oppression.

Chapter 2 asserts that efforts to expand housing opportunities for formerly incarcerated women should also take into account the significance of navigating motherhood for prospective living arrangements. Affordable housing to accommodate formerly incarcerated individuals is lacking not only in congested cities like New York City, but across the United States as a whole.[25] While several housing programs exist across the country for the general population and the formerly incarcerated, the mothers I spoke with received inadequate support both during and after incarceration in finding housing and managing the array of housing requirements when seeking custody of underage children. More attention should be given to viable pathways whereby women may secure suitable housing for themselves and their children. Such pathways would not only support women's reentry but also work to detangle their involvement in carceral systems from their children's placement in the foster care system or other informal placements with family members.

Chapter 3 argues that while "ban the box" prohibitions are a step toward acknowledging discriminatory labor market practices toward individuals with criminal records, this sometimes prolongs the inevitable denial of hire and does not undo the harm done or offset employment obstacles post-incarceration. In examining high unemployment rates among formerly incarcerated individuals, some research emphasizes their employability by highlighting things such as poor communication skills and limited education and work experience.[26] This focus on employability essentially blames them for unemployment by overlooking the negative role and impact of oppression and penal control in their circumstances, essentially "demonizing people with problems as problems."[27]

In addition to having more employers that hire women with criminal records, as generally discussed by criminologists, chapter 3 suggests that work opportunities may be more accessible to formerly incarcerated mothers if these employers uphold family-friendly policies. Such family-friendly policies should account for maternal roles and obligations, without using maternal circumstances to justify negative evaluations of mothers. This would be especially beneficial for formerly incarcerated mothers since they, like other mothers, may seek employment that is specifically conducive to their maternal role, especially when they have dependent children. Yet as highlighted throughout this book, formerly incarcerated mothers do motherwork within complicated living and custodial arrangements after incarceration. Even though obtaining employment is a notable accomplishment after incarceration, having a job with unpredictable schedules, extended work hours into the night, mandatory weekends, and little flexibility during family emergencies introduces additional problems in navigating complicated mother-child relationships and arrangements post-incarceration. Not only is there a need for more work opportunities that are receptive to employing formerly incarcerated individuals, but we also need jobs that remove these maternal barriers to employment.

Chapter 4 notes the role of US drug policies in criminalizing substance use and incarcerating mothers of color for mere drug possession or committing minor nonviolent offenses while under the influence.[28] This chapter suggests there is a need for anti-carceral and anti-oppressive approaches to substance use. Given the nexus between welfare systems of care and carceral systems of penal control, reentry programs and social service providers are in a unique and complicated position. They may engage in supportive practices that empower mothers of color through reentry and recovery while navigating motherhood, or they may function as another form of supervision and as enforcers of state control, contributing to mothers' systematic oppression. *Invisible Mothers* demonstrates that these two roles are not necessarily mutually exclusive, and they often overlap.[29]

Narratives in this book show how reentry and treatment programs functioned as supervisory units, forcing mothers of color to continue being intermingled with and dictated to by punitive forms of control and punishment. For instance, narratives in chapter 4 suggest social service providers in these programs were tasked with assessing mothers' perceived failure based on excessive standards and punitive guidelines that encourage reprimand. A challenge for mothers was the use of scare tactics and warnings highlighting unfortunate circumstances and reiterating the negative consequences of setbacks for mothers' children and reentry goals. These warnings and scare tactics functioned as another form of surveillance, grounded in doubt about the mothers' progress and emphasizing conflicts in post-incarceration mothering. Social service providers are complicit in this hypersurveillance when they emphasize women's accountability and "discursively uphold and maintain the carceral state by pathologizing women's issues."[30] In fact, professor Annette Appell discovered that the "training for most therapists involves so much mother-blame and women-blame."[31] Chapter 4 illustrates how blaming mothers for their circumstances fuels narratives that problematize the women rather than their social-structural marginalization, via a hierarchical undertone that these women must be "fixed" or corrected.[32] Such a risk management approach is not sufficient or adequate to support the reentry process.[33] Rather than focusing solely on the management and prevention of "bad" acts, social service providers should treat their role as more of an equal partner working collaboratively with the mothers to tackle common post-incarceration obstacles.[34]

AREAS FOR FUTURE RESEARCH

At various points throughout this book, I have highlighted potential areas for future research stemming from the women's narratives and experiences. I advise researchers to further examine the intraracial and interethnic nuances in social interactions during reentry, to consider the role of cultural values and the impact of cultural transgressions on receiving support from family and local communities, to research women's experiences mothering infants and toddlers while in reentry, and to explore mothers' intentions and actions in reentry compared to how these are viewed and received by their children.

Intraracial and Interethnic Stereotypes during Reentry

This book predominantly demonstrates shared intraracial experiences, in that the mothers had common interests in "being there" for their children post-incarceration and encountered shared obstacles in obtaining work as criminalized (m)others of color. Though criminologists typically study African Americans and West Indians of African descent collectively under a Black racial category, *Invisible Mothers* shows that they confronted distinct ethnicity-based stereotypes during their search for work and within the workplace. While West Indians and Latinxs were paralleled with each other in terms of cultural values about hard work and earned benefits, the mothers believed West Indians were generally the "model minorities" based on their perceived work ethic compared to that of African Americans. As shown in chapter 3, these interethnic stereotypes about work ethic also contributed to some quarrels between these groups. While existing research discusses white employers' perceptions and treatment of each ethnic group, the question remains of whether underrepresented groups miss out on work opportunities post-incarceration when Black employers also have their own interethnic reservations about or preferences for certain groups.[35] The mothers' narratives suggest such interethnic stereotypes and disproportionate treatment were a reality.

Future research should further explore the different interethnic experiences in the labor market and in the workplace that were said to stem from public perceptions of work ethic. Racial classifications along a Black/white dichotomy obscure the unique challenges across ethnic groups. I urge researchers to be cognizant of limitations in their research that result from homogenizing the Black experience without addressing ethnic nuances, which may appear small in nature but can have large effects on the life experiences of those in reentry.[36] *Invisible Mothers* specifically focuses on African American, West Indian, and Latina mothers since they are predominant ethnic groups in New York City, where they were interviewed. This book does not specifically suggest studying these same three ethnic groups in all geographic areas, given that cities and states differ drastically in their racial-ethnic makeup; instead, scholars should tailor their research to the racial-ethnic makeup of any areas they are studying. Examining reentry experiences across racial-ethnic groups allows for a better understanding of societal barriers to gaining or maintaining employment, along with the nature of mothers' (in)visibility in the labor market and within the workplace.

Cultural Values in Family and Communal Support

Social support is crucial in overcoming social-structural reentry barriers and in navigating motherhood post-incarceration; *Invisible Mothers* highlights nuances in who provides social support and when this support is given (or not). For instance, West Indian and Latina mothers shared common cultural values about earning one's monetary and tangible benefits and, in turn, honoring the family and community. Compared to the African American mothers I interviewed, they were more likely to discuss family disapproval of behaviors deemed culturally unacceptable, like engaging in substance use, committing certain crimes (like money crimes), and getting incarcerated. Chapter 3 shows that regardless of their reasons or their survival mechanisms through hardship, committing money crimes contradicted notions of honorable hard work and was grounds for West Indian and Latinx family members to potentially withhold support. Consistent with other research, chapter 4 discusses how substance use and incarceration were often perceived as a cultural transgression within the West Indian community, triggering emotional and financial detachment from them while navigating life under penal control.[37] These narratives demonstrate some nuances in social support networks and the importance of exploring nuances to understand what helps and hinders women's efforts to maintain sobriety and reenter the community after incarceration.

Future research should further examine the role of cultural values and the impact of cultural transgressions on receiving financial help and emotional support from family and local communities. Perceptions of (un)acceptable behaviors and a reluctance to aid women who engage in these actions may have serious implications when women need tangible and emotional support post-incarceration. This population may possibly feel more discouraged from seeking assistance in their reentry and recovery given the substantial stigma within their families and ethnic communities. If so, reentry and treatment programs may have additional work on their hands to ensure these women have a suitable support network post-incarceration. Although closer examination may help improve outreach efforts to West Indian women in the criminal legal system, researchers may likely encounter obstacles in recruiting them to discuss their lived experiences. I experienced these obstacles firsthand in my recruitment efforts to interview formerly incarcerated mothers of color. I learned from informal discussions with West Indian community members that the West Indian population in carceral systems is "so down low" because of the "high level of intolerance" for substance use and incarceration. This perceived "intolerance" described by community members underscores the need for additional research on the intraracial and interethnic nuances in reentry experiences. Thus, to avoid barriers in trying to recruit formerly incarcerated West Indian women, it may be more feasible for criminologists to conduct interviews or focus groups with the larger ethnic population about the cultural mechanisms at play in providing or denying social support to those with substance use histories and in the criminal legal system.

Mothering Infants and Toddlers during Reentry

Invisible Mothers raises important questions for future research about how post-incarceration mothering is experienced by mothers of children who are an average of 19 years old.[38] It may be valuable for future research to focus more attention on formerly incarcerated mothers with children who are younger in age and to be more inclusive of infants (up to 12 months old) and toddlers (ages 1 to 3). Mothering is not context-free and is shaped by social and practical factors in women's lives like finances, maternal obligations, and social support. Women typically face increased maternal expectations from society and increased demands from children during the early developmental stages, which can make mothers especially vulnerable to emotional turmoil while dealing with oppressive carceral systems.[39] In her book *Of Woman Born*, Adrienne Rich discusses her own experiences with motherhood and includes entries from her personal journal to illustrate feelings of entrapment since her needs were positioned in a losing battle against the needs of her children. Although Rich was not a mother in reentry, such feelings of entrapment when balancing mothers' needs with the needs of small children is likely exacerbated when these mothers are navigating reentry barriers. Future research interviewing mothers of color about post-incarceration motherhood with infants and toddlers would be an excellent complement to this book in exploring how carceral involvement shapes their motherwork and how navigating motherhood at this developmental stage shapes the reentry process.

MATCHED MOTHER-CHILD PERSPECTIVES

As a complement to this book on formerly incarcerated mothers of color, it may be especially fruitful to explore how post-incarceration motherhood is understood and experienced from the perspective of both major parties involved: the mothers and their children. The mothers hinted at the adjustments that their children underwent, but it is unclear if the mothers' beliefs are in line with their children's views. While women may share their maternal decisions and express their intentions behind these decisions, their children may have different interpretations of their mothers' actions and the mother-child relationships. For instance, sociologist Jane Siegel suggests mothers' post-release expectation to "put on the mantle of motherhood" may create conflicts for their children if children have grown accustomed to temporary caregivers or witnessed their mothers struggling post-incarceration.[40] *Invisible Mothers* suggests that the saying "time heals all wounds" did not always apply. In fact, it was more common for mothers to lack communication with adult children than with underage children. Despite trying to improve communication and rebuild relationships, the mothers believed they didn't have contact with adult children because these children were unable to recuperate from troubled pasts and were less receptive to the mothers' efforts.

While this book presents mothers' thoughts about their children's perspectives, the work of other scholars who directly examine matched mother-child perspectives are a great complement to this book. Future research on matched mother and child relationships could further explore mothers' intentions and actions post-incarceration in relation to how these are viewed and received by their children. Given the mothers' discussions about the impact of oppressive structural systems on their lives as invisible mothers and visible (m)others, this research approach may comparatively demonstrate how these oppressive circumstances are understood from differing perspectives.

CLOSING REMARKS

People of color, and more specifically women of color, "have never been powerless. The question is how do they identify and more effectively use the forms of power that exist within communities to hold back the flood gates that seem to persistently threaten their survival."[41] *Invisible Mothers* acknowledges the social-structural positionality of women of color and highlights the intersectionality of gender, motherhood, racial-ethnic background, and criminalization. In doing so, this book, as a form of matricentric feminism, centers mothers' experiences, demonstrating how mothers make use of shared mothering from family and community networks and how they mentally handle disempowerment, hypersurveillance, and criminalization within the carceral state. Personal narratives essentially helped mothers "make meaning out of their lives" and remain resilient in their motherwork post-incarceration.[42] They saw themselves as mothers, and they deserve to be seen as such. Listening to and understanding formerly incarcerated women as visible mothers is more constructive in helping them and addressing systemic oppression than the carceral focus on managing, controlling, and punishing "bad behaviors."[43] I encourage readers to reflect on the experiences of formerly incarcerated mothers, to consider the influence of motherhood in women's reentry, to acknowledge the nuances of social perceptions and treatment across racial-ethnic groups, and to incorporate this knowledge into anti-oppressive efforts. Until then, colorblind and gender-neutral reentry programs will continue to function as enforcers of state control and will remain limited in assisting formerly incarcerated mothers of color.

Research Design

The state of New York, and New York City more specifically, is often described as one of the landing grounds in the United States for Latinxs and West Indians.[1] Like many other families, my parents immigrated to the United States and focused their eyes on New York City for more opportunities and better living conditions than are offered in our home country of Honduras. As an Afro-Latina woman raised in New York City, I admire the diversity of the city, but at a young age I was also cognizant of the city's ethnic enclaves, in which underrepresented ethnic groups largely lived in small pockets throughout the city. A bus line through Manhattan could literally expose bus riders to the Asian enclave of Chinatown, followed by the predominantly white area of the Upper East Side, through the predominantly African American community of Harlem, into the largely Latinx area of Washington Heights.[2] My early awareness of the drastic differences between these ethnic enclaves, along with my early exposure to carceral interventions in underrepresented neighborhoods like mine, as discussed in the book's introduction, collectively sparked my personal interest in the carceral experiences of various underrepresented racial-ethnic groups. Based on interviews I conducted in New York City, *Invisible Mothers* is devoted to enhancing the visibility of traditionally silenced individuals in the criminal legal system by highlighting the voices, challenges, and needs of formerly incarcerated African American, West Indian, and Latina mothers.

To find formerly incarcerated African American, West Indian, and Latina mothers who were willing to be interviewed, I left flyers and gave short oral presentations at local reentry programs, coalition meetings, and events that were for or about women and mothers in carceral systems. I intentionally chose not to recruit mothers through the criminal legal system or its personnel, such as parole officers or probation officers. Doing so can hinder people's willingness to be interviewed and, if interviewed, may limit how much they share if they believe there is some aspect of legal oversight involved. To ensure that willing mothers felt comfortable discussing their personal experiences, I maintained no affiliation with the criminal legal system and introduced myself as an independent research scholar during any communications.

Between November 2014 and October 2015, I interviewed a total of 37 formerly incarcerated African American, West Indian, and Latina mothers with varying degrees of contact with their children. All things considered, the mothers learned about the research project in a number of ways. I gave four informal presentations, including one tabling session, which yielded 14 interviews. Nine women called me about an interview after seeing a posted flyer. In addition to the two mothers I recruited directly through personal contacts, six learned of the research project by word of mouth from other mothers I had previously interviewed. Finally, I do not know if the remaining six mothers learned of the study via flyer or by word of mouth.

In the first month of conducting interviews (November 2014), I recruited primarily at a nonprofit organization that provides formerly incarcerated mothers with resources like supportive housing for the mothers and their children, job readiness workshops, an after-school program for their children, and access to donated clothing. I interviewed the first 9 mothers at the program location while identifying and confirming other locations to interview more mothers. In order to be interviewed, formerly incarcerated women needed to self-identify as mothers, which was necessary for exploring their narratives about the institution of motherhood, about doing motherwork, and about how they navigated motherhood post-incarceration. I met several formerly incarcerated women who did not have biological children but who self-identified as mothers to their pet dogs and cats. To maintain consistency, I limited my interviews to mothers with biological children. Though I only interviewed biological mothers, they were asked if there were other children whom they helped care for and raise, either previously or at the time of the interview. This allowed for consideration of maternal involvement in the lives of other children despite the focus on mothers' relationships with biological children.

I used a purposive sampling strategy with the objective of interviewing a balanced number of formerly incarcerated African American, West Indian, and Latina mothers. Despite my goal of interviewing the same number of mothers across racial-ethnic background, I found it difficult to recruit West Indian mothers. The majority of my first 9 interviews were with African American mothers. In an attempt to interview more West Indian mothers, I traveled to highly populated West Indian communities in New York City, including Flatbush (in the borough of Brooklyn) and Jamaica (in the borough of Queens). I used this opportunity to post flyers in storefronts, provide flyers to daycare personnel, and leave flyers at various nonprofit organizations and health centers that provided generic services to community residents. These efforts were also supplemented by numerous calls and emails to representatives at these organizations and health centers. Through these particular efforts, I managed to interview 6 additional West Indian mothers. In the end, I interviewed 8 mothers who identified with a West Indian background, 15 who identified as Latinas, 21 who identified as African American, and 1 mother who identified as Black but could not describe an ethnicity with which she identified.[3]

I also sought to purposefully recruit formerly incarcerated women with varying degrees of contact with their children: mothers living with their children, mothers not living with their children but in contact with them, and mothers without contact with their children. In the first few months of interviewing I only interviewed 3 mothers who did not have contact with a child. Yet I found these interviews quite revealing, especially with regard to how these mothers framed their narratives around the "good times" in their mother-child relationships or focused on the children with whom they had contact or could potentially develop contact. To recruit more formerly incarcerated mothers without contact with a child, I left flyers at legal information centers associated with Family Court and also relied on word of mouth from mothers I had previously interviewed. Through these efforts, I was able to recruit 6 additional mothers who did not have contact with either their only child or at least one of multiple children. Of these, 2 learned of the study from other mothers I had previously interviewed, 3 saw flyers posted at housing programs and the courthouse, and 1 was informed of the study by the program coordinator at a women's reentry program. In the end, almost a quarter of the mothers had no communication with a child, approximately one-third lived with at least one of their children, and over three-quarters maintained contact with children without physically living together.[4]

INTERVIEW PROCEDURES

Once mothers demonstrated an interest in being interviewed, we arranged a meeting time and location. No one declined to be interviewed, and no one withdrew from the interview once it was underway. In accordance with their preferences, mothers were interviewed at programs used for recruitment (N = 11); in their homes or the home of a family member (N = 4); at shelters (N = 2); at schools where they were enrolled or employed, or that they were familiar with (N = 3); and at local eateries such as cafés, McDonald's, Burger King, and iHop (N = 17). The interviews lasted from 39 minutes to 2.5 hours, with an average of approximately 1.5 hours' duration. Of the 37 mothers who were interviewed, only 2 opted not to be audio-recorded; in these cases, I typed up their narratives on a laptop computer during the interviews. All other interviews were audio-recorded and transcribed.

The Interview Guide

The semistructured interview guide consisted of questions pertaining to the women's perceptions of motherhood, interpretations of mothering, and insights regarding the expectations placed on them as mothers. In addition, our discussions probed the place of motherhood in women's desires, decisions and behaviors related to post-incarceration living arrangements, employment, recovery from substance use, child custody, and child-rearing practices. Due to the importance of previous life circumstances for understanding the navigation of motherhood and reentry into the community post-incarceration, the interview guide included questions about life before and during incarceration in order to consider factors that may have had an impact on post-incarceration motherhood. Once mothers noted their ethnic identities, I probed deeper into their nationalities and relevant experiences with living and visiting the countries mentioned and whether they were foreign-born or native-born with ethnic ties to another country. I also asked the women about personal experiences and decisions associated with their ethnicities. Finally, I asked mothers to describe their neighborhoods and the presence and use of services in their neighborhoods in order to obtain an understanding of the communities where they lived and the community role in navigating motherhood during reentry.

Interview Language(s)

Interviews could have been conducted in either English or Spanish depending on the mothers' preferences, but all interviews were conducted in English. This may be so for a number of reasons. First, given my appearance as a brown-skinned woman, I am often mistaken for someone who is not a native Spanish speaker, and this confusion may have discouraged mothers from approaching me at recruitment events if Spanish was their primary language. Second, I recruited largely at locations where English was the dominant language spoken, albeit with bilingual personnel available. This remained true despite my deliberate recruitment in predominantly Spanish-speaking neighborhoods. Third, even though I posted and distributed both English- and Spanish-language flyers at each recruitment location, I received no calls from mothers who only spoke Spanish. This may be tied to the previous point regarding recruitment at locations that were predominantly English speaking. Finally, while no mothers called who did not speak English, some of the mothers were fluent in both English and Spanish. When I received calls from bilingual mothers, our interviews were conducted in the language spoken at the time of scheduling, English.

Even though all interviews were conducted in English, 6 mothers incorporated other languages or dialects into their interviews, which was typically done when telling a story. One Haitian mother, Marie, occasionally spoke Haitian Creole during her interview, and I consulted three Haitian colleagues for an accurate translation of these accounts. One mother, Jesenia, incorporated both Spanish and Italian, yet only spoke one Italian word during her interview. One mother, Vanessa, did not speak Spanish or Garifuna,[5] but in demonstrating her knowledge of a few Garifuna words, she and I simultaneously said "good afternoon" in Garifuna: *buiti rabanweyu.* Three mothers—Priscilla, Francesca, and Emma—spoke Spanish at some point during their interviews. What I found particularly interesting was that Emma occasionally incorporated Spanish-language conversations into her interview, but upon the conclusion of the interview, we spoke using an interchange between English and Spanish (informally known as "Spanglish"). She was one of the two mothers who opted out of being audio-recorded. I wondered if she felt more comfortable speaking Spanglish after the interview, given that it was more of a conversation in which I was not typing as she spoke. I don't know whether she would have spoken in Spanglish during the interview if it were audio-recorded.

Compensation

Mothers were compensated for their time, which was beneficial during recruitment as an additional incentive.[6] They were given either a $25 metro card or a $25 gift card to the Pathmark supermarket, Duane Reade/Walgreens pharmacy, or Staples office supply store. They had the opportunity to choose from a selection of retailers that best accommodated their interests or to choose a metro card to use in New York City's extensive public transit system. The most frequently requested compensation was the Duane Reade/Walgreens gift card, with 19 requests, followed by 10 requests for metro cards, 7 requests for Pathmark gift cards, and 1 request for a Staples gift card. The mothers often explained their interest in particular options, for instance, noting that the Duane Reade/Walgreens gift card could be used at the store's pharmacy and the metro card could be used for transportation to and from work. At the conclusion of some interviews, women prepared to use the gift cards they had just received. Bianca, who lived in a shelter with her daughter, requested a Pathmark gift card and asked her teenage daughter to prepare for their grocery shopping at the end of our interview. In two instances, I was present as they made their purchases. Karen used her Pathmark gift card to purchase milk for her grandson, and Regina used her Duane Reade/Walgreens gift card to buy several personal items including a card for Mother's Day, which was the day after our interview.

DATA ANALYSIS

I analyzed the 37 interviews using grounded theory techniques: an inductive approach that does not impose preconceived theories or themes from other external research but instead allows for discovering interrelated concepts and thematic patterns that surface naturally within and across interviews.[7] I adopted this particular approach for data analysis to understand the mothers' realities as they experienced them and understood them and to ensure that the conclusions presented in this book are grounded in the mothers' narratives.

During data analysis, I meticulously engaged in initial line-by-line coding. Interviews were initially coded into broad preliminary codes including, for example, "Race and Ethnicity," with any direct discussions of race or ethnicity as it relates to personal or vicarious experiences noted as such; "Mothers and Motherhood" vis-à-vis interpretations of mothering with parallels and contrasts with other groups; and "Aspects of Living," which included eight components:

1. Substance Use and Recovery (Drugs, Alcohol, and Money)
2. Childrearing Practices and Parenting During Reentry
3. Custody and Living Arrangements of Children
4. Education
5. Employment (and Funds)

6. Family Relations (Non-Children)
7. Housing and Living Arrangements of Mothers
8. Intimate Partners

I then conducted a more focused coding within these broader areas. I gave special attention to repetitions within and across the interviews as indicative of interrelated thematic patterns, which is a technique also described as the constant comparative method.[8] Using this approach, I further refined initial codes. For instance, "Mothers and Motherhood" was refined into more conceptual themes regarding mothers' experiences in relation to nonmothers and fathers, notions of "bad" versus "good" mothers, and the construction of fictive mothers, to name a few. In addition, "Race and Ethnicity" was further refined into more conceptual themes regarding the family and community responses to incarceration and drugs.

The mothers' narratives in early interviews led me to engage in theoretical sampling to expand upon my initial analysis of the interviews and to gain a better understanding of emerging themes. Even though I began with a purposive sampling approach to interviewing formerly incarcerated West Indian, African American, and Latina mothers, I continued with a more specified theoretical sampling approach that "directs you where to go" in interviewing more mothers.[9] This back and forth between conducting interviews and analyzing interviews is consistent with grounded theory techniques, which begin early in the interview process and help further data collection.[10] I found this approach to be especially helpful in reaching additional mothers to expand on emerging themes in early interviews as they related to mothers navigating the shelter system and mothers without contact with children.

I subsequently did a third round of coding while writing each chapter. This round of coding was instrumental in comparative analyses across mothers' racial-ethnic background and mothers' degree of contact with children, including other relevant aspects like their children's age and dependency. I was able to gain a deeper understanding of heterogeneity among formerly incarcerated mothers of color as they navigated motherhood post-incarceration. During this stage of coding, I also accounted for deviant narratives within prevalent themes in order to obtain a better understanding of the circumstances influencing any departures from major themes.

I used NVivo 10 data analysis software during each stage of coding. The NVivo 10 software helped me organize the mothers' narratives into major themes, then subthemes, with logs of the frequency of references along with their significance across interviews, and also to make links to the field notes I wrote for each of the interviews. Using this software was also helpful in organizing the comparative analyses embedded in the research design exploring across racial-ethnic groups and mothers' degree of contact with children, as well as the comparisons that naturally emerged during interviews (like adult versus underage children or dependent children versus independent children). In this way, the software helped me keep track of the nuances found across the 37 interviews.

RESEARCH LIMITATIONS

Although the goal was to interview a comparative number of formerly incarcerated mothers across racial-ethnic groups, the 37 mothers included a smaller number of West Indian than Latina and African American mothers. Scholars are well aware of common recruitment issues in qualitative research, but the difficulties I experienced in meeting and interviewing formerly incarcerated West Indians mothers may also speak to the stigma about incarceration within the West Indian community. During my attempts to recruit West Indian mothers, I received input from third parties about the carceral stigma in this community and the reluctance to discuss carceral involvement. Initial interviews and informal discussions with West Indian colleagues and service providers within nonprofit organizations sparked discussions of cultural values and family's disengagement from those who were incarcerated or had histories of substance use. This information suggested that it would be difficult to interview an equal number of mothers from each racial-ethnic group but also that the interviews I was able to conduct with West Indian mothers would be vital for understanding their reentry, their mothering experiences post-incarceration, and the unique obstacles they faced as West Indian mothers in the criminal legal system. Despite interviewing fewer West Indian mothers, I believe I reached a point of saturation in which their interviews were no longer bringing up new information that was unique to their racial-ethnic background. Of the 8 mothers I interviewed who identified with a West Indian background, I found that their interviews were rich in narrative about their obstacles navigating motherhood post-incarceration and the racial-ethnic nuances they experienced reentering the community, which are discussed throughout this book.[11]

Given my focus on the mothers' ethnic backgrounds, the extent of mixed ethnic identities should be addressed. To some degree, the number of ethnically mixed mothers made it challenging to parse out ethnic differences among the women, as it is difficult to compare experiences between women who identity with solely one ethnic background and women who identify with more than one. Scholars like Mary Waters have written about the challenges associated with measuring race and ethnicity given high immigration rates and interethnic relations.[12] Despite research challenges concerning interethnic identifications, scholars must continue to research racial and ethnic groups in order to examine and highlight inequalities or risks they encounter in society. *Invisible Mothers* contributes to existing research by going beyond the mere *measurement* of racial/ethnic identities and, instead, drawing from individuals' narratives to qualitatively explore the role of ethnicity in their experiences. Despite identifying with more than one ethnicity, participants often described a particular "side" with which they identified more or had more familial interactions. This allowed for a better understanding of their experiences, particularly as it related to cultural ideals and familial assistance. More importantly, when the mothers discussed an experience that was specifically associated with their ethnicity or the ethnicity of others, the specific ethnic association was often identified. For instance, Jesenia's father was Latino and her mother was white. Born in Puerto

Rico and mostly raised in New York City, Jesenia did not consider herself mixed or white but referred to herself as a Latina mother. These explicit accounts were crucial in exploring the role of ethnicity in the experiences of ethnically mixed mothers and permitted for discussions of this throughout the book.

In addition, some scholars argue that it is best to interview research participants with a wide range of time incarcerated.[13] For instance, research suggests that the length of mothers' incarceration can influence the meaning or value of maternal identities and may shape the significance of their motherwork in compensating for the physical separation from children: "Mothers with longer terms actually appeared to consider their mother identities *more important* than women with shorter sentences. Given that these women will be separated from their children for longer periods of time, maintenance of the mothering role may require that it be invoked often and intensely if it is to be maintained at all."[14] Among the mothers I interviewed, there was variation in the length of their last incarceration, from as little as seven days to as long as five years. Even though I did not interview mothers with periods of incarceration exceeding five years, the length of incarceration did not arise as something that drastically shaped post-incarceration experiences as mothers. Instead, the mothers I interviewed emphasized the number of times they were incarcerated and the influence of multiple incarcerations on mother-child relationships. Given that their narratives emphasized the impact of multiple incarcerations, with less attention paid to the impact of incarceration length, and since 57% of the 37 mothers had been incarcerated more than once, I did not believe it was necessary to further sample women who had experienced longer sentences.

Despite these research limitations, *Invisible Mothers* is well-suited to expose the marginalization of African American, West Indian, and Latina mothers as they navigate motherhood and reenter the community after incarceration. This book illustrates how social institutions render mothers of color invisible when it concerns establishing and upholding equity across social groups, while these mothers simultaneously become visible (m)others to politicians, law enforcers, and the general public, who criminalize and penalize them for surviving their marginalization. All things considered, the mothers' narratives presented in this book highlight how reentering the community post-incarceration as African American, West Indian, and Latina mothers makes navigating motherhood more difficult, and conversely, how navigating motherhood as visible (m)others complicates their reentry process after release. It is my hope that readers will incorporate the knowledge gained throughout this book into advocating for and supporting anti-oppressive efforts.

Summary of the Mothers

Table 1 includes demographic characteristics of the mothers, such as their ages, the lengths of their last incarcerations, time since their release, ethnic backgrounds, degrees of contact with their children, and employment status.

TABLE I   PSEUDONYMS AND DEMOGRAPHIC CHARACTERISTICS OF THE MOTHERS

Participant	Age in years	Time last incarcerated (time in weeks)	Time since release (time in weeks)
Ana	41	7 months (30.1 weeks)	1 year, 2 months (60.7 weeks)
Bernadette	63	3 months (12.9 weeks)	14 years (729.4 weeks)
Bianca	47	8 months (34.4 weeks)	2 years (104.2 weeks)
Carolina	41	3 years (156.3 weeks)	1.5 months (6.5 Weeks)
Dolores	53	6 months (25.8 weeks)	2 weeks
Donna	41	2 years, 10 months (147.2 weeks)	2.5 weeks
Emily	44	1 year, 8 months (86.5 weeks)	7 years (364.7 weeks)
Emma	51	2.5 years (130.3 weeks)	4 years (208.4 weeks)
Francesca	49	2 years (104.2 weeks)	11 years (573.1 weeks)
Henrietta	62	10 months (43 weeks)	6 years (312.6 weeks)
Jesenia	26	66 days (9.4 weeks)	1 year, 4 months (69.3 weeks)
Josefina	42	88 days (12.6 weeks)	10 weeks
Karen	49	32 days (4.6 weeks)	10 weeks
Kerry-Ann	42	2.5 years (130.3 weeks)	10 years, 5 months (542.5 weeks)
Latoya	57	13 months (55.9 weeks)	4 years, 4 months (225.6 weeks)
Laura	58	2 years (104.2 weeks)	3 years, 3 months (169.2 weeks)
Lucinda	59	2 years (104.2 weeks)	4 years (208.4 weeks)
Lucy	43	30 days (4.3 weeks)	16 years (833.6 weeks)
Madison	25	4 years (208.4 weeks)	1 year, 4 months (69.3 weeks)

Ethnicity	Children living with	Children not living with, but in contact	Children without contact	Work
Latina; other	3 1 adult; 2 minors			No
African American		4 Adults	2 Adults	No
African American	1 Minor	1 Adult		No
Latina		2 Minors		No
African American		3 Adults		No
African American		1 Minor		Intern
Latina; other		1 Adult	2 Adults	No
Latina; other		2 Adults		No
African American; Latina; other		1 Adult		Yes
African American		3 Adults		No
Latina; other			1 Minor	No
Latina	1 Adult	2 Adults	2 Minors	Yes
African American		2 Adults		Yes
West Indian	2 1 adult; 1 minor			Yes
unknown	2 1 adult; 1 minor			No
Latina; other			1 Adult	Yes
African American		3 Adults		No
African American; Latina	2 1 adult; 1 minor	2 Adults		No
African American	2 Minors			Intern

TABLE I (*Continued*)

Participant	Age in years	Time last incarcerated (time in weeks)	Time since release (time in weeks)
Makayla	28	1 year, 10 months (95.1 weeks)	2 years (104.2 weeks)
Marcia	38	40 days (5.7 weeks)	1 year, 4 months (69.3 weeks)
Marie	43	11 months (47.3 weeks)	7 months (30.1 weeks)
Natalie	31	7 months (30.1 weeks)	6.5 months (28 weeks)
Odessa	32	6 months (25.8 weeks)	11 years (573.1 weeks)
Onika	44	5 years (260.5 weeks)	4 years (208.4 weeks)
Paloma	37	2 years, 9 months (142.9 weeks)	5 years (260.5 weeks)
Priscilla	42	1 year (52.1 weeks)	5 years (260.5 weeks)
Qiana	24	1 year (52.1 weeks)	2.5 weeks
Rashida	54	40 days (5.7 weeks)	1 year, 3 months (65 weeks)
Regina	38	8 weeks	4 weeks
Shanise	56	2 years (104.2 weeks)	1 year, 10 months (95.1 weeks)
Tia	34	8 months (34.4 weeks)	2 months (8.6 weeks)
Valerie	45	7 days (1 week)	1.5 weeks
Vanessa	25	3 months (12.9 weeks)	2 years, 2 months (112.8 weeks)
Vera	45	8 months (34.4. weeks)	6 months (25.8 weeks)
Wyndolyn	48	3 months (12.9 weeks)	2 weeks
Yvette	45	4 months (17.2 weeks)	11 months (47.3 weeks)
Average	43	1 year, 3 months	3 years, 4 months

Ethnicity	Children living with	Children not living with, but in contact	Children without contact	Work
African American	1 Minor			No
Latina; other		4 Minors		No
West Indian		1 Minor		No
African American		3 Minors		No
Latina; West Indian; other		1 Minor		Yes
African American; West Indian	1 Adult	1 Adult	1 Adult	Yes
Latina	1 Minor	2 1 adult; 1 minor	7 Minors	No
Latina	2 Minors	1 Adult		Intern
African American; Latina; other		1 Minor		Yes
African American; West Indian		3 Adults		Intern
African American		5 3 adults; 2 minors		No
African American		1 Adult		No
West Indian		4 Minors		No
African American; other		2 1 adult; 1 minor	2 Adults	No
Latina; West Indian	1 Minor			No
African American; West Indian	1 Adult	1 Adult		No
African American		2 Adults	1 Adult	No
African American		3 2 adults; 1 minor		No
—	—	—	—	—

Notes

INTRODUCTION

1. Travis (2005).
2. Carson (2020); Kaeble (2018); Zeng (2020).
3. Bush-Baskette (2010).
4. Glaze and Maruschak (2008).
5. Dallaire et al. (2010); Hagan and Foster (2012); Siegel (2011); Turney and Wildeman (2015); Wildeman and Turney (2014).
6. Minaker and Hogeveen (2015).
7. Collins (2009, pp. 25–26).
8. This book draws from existing discussions about the visibility and intersectional invisibility of women of color (Jordan-Zachery, 2008; Mowatt et al., 2013; Purdie-Vaughns and Eibach, 2008).
9. O'Reilly (2019).
10. O'Reilly (2019); Rich (1995).
11. O'Reilly (2019, p. 16).
12. Hays (1996).
13. Hays (1996, p. 8); see also McMahon (1995).
14. Browne and Misra (2003, p. 488).
15. Potter (2013).
16. Collins (2009, p. 29).
17. Browne and Giampetro-Meyer (2003); Byron (2010); Crosby et al. (2004); Williams (2001).
18. Ritchie (2017, pp. 169–170).
19. Collins (2009).

20. For a review, see Garcia-Hallett and Kovacs (2020).

21. Consistent with Nancy Foner's (2001, p. 3) work, *African Americans* refers to North Americans of African ancestry, while *West Indians* refers to people from the Anglophone Caribbean region, though I also include those from Haiti since this was consistent with self-identification during interviews and in dialogues with community members during recruitment.

22. Ritchie (2017, p. 12).

23. Collins (2009).

24. Davis (1981, p. 7); see Collins (2009).

25. Foner (2001); Henry (1998); see also Bobb and Clarke (2001).

26. Premdas (1995, p. 249); see also Foner (2001); Reddock, (2001); Waters (1999).

27. Reddock (2001).

28. Reddock (2001).

29. Waters (1999).

30. Palmer (2010).

31. Palmer (2010).

32. López and Chesney-Lind (2014); Romero (2008).

33. Bridges (2007); Collins (2009).

34. Romero (2008).

35. Hondagneu-Sotelo and Avila (1997, p. 551).

36. Collins (2009, p.79).

37. Minaker and Hogeveen (2015, p. 8).

38. Collins (2009); Roberts (2016).

39. Hayward and DePanfilis (2007); Phillips et al. (2010); Raimon et al. (2009); Roberts (2012).

40. Harris (2012).

41. Ritchie (2017, p. 15).

42. Bronson and Carson (2019); US Census Bureau (2019).

43. Bronson and Carson (2019); US Census Bureau (2019).

44. Garcia-Hallett (2019a).

45. See Bush-Baskette (2010).

46. Carson (2020).

47. Kopak and Hoffmann (2014).

48. For a discussion of disproportionate drug offense arrests of people of color and in communities of color, see Bush-Baskette (2010); Mauer (2009).

49. Minaker and Hogeveen (2015, p. 8).

50. Glaze and Maruschak (2008).

51. Flavin (2001).

52. Flavin (2001, p. 630).

53. Byrne and Trew (2008); Ferraro and Moe (2003); Garcia-Hallett (2019a).

54. Byrne and Trew (2008, p. 249).

55. Mumola (2000).

56. Mumola (2000); Siegel (2011).

57. Mumola (2000).

58. Enos (2001); Jensen and DuBeck-Biondo (2005); Siegel (2011); Wakefield and Garcia-Hallett (2017).

59. Jensen and DuBeck-Biondo (2005).

60. Berry and Eigenberg (2003).

61. Sufrin (2018).

62. Sufrin (2018, p. 62).

63. Brown and Bloom (2009); Covington (2003); Hayes (2009); Kreager et al. (2010); Leverentz (2014); Michalsen (2011); Sharpe (2015).

64. Richie (2001, p. 381).

65. Gurusami (2019).

66. Garcia-Hallett (2019b).

67. Steffensmeier et al. (2010); Steffensmeier et al. (2011).

68. For examples, see Durose et al. (2014); Minton (2013); For a review of limitations of the Black/white dichotomy and the promise of unpacking this dichotomy in reentry research, see Garcia-Hallett and Kovacs (2020).

69. Garcia-Hallett and Kovacs (2020).

70. In addition, one mother named Paloma had seven children who had been adopted and whose ages she was not sure of, but who were all minors.

71. Garcia-Hallett (2019a).

72. Glaze and Maruschak (2008); Mumola (2000); Siegel (2011).

73. Miller and Stuart (2017).

74. Roberts (1993, pp. 4-5).

75. Phillips et al. (2010); Roberts (2012).

76. Hayward and DePanfilis (2007); Phillips et al. (2010); Raimon et al. (2009); Roberts (2012).

77. Browne (2000); Browne and Giampetro-Meyer (2003); Browne and Misra (2003); Roscigno and Bobbitt-Zeher (2007).

78. National Employment Law Project (2016); Pager (2003).

79. Ifatunji (2016); Ortiz and Roscigno (2009).

CHAPTER 1. MOTHERWORK

1. The stratification of skin tone may expose people of color to colorism, in which those with darker skin are viewed as subordinate and treated more negatively than those of lighter skin color (Hunter, 2007).

2. Said by Dr. Ruby Tapia at the Carceral State Project's 2018–2019 Symposium.

3. Alexander (2012, p. 164).

4. Embrick (2015); see also Williams and Battle (2017).

5. King et al. (2015).

6. Foucault (1977).

7. Jefferson (2018).

8. Mitchell and Davis (2019); Turner (2020).

9. Gurusami (2019, p. 129).

10. Foner (2001); Hughes (2003); Phinney and Chavira (1995); Waters (1999).

11. Foner (2001, p. 16).

12. Colen (2006); Collins (2009); Odum (2017).

13. Collins (2009); Davis (1998); Hancock (2004); Lubiano (1992); McCorkel (2013).

14. Hays (1996).

15. Battle (2016); Correctional Association of New York (2013); Raimon et al. (2009); Roberts (2012).

16. Bermúdez et al. (2014); Collins (2009); Odum (2017); Smith (1962); Stack and Burton (1994).

17. See Bemiller (2010); Berry and Eigenberg (2003); Hondagneu-Sotelo and Avila (1997).

18. Hays (1996).

19. Enos (1998).

20. Brody (2017); Hansen et al. (2002); Panettieri and Hall (2008); Simkin et al. (2018); Ward and Wolf-Wendel (2012).

21. Leverentz (2014); Michalsen (2011); Sharpe (2015).

22. Interestingly, however, the distinguishing factor of maternal responsibilities was only noted when mothers had contact with either their only child or at least one of their multiple children. Those who did not have contact with their only child made no mention of maternal responsibilities or concerns that distinguished mothers from non-mothers in their reentry.

23. Glaze and Maruschak (2008); Mumola (2000).

24. Leverentz, 2014; Michalsen (2011).

25. Easterling et al. (2019); Hondagneu-Sotelo and Avila (1997); Walsh and Nieves (2018).

26. Garcia-Hallett (2019a).

27. Wildeman and Turney (2014). For a review, see Wakefield and Garcia-Hallett (2017).

28. McCorkel (2004, 2013); McKim (2017); Roberts (2012); Sered and Norton-Hawk (2014).

29. Colen (2006); Collins (2009); Odum (2017).

30. Collins (2009); Hill (2003); Jambunathan et al. (2000); Mendoza et al. (2018); Smith (1962); Stack and Burton (1994).

31. Chamberlain (2003, p. 63).

32. Pruchno (1999).

33. Collins (2009); Hill (2003).

34. Thornton (1998, p. 51).

35. Hays (1996).

36. Christopher (2012, pp. 87–88) found that employed mothers justified employment by highlighting individual benefits and "challenging the notion that children's needs should always come first." Transnational mothers work and/or live in a different country than their country of origin where their children reside (Colen, 2006; Hondagneu-Sotelo & Avila, 1997). In their work on transnational mothers, Hondagneu-Sotelo and Avila (1997, p. 562) discovered: "Rather than replacing caregiving with breadwinning definitions of motherhood, they appear to be expanding their definitions of motherhood to encompass breadwinning that may require long-term physical separations."

37. Gustafson (2013, p. 8).

CHAPTER 2. CUSTODY AND HOUSING

1. In New York City, the Administration for Children's Services (ACS) oversees child welfare programs.

2. Hayward and DePanfilis (2007); Phillips et al. (2010); Raimon et al. (2009); Roberts (2012).

3. Roberts (2012).

4. Phillips et al. (2010); Roberts (2012).

5. Garcia-Hallett (2019b); Gurusami (2019); Roberts (2012).

6. Moynihan (1965).

7. Barnes and Stringer (2014); Baunach (1985).

8. Hayward and DePanfilis (2007); Wells and Guo (1999).

9. Collins (2009); Hondagneu-Sotelo and Avila (1997); Odum (2017); Stack and Burton (1994).

10. Collins (2009).

11. Collins (2009); Hill (2003); Jambunathan et al. (2000); Pruchno (1999); Smith (1962); Stack and Burton (1994).

12. However, refer to chapter 3 for a discussion on reluctance from family members and ethnic communities to support mothers after cultural values about legitimate work had seemingly been ignored; refer to chapter 4 for a discussion of distinctions in familial acceptance and assistance when mothers had histories of substance use.

13. Reilly (2003).

14. Leathers (2005); Reilly (2003).

15. Collins (2009).

16. Bresler and Lewis (1983); Enos (2001).

17. Garcia-Hallett (2019a).

18. According to New York Social Services Law SOS Section 371 (4-a): "'Neglected child' means a child younger than age 18 whose physical, mental, or emotional condition has been impaired or is in imminent danger of becoming impaired as a result of the failure of his or her parent or other person legally responsible for his or her care to exercise a minimum degree of care . . . by misusing a drug or drugs, or by misusing alcoholic beverages to the extent that he or she loses self-control of his or her actions, or by any other acts of a similarly serious nature requiring the aid of the court; provided, however, that where the respondent is voluntarily and regularly participating in a rehabilitative program, evidence that the respondent has repeatedly misused a drug or drugs or alcoholic beverages to the extent that he or she loses self-control of his or her actions shall not establish that the child is a neglected child in the absence of evidence establishing that the child's physical, mental, or emotional condition has been impaired or is in imminent danger of becoming impaired" (Child Welfare Information Gateway, 2016, p. 22).

19. Thomas and Bauer (2019).

20. Appell (1998, p. 377).

21. Robison and Miller (2016, p. 332).

22. Reviere et al. (2020, p. 88).

23. Enos (1998, p. 64); see also Correctional Association of New York (2013).

24. Roscigno and Bobbitt-Zeher (2007); Roscigno et al. (2009); Thacher (2008).

25. Quets et al. (2016, p. 8).

26. Massey and Lundy (2001, p. 461).

27. Correctional Association of New York (2013); Department of Housing and Urban Development (2016); Quets et al., (2016); Thacher (2008).

28. Department of Housing and Urban Development (2016).

29. Department of Housing and Urban Development (2016).

30. *Connections: A Guide for Formerly Incarcerated People in New York City* is a free guide that serves as a reentry resource for information on housing, education, financial assistance, substance use programs, legal services, and immigration—to name a few topics. The guide is available through the New York Public Library, which provides a PDF version on its website (https://www.nypl.org/help/community-outreach/correctional-services). While print copies of the book are also available to incarcerated individuals pending release, there is limited printing of the book, and priority is given to those approaching release. In addition, the Spanish version of *Connections* is only available as a PDF document, so incarcerated individuals must submit a mailed request for access to the guide. Yet at the time of this study, incarcerated Spanish speakers were only allowed to request a maximum of forty pages to be printed at a time, and there was also a one-year lag in the Spanish translation of the annual guide.

31. Smiley and Middlemass (2020).

32. Michalsen (2011).

33. Haney (2010); McCorkel (2004); Sered and Norton-Hawk (2014).

34. Stern (2020).

35. Brown and Bloom (2009, p. 319).

36. Savarese (2015, p. 105).

37. Enos (2001); Stenius et al. (2005).

38. This is consistent with research by Enos (2001); Leverentz (2014); Michalsen (2011); Richie (2001); and Sharpe (2015).

39. Richie (2001, p. 379).

CHAPTER 3. EMPLOYMENT AND FINANCES

1. Holzer et al. (2004).

2. New York City Bar (n.d., p. 4).

3. Holzer et al. (2004); Pager (2003).

4. Flake (2015); Shimizu (2018).

5. Stevenson (1993) uses the term "double minority," while other scholars have used terms like "multiple marginality" (Turner, 2002) and "double-bind syndrome" (Stanley, 2006), to highlight the marginalization of women of color across both gender and race/ethnicity.

6. England and Browne (1992).

7. Applicants' interests and self-selection into certain fields can potentially influence some of these hiring disparities, but gendered job segregation is primarily affected by employers' stereotypes, assumptions, and responses to women's competencies (Browne and Giampetro-Meyer, 2003; Browne and Misra, 2003).

8. Browne and Giampetro-Meyer (2003); Morrison et al. (1987).

9. See Reid et al. (2000).

10. Browne (2000); England and Browne (1992); Roscigno and Bobbitt-Zeher (2007).

11. Bendick et al. (1994); Bendick et al. (1991); Browne (2000); Browne and Misra (2003).

12. Ortiz and Roscigno (2009).

13. Bound and Dresser (1999); Browne (2000); Browne and Misra (2003).

14. Maruna, 2001

15. National Employment Law Project, 2016

16. Although it is possible that these disparities can be a function of the smaller sample of West Indian mothers, these ethnic differences in labor force participation are generally consistent with the broader New York City population, where the mothers lived. In New York City, 68% of West Indian women report being in the labor force, which is higher than the percentage of Latina women (55%) and women referred to as "Black or African American alone" (60%) (US Census Bureau, 2013; see also Model, 1995).

17. Bobb and Clarke (2001, p. 234).

18. See Shaw-Taylor and Tuch (2007).

19. Clerge (2014); Ifatunji (2016); Waters (1999).

20. Waters (1999).

21. Bobb and Clarke (2001); Model (1995); Waters (1999).

22. Foner (1985); see also Gopaul-McNicol (1993).

23. Model (1995).

24. Waters and Kasinitz (2010); see also Rogers (2001).

25. Waters (1999).

26. Foner (1985); Gopaul-McNicol (1993); Rogers (2006); Waters and Kasinitz (2010).

27. Model (2001, p. 53).

28. Rogers (2004).

29. Williams (2003, p. 1).

30. Cahusac and Kanji (2014); Crosby et al. (2004); Williams (2001, 2003).

31. Byron (2010); Byron and Roscigno (2014); Halpert et al. (1993).

32. While this study demonstrates employers' assumptions about women of color as single mothers and therefore incompetent, it also suggests that women of color may be seen as hard-working "matriarchs" who would do anything to support their family. Yet this was viewed negatively as women of color who were desperate for a paycheck.

33. Harris (2020).

34. See Edin and Lein (1997); Scott et al. (2004).

35. Williams (2001, p. 70).

36. Edin and Lein (1997).

37. The number of unemployed mothers excludes four mothers who interned at the not-for-profit reentry programs that they were participants of, an opportunity given to them to gain work experience.

38. Brown and Bloom (2009); Harris (2020); La Vigne et al. (2009); Patel and Philip (2012).

39. Hawkins et al. (2006).
40. Fournier and Herlihy (2006, pp. 170–171).
41. Fournier and Herlihy (2006); Hallett (2012); Waters (1999).
42. Waters (1999).
43. Garcia-Hallett (2019b).
44. Beckhusen et al. (2012); Bhuyan and Velagapudi (2013); Morales et al. (2012).
45. See Beckhusen et al. (2012); Toussaint-Comeau (2008). Despite the potential benefits of ethnic enclaves, Garcia-Hallett et al. (2020) suggest that ethnic enclaves may simultaneously expose residents to disproportionate criminalization by law enforcement because of their high visibility as targets.
46. Chamberlain and Wallace (2016); Lynch and Sabol (2001); Wallace (2015).
47. Boswell and Wedge (2002); Fried and Fried (1996).
48. Fried and Fried (1996, p. 121).
49. Nieva and Pulido (2014); Smith (2010).
50. Beckhusen et al. (2012); Garcia-Hallett et al. (2020); Toussaint-Comeau (2008).

CHAPTER 4. LIFE IN RECOVERY

1. Braithwaite et al. (2005).
2. The mother who described herself as previously abusing or craving money was Latoya. Her craving for money was equated to drugs and alcohol given the "high" she received from getting money and the physical symptoms of withdrawal she had when she was unable to "get over" on local businesses or organizations. Thus, she was included among the group of mothers with substance use histories with drugs and alcohol.
3. Braithwaite et al. (2005); Greenfeld and Snell (1999); Snell and Morton (1994).
4. Garcia-Hallett (2019a); Glaze and Maruschak (2008); Mumola and Karberg (2006).
5. Glaze and Maruschak (2008).
6. Freiburger (2011).
7. Phillips et al. (2010).
8. Christopher (2012); Colen (2006); Hondagneu-Sotelo and Avila (1997).
9. Roberts (1991).
10. Alexander (2012).
11. Caplan (1998); Jackson and Mannix (2004).
12. Garcia (2016).
13. Falkin and Strauss (2003); Strauss and Falkin (2001).
14. Falkin and Strauss (2003).
15. Cooper-Sadlo et al. (2019); Mitchell and Davis (2019).
16. Kleinman and Lukoff (1978).
17. Djumalieva et al. (2002); Jean-Louis et al. (2001); Kleinman and Lukoff (1978).
18. Djumalieva et al. (2002); Sargent and Harris (1992).

19. Jean-Louis et al. (2001).

20. Brown and Bloom (2009); Haney (2013); McCorkel (2004); Sered and Norton-Hawk (2014).

21. Burns and Peyrot (2003); McKim (2017); Sered and Norton-Hawk (2014).

22. Burns and Peyrot (2003).

23. Carr (2010); McKim (2017); Whalley and Hackett (2017).

24. McCorkel (2004).

25. Carr (2010).

26. Kerrison (2018, p. 140); see also McKim (2017).

27. Mauer (2009 2013); Sabol et al. (2009).

28. Elliot et al. (2005).

29. Nelson-Zlupko et al. (1996).

30. Irwin (1995).

31. Dervin (2012); Jensen (2011).

32. Peter D. Hart Research Associates Inc. (1998).

33. See Aiello and McQueeny (2016).

34. See the 2005 New York/New York III Supportive Housing Agreement, made on November 3, 2005, and in effect through June 30, 2016, which includes the period of data collection for this study.

35. Jean-Louis et al. (2001, p. 116).

CONCLUSION

1. Lorde (1984, p. 42).

2. Brown and Bloom (2009); Covington (2003); Hayes (2009); Leverentz (2014); Sharpe (2015).

3. For a review of cognitive dissonance and reducing dissonance, see McGrath (2017).

4. Middlemass (2020, p. 145).

5. Williams et al. (2020).

6. States spend more to investigate families suspected of neglect and abuse than is spent on providing families with in-home services from community-based agencies contracted with the Administration for Children's Services (ACS) (Thomas and Bauer, 2019).

7. Newsome (2003); Ritchie (2017); see also Miller and Stuart (2017).

8. For single mothers, see Meier et al. (2016). For primiparas and first-time mothers, see Krieg (2007) and Reece (1995). For teenage and older mothers, see Larson (2004) and Reece (1995). For working mothers in a variety of fields, see Kelly et al. (1994) and Novich and Garcia-Hallett (2018).

9. Gustafson (2013, p. 1).

10. Hays (1996); McMahon (1995).

11. This is consistent with research by Easterling et al. (2019, p. 534), describing "suspended moms" as justice-involved mothers who "were experiencing a shift in focus from the family to the individual. Instead of focusing on the family unit, they were drawn to focus on themselves."

12. Easterling et al. (2019); Enos (2001); Jensen and DuBeck-Biondo (2005).

13. Jensen and DuBeck-Biondo (2005).

14. Easterling et al. (2019, p. 532).

15. Williams et al. (2021).

16. Brown and Bloom (2009); Haney (2013); McCorkel (2004); Sered and Norton-Hawk (2014).

17. Brown and Bloom (2009); Haney (2013); McCorkel (2004).

18. Helgeson and Gottlieb (2000).

19. Helgeson and Gottlieb (2000).

20. Goffman (1963).

21. Helgeson and Gottlieb (2000, p. 225).

22. Collins (2009); Odum (2017).

23. Whalley and Hackett (2017, p. 465).

24. Heiner and Tyson (2017); Kim (2020); Whalley and Hackett (2017).

25. During the month this study began, approximately 60,352 people were sleeping in New York City shelters, and the mayor, Bill de Blasio, had an agenda to tackle the city's extreme homelessness.

26. For example, Alós et al. (2015).

27. Lipsitz (2011, p. 1761).

28. Kopak and Hoffmann (2014).

29. Heiner and Tyson (2017).

30. Hackett (2015, p. 37).

31. Appell (1998, p. 139).

32. Carlton (2018); Carlton and Russell (2018).

33. Ward and Maruna (2007).

34. See Blakey (2018).

35. See Foner (1985); Model (1995); Waters (1999).

36. Garcia-Hallett and Kovacs (2020).

37. See also Jean-Louis et al. (2001).

38. Their children's average age excludes seven underaged children whose exact ages were unknown by their mother, Paloma.

39. Brown (2011); Rich (1995).

40. Siegel (2011).

41. Thornton (1998, p. 63).

42. McAdams (2008, p. 242); Miller et al. (2015).

43. Ward and Maruna (2007).

APPENDIX A. RESEARCH DESIGN

1. Kent (2007); Waters (1999).

2. The New York City bus line M101, M102, M103.

3. As discussed in the introduction, some mothers identified with more than one ethnicity, shaping the overlap in numbers for ethnic representation.

4. As discussed in the introduction, mothers had an average of two to three children, shaping the overlap in numbers for the various degrees of mothers' contact with children.

5. The Garifuna language belongs to the Arawak language family and is the language of the Garifuna people in Honduras, Guatemala, Belize, and Nicaragua.

6. Mothers were compensated using funds received from the 2014 American Society of Criminology's Graduate Fellowship for Ethnic Minorities (currently known as the Ruth Peterson Fellowship for Racial and Ethnic Diversity).

7. Charmaz (2006); Floersch et al. (2010); Lal et al. (2012).

8. Ryan and Bernard (2003).

9. Charmaz (2006, p. 100).

10. Charmaz (2006).

11. See the introduction for a review of controlling images about West Indian, African American, and Latina women and mothers. See chapter 1 for a discussion about mothering under a carceral siege in communities of color and racial-ethnic nuances in how much they must protect their children from social exclusion and marginalization. See chapters 3 and 4 for discussions of cultural beliefs among the West Indian population and the impact of perceived cultural transgressions on family and community support.

12. Waters (2000).

13. This may also be conflated with time since release. Specifically, some scholars argue that it is best to have recently released participants as well as participants with more time since their last incarceration, given that reentry obstacles may vary based on the amount of time post-incarceration (see Durose et al., 2014). Though it was not an intentional part of my study design, I recruited study participants with a wide range of time since their last incarceration, from as short as 1.5 weeks to as long as 16 years since their release (for an in-depth breakdown and summary of the mothers, see appendix B).

14. Barnes & Stringer (2014, p. 16).

References

Aiello, B., & McQueeny, K. (2016). "How can you live without your kids?": Distancing from and embracing the stigma of "incarcerated mother". *Journal of Prison Education and Reentry*, 3(1), 32–49.

Alexander, M. (2012). *The new Jim Crow: Mass incarceration in the age of colorblindness*. The New Press.

Alós, R., Esteban, F., Jódar, P., & Miguélez, F. (2015). Effects of prison work programmes on the employability of ex-prisoners. *European Journal of Criminology*, 12(1), 35–50.

Appell, A. R. (1998). On fixing "bad" mothers and saving their children. In M. Ladd-Taylor & L. Umansky (Eds.), *"Bad" mothers: The politics of blame in twentieth-century America* (pp. 356–380). New York University Press.

Barnes, S. L., & Stringer, E. C. (2014). Is motherhood important? Imprisoned women's maternal experiences before and during confinement and their postrelease expectation. *Feminist Criminology*, 9(1), 3–23.

Battle, N. T. (2016). From slavery to Jane crow to Say Her Name: An intersectional examination of black women and punishment. *Meridians*, 15(1), 109–136.

Baunach, P. J. (1985). *Mothers in prison*. Transaction Books.

Beckhusen, J., Florax, R. J. G. M., de Graaff, T., Poot, J., & Waldorf, B. (2012). *Living and working in ethnic enclaves: Language proficiency of immigrants in U.S. metropolitan areas* (Discussion paper series, Forschungsinstitut zur Zukunft der Arbeit, No. 6363).

Bemiller, M. (2010). Mothering from a distance. *Journal of Divorce & Remarriage*, 51(3), 169–184.

Bendick, M., Jr., Jackson, C. W., & Reinoso, V. A. (1994). Measuring employment discrimination through controlled experiments. *The Review of Black Political Economy, 23*(1), 25–48.

Bendick, M., Jr., Jackson, C. W., Reinoso, V. A., & Hodges, L. E. (1991). Discrimination against Latino job applicants: A controlled experiment. *Human Resource Management, 30*(4), 469–484.

Bermúdez, J. M., Zak-Hunter, L. M., Stinson, M. A., & Abrams, B. A. (2014). "I am not going to lose my kids to the streets": Meanings and experiences of motherhood among Mexican-origin women. *Journal of Family Issues, 35*(1), 3–27.

Berry, P. E., & Eigenberg, H. M. (2003). Role strain and incarcerated mothers: Understanding the process of mothering. *Women & Criminal Justice, 15*(1), 101–119.

Bhuyan, R., & Velagapudi, K. (2013). From one "dragon sleigh" to another: Advocating for immigrant women facing violence in Kansas. *Affilia: Journal of Women and Social Work, 28*(1), 65–78.

Blakey, J. M. (2018). Trauma-informed care with legally mandated involuntary clients. In R. H. Rooney & R. G. Mirick. (Eds.), *Strategies for work with involuntary clients* (pp. 139–164). Columbia University Press.

Bobb, B. F. B., & Clarke, A. Y. (2001). Experiencing success: Structuring the perception of opportunities for West Indians. In N. Foner (Ed.), *Islands in the city: West Indian migration to New York* (pp. 216–236). University of California Press.

Boswell, G., & Wedge, P. (2002). *Imprisoned fathers and their children.* Jessica Kingsley.

Bound, J., & Dresser, L. (1999). Losing ground: The erosion of the relative earnings of African American women during the 1980s. In I. Browne (Ed.), *Latinas and African American women at work: Race, gender, and economic inequality* (pp. 61–104). Russell Sage Foundation.

Braithwaite, R. L., Treadwell, H. M., & Arriola, K. R. (2005). Health disparities and incarcerated women: A population ignored. *American Journal of Public Health, 95*(10), 1679–1681.

Bresler, L., & Lewis, D. K. (1983). Black and white women prisoners: Differences in family ties and their programmatic implications. *The Prison Journal, 63*(2), 116–123.

Bridges, K. M. (2007). Wily patients, welfare queens, and the reiteration of race in the U.S. *Texas Journal of Women and the Law, 17*(1), 1–66.

Brody, L. S. (2017). *The fifth trimester: The working mom's guide to style, sanity, & success after baby.* Knopf Doubleday Publishing Group.

Bronson, J., & Carson, E. A. (2019). Prisoners in 2017. *Bureau of Justice Statistics Bulletin* (NCJ 252156). U.S. Department of Justice.

Brown, I. (2011). *A sociological analysis of maternal ambivalence: Class and race differences among new mothers* [Doctoral dissertation]. Rutgers University–New Brunswick.

Brown, M., & Bloom, B. E. (2009). Colonialism and carceral motherhood: Native Hawaiian families under corrections and child welfare control. *Feminist Criminology, 4*(2), 151–169.

Browne, I. (2000). Employment and earnings among Latinas and African American women. In I. Browne (Ed.), *Latinas and African American women at work: Race, gender, and economic inequality* (pp. 1–31). Russell Sage Foundation.

Browne, I., & Misra, J. (2003). The intersection of gender and race in the labor market. *Annual Review of Sociology, 29,* 487–513.

Browne, M. N., & Giampetro-Meyer, A. (2003). Many paths to justice: The glass ceiling, the looking glass, and strategies for getting to the other side. *Hofstra Labor & Employment Law Journal, 21*(1), 61–107.

Budig, M. J., & England, P. (2001). The wage penalty for motherhood. *American Sociological Review, 66*(2), 204–225.

Burns, S. L., & Peyrot, M. (2003). Tough love: Nurturing and coercing responsibility and recovery in California drug courts. *Social Problems, 50*(3), 416–438.

Bush-Baskette, S. (2000). The war on drugs and the incarceration of mothers. *Journal of Drug Issues, 30*(4), 919–928.

Bush-Baskette, S. (2010). *Misguided justice: The war on drugs and the incarceration of Black women.* iUniverse.

Byrne, C. F., & Trew, K. J. (2008). Pathways through crime: The development of crime and desistance in the accounts of men and women offenders. *The Howard Journal, 47,* 238–258.

Byron, R. A. (2010). Discrimination, complexity, and the public/private sector question. *Work and Occupations, 37*(4), 435–475.

Byron, R. A., & Roscigno, V. J. (2014). Relational power, legitimacy, and pregnancy discrimination. *Gender & Society, 28*(3), 435–462.

Cahusac, E., & Kanji, S. (2014). Giving up: How gendered organizational cultures push mothers out. *Gender, Work & Organization, 21*(1), 57–70.

Caplan, P. J. (1998). Mother-blaming. In M. Ladd-Taylor & L. Umansky (Eds.), *"Bad" mothers: The politics of blame in twentieth-century America* (pp. 127–144). New York University Press.

Carlton, B. (2018). Penal reform, anti-carceral feminist campaigns and the politics of change in women's prisons, Victoria, Australia. *Punishment & Society, 20*(3), 283–307.

Carlton, B., & Russell, E. K. (2018). *Resisting carceral violence: Women's imprisonment and the politics of abolition.* Palgrave Macmillan.

Carr, E. S. (2010). *Scripting addiction: The politics of therapeutic talk and American sobriety.* Princeton University Press.

Carson, E. A. (2020). Prisoners in 2018. Bureau of Justice Statistics Bulletin (NCJ 253516). U.S. Department of Justice.

Chamberlain, A. W., & Wallace, D. (2016). Mass reentry, neighborhood context and recidivism: Examining how the distribution of parolees within and across neighborhoods impacts recidivism. *Justice Quarterly, 33*(5), 912–941.

Chamberlain, M. (2003). Rethinking Caribbean families: Extending the links. *Community, Work & Family, 6*(1), 63–76.

Charmaz, K. (2006). *Constructing grounded theory: A practical guide through qualitative analysis.* Sage.

Child Welfare Information Gateway. (2016). *Parental drug use as child abuse.* US Department of Health and Human Services, Children's Bureau.

Christopher, K. (2012). Extensive mothering: Employed mothers' constructions of the good mother. *Gender & Society*, 26(1), 73–96.

Clerge, O. (2014). Toward a minority culture of mobility: Immigrant integration into the African-American middle class. *Sociology Compass*, 8(10), 1167–1182.

Colen, S. (2006). "Like a mother to them": Stratified reproduction and West Indian childcare workers and employers in New York. In E. Lewin (Ed.), *Feminist anthropology: A reader* (pp. 380–396). Blackwell Publishing.

Collins, P. H. (1994). Shifting the center: Race, class, and feminist theorizing about motherhood. In E. N. Glenn, G. Chang, & L. R. Forcey (Eds.), *Mothering: Ideology, experience, and agency* (pp. 45–65). Routledge.

Collins, P. H. (2005). Black women and motherhood. In C. Wiedmer & S. Hardy (Eds.), *Motherhood and space: Configurations of the maternal through politics, home, and the body* (pp. 149–159). Palgrave Macmillan.

Collins, P. H. (2009). *Black feminist thought: Knowledge, consciousness, and the politics of empowerment*. Routledge Classics.

Cooper-Sadlo, S., Mancini, M. A., Meyer, D. D., & Chou, J. L. (2019). Mothers talk back: Exploring the experiences of formerly incarcerated mothers. *Contemporary Family Therapy*, 41(1), 92–101.

Correctional Association of New York. (2013). *A place to call my own: Women and the search for housing after incarceration*. http://www.correctional association.org/wp-content/uploads/2013/10/CA-AP2CMO-FINAL-print -ready-August-8-2013.pdf

Covington, S. (2003). A woman's journey home: Challenges for female offenders and their children. In J. Travis & M. Waul (Eds.), *Prisoners once removed: The impact of incarceration and reentry on children, families, and communities* (pp. 67–104). The Urban Institute Press.

Crosby, F. J., Williams, J. C., & Biernat, M. (2004). The maternal wall. *Journal of Social Issues*, 60(4), 675–682.

Dallaire, D. H., Ciccone, A., & Wilson, L. C. (2010). Teachers' experiences with and expectations of children with incarcerated parents. *Journal of Applied Developmental Psychology*, 31(4), 281–290.

Davis, A. Y. (1981). *Women, race & class*. Vintage Books.

Davis, A. Y. (1998, September 10). *Masked racism: Reflections on the prison industrial complex*. Colorlines. https://www.colorlines.com/articles/masked -racism-reflections-prison-industrial-complex

Department of Housing and Urban Development. (2016, April 4). *Office of General Counsel Guidance on Application of Fair Housing Act Standards to the Use of Criminal Records by Providers of Housing and Real Estate-Related Transactions*. http://portal.hud.gov/hudportal/documents/huddoc ?id=HUD_OGCGuidAppFHAStandCR.pdf

Dervin, F. (2012). Cultural identity, representation and othering. In J. Jackson (Ed.), *The Routledge handbook of language and intercultural communication* (pp. 181–194). Routledge.

Djumalieva, D., Imamshah, W., Wagner, U., & Razum, O. (2002). Drug use and HIV risk in Trinidad and Tobago: Qualitative study. *International Journal of STD & AIDS*, 13(9), 633–639.

Durose, M. R., Cooper, A. D., & Snyder, H. N. (2014). Recidivism of prisoners released in 30 states in 2005: Patterns from 2005 to 2010. *Bureau of Justice Statistics Special Report* (NCJ 244205). US Department of Justice.

Easterling, B. A., Feldmeyer, B., & Presser, L. (2019). Narrating mother identities from prison. *Feminist Criminology*, 14(5), 519–539.

Edin, K., & Lein, L. (1997). Work, welfare, and single mothers' economic survival strategies. *American Sociological Review*, 62(2), 253–266.

Elliott, D. E., Bjelajac, P., Fallot, R. D., Markoff, L. S., & Reed, B. G. (2005). Trauma-informed or trauma-denied: Principles and implementation of trauma-informed services for women. *Journal of Community Psychology*, 33(4), 461–477.

Embrick, D. G. (2015). Two nations, revisited: The lynching of black and brown bodies, police brutality, and racial control in "post-racial" Amerikkka. *Critical Sociology*, 41(6), 835–843.

England, P., & Browne, I. (1992). Trends in women's economic status. *Sociological Perspectives*, 35(1), 17–51.

Enos, S. (1998). Managing motherhood in prison: The impact of race and ethnicity on child placements. *Women & Therapy*, 20, 57–72.

Enos, S. (2001). *Mothering from the inside: Parenting in a women's prison.* State University of New York Press.

Euser, S., Alink, L. R., Tharner, A., van IJzendoorn, M. H., & Bakermans-Kranenburg, M. J. (2013). The prevalence of child sexual abuse in out-of-home care: A comparison between abuse in residential and in foster care. *Child Maltreatment*, 18(4), 221–231.

Falkin, G. P., & Strauss, S. M. (2003). Social supporters and drug use enablers: A dilemma for women in recovery. *Addictive Behaviors*, 28(1), 141–155.

Ferraro, K. J., & Moe, A. M. (2003). Mothering, crime and incarceration. *Journal of Contemporary Ethnography*, 32(1), 9–40.

Finzen, M. E. (2005). Systems of oppression: The collateral consequences of incarceration and their effects on black communities. *Georgetown Journal on Poverty Law & Policy*, 12(2), 299–324.

Flake, D. F. (2015). When any sentence is a life sentence: Employment discrimination against ex-offenders. *Washington University Law Review*, 93(1), 45–102.

Flavin, J. (2001). Of punishment and parenthood: Family-based social control and the sentencing of Black drug offenders. *Gender and Society*, 15(4), 611–633.

Floersch, J., Longhofer, J. L., Kranke, D., & Townsend, L. (2010). Integrating thematic, grounded theory and narrative analysis: A case study of adolescent psychotropic treatment. *Qualitative Social Work*, 9(3), 407–425.

Foner, N. (1985). Race and color: Jamaican migrants in London and New York City. *The International Migration Review*, 19(4), 708–727.

Foner, N. (2001). West Indian migration to New York: An overview. In N. Foner (Ed.), *Islands in the city: West Indian migration to New York* (pp. 1–22). University of California Press.

Foucault, M. (1977). *Discipline & punish: The birth of the prison.* Vintage Books.

Fournier, A. M., & Herlihy, D. (2006). *The zombie curse: A doctor's 25-year journey into the heart of the AIDS epidemic in Haiti.* Joseph Henry Press.

Freiburger, T. L. (2011). The impact of gender, offense type, and familial role on the decision to incarcerate. *Social Justice Research,* 24, 143–167.

Fried, S., & Fried, P. (1996). *Bullies & victims: Helping your child survive the schoolyard battlefield.* M. Evans and Company.

Garcia, J. (2016). The importance of the mentor-mentee relationship in women's desistance from destructive behaviors. *International Journal of Offender Therapy and Comparative Criminology,* 60(7), 808–827.

Garcia-Hallett, J. (2019a). Maternal identities and narratives of motherhood: A qualitative exploration of women's pathways into and out of offending. *Feminist Criminology,* 14(2), 214–240.

Garcia-Hallett, J. (2019b). "We're being released to a jungle": The state of prisoner reentry and the resilience of women of color. *The Prison Journal,* 99(4), 459–483.

Garcia-Hallett, J., & Kovacs, K. P. (2020). The promise of unpacking the Black/white dichotomy for reentry research. In A. Leverentz, E. Chen, & J. Christian (Eds.), *Beyond recidivism: New approaches to research on prisoner reentry and reintegration* (pp. 135–150). New York University Press.

Garcia-Hallett, J., Like, T., Torres, T., and Irazábal, C. (2020). Latinxs in the Kansas City Metro area: Policing and criminalization in ethnic enclaves. *Journal of Planning Education and Research,* 40(2), 151–168.

Glaze, L. E., & Maruschak, L. M. (2008). Parents in prison and their minor children. *Bureau of Justice Statistics Special Report* (NCJ 222984). U.S. Department of Justice.

Goffman, E. (1963). *Stigma: Notes on the management of spoiled identity.* Simon & Schuster.

Gopaul-McNicol, S. (1993). *Working with West Indian families.* Guilford Press.

Greenfeld, L. A., & Snell, T. L. (1999). Women offenders. *Bureau of Justice Statistics Special Report* (NCJ 175688). U.S. Department of Justice.

Gurusami, S. (2019). Motherwork under the state: The maternal labor of formerly incarcerated black women. *Social Problems,* 1(1), 128–143.

Gustafson, D. L. (2013). Framing the discussion. In D. L. Gustafson (Ed.), *Unbecoming mothers: The social production of social absence* (pp. 1–21). Routledge.

Hackett, C. M. (2015). *"Helping women help themselves": An ethnography of carceral empowerment and the neoliberal rehabilitative ideal at a recovery center for criminalized women* [Doctoral dissertation]. University of Colorado at Boulder.

Hagan, J., & Foster, H. (2012). Children of the American prison generation: Student and school spillover effects of incarcerating mothers. *Law & Society Review,* 46(1), 37–69.

Hallett, M. C. (2012). "Better than white trash": Work ethic, Latinidad and whiteness in rural Arkansas. *Latino Studies,* 10(1–2), 81–106.

Halpert, J. A., Wilson, M. L., & Hickman, J. L. (1993). Pregnancy as a source of bias in performance appraisals. *Journal of Organizational Behavior,* 14(7), 649–663.

Hancock, A. (2004). *The politics of disgust: The public identity of the welfare queen.* New York University Press.

Haney, L. A. (2010). *Offending women: Power, punishment, and the regulation of desire.* University of California Press.

Haney, L. A. (2013). Motherhood as punishment: The case of parenting in prison. *Signs: Journal of Women in Culture and Society,* 39(1), 105–130.

Hansen, R., Hansen, J., & Pollycove, R. (2002). *Mother nurture: A mother's guide to health in body, mind, and intimate relationships.* Penguin Books.

Hardesty, M., & Black, T. (1999). Mothering through addiction: A survival strategy among Puerto Rican addicts. *Qualitative Health Research,* 9(5), 602–619.

Harris, A. (2020). Framing the system of monetary sanctions as predatory: Policies, practices, and motivations. *UCLA Criminal Justice Law Review,* 4(1), 1–8.

Harris, A. P. (2012). Critical race theory. In *The selected works of Angela P. Harris.* University of California, Davis.

Hatfield, T. (2017). Mother-blaming. In J. Carlson & S. Dermer (Eds.), *The SAGE encyclopedia of marriage, family, and couples counseling* (Vol. 3, pp. 1105–1107). Sage Publications.

Hawkins, D. N., Amato, P. R., & King, V. (2006). Parent-adolescent involvement: The relative influence of parent gender and residence. *Journal of Marriage and Family,* 68(1), 125–136.

Hayes, M. (2009). The lived experience of mothering after prison. *Journal of Forensic Nursing,* 5(4), 228–236.

Hays, S. (1996). *The cultural contradictions of motherhood.* Yale University Press.

Hayward, R. A., & DePanfilis, D. (2007). Foster children with an incarcerated parent: Predictors of reunification. *Children and Youth Services Review,* 29, 1320–1334.

Heiner, B. T., & Tyson, S. K. (2017). Feminism and the carceral state: Gender-responsive justice, community accountability, and the epistemology of anti-violence. *Feminist Philosophy Quarterly,* 3(1). https:// doi.org/10.5206/fpq /2016.3.3

Helgeson, V. S., & Gottlieb, B. H. (2000). Support groups. In S. Cohen, L. G. Underwood, & B. H. Gottlieb (Eds.), *Social support measurement and intervention: A guide for health and social scientists* (pp. 221–245). Oxford University Press.

Henry, F. (1998). Race and racism in Trinidad and Tobago: A comment. *Caribbean Dialogue,* 3(4), 45–48.

Hill, R. B. (2003). *The strengths of Black families* (2nd ed.). University Press of America.

Holzer, H. J., Raphael, S., & Stoll, M. A. (2004). Will employers hire former offenders? Employer preferences, background checks, and their determinants. In M. Patillo, D. Weiman, & B. Western (Eds.), *The social effects of mass incarceration* (pp. 205–243). Russell Sage Foundation.

Hondagneu-Sotelo, P., & Avila, E. (1997). "I'm here, but I'm there": The meanings of Latina transnational motherhood. *Gender & Society,* 11(5), 548–571.

Hughes, D. (2003). Correlates of African American and Latino parents' messages to children about ethnicity and race: A comparative study of racial socialization. *American Journal of Community Psychology*, 31(1/2), 15–33.

Hunter, M. (2007). The persistent problem of colorism: Skin tone, status, and inequality. *Sociology Compass*, 1(1), 237–254.

Ifatunji, M. A. (2016). A test of the Afro Caribbean model minority hypothesis: Exploring the role of cultural attributes in labor market disparities between African Americans and Afro Caribbeans. *Du Bois Review: Social Science Research on Race*, 13(1), 109–138.

Irwin, K. (1995). Ideology, pregnancy and drugs: Differences between crack-cocaine, heroin and methamphetamine users. *Contemporary Drug Problems*, 22, 613–638.

Jackson, D., & Mannix, J. (2004). Giving voice to the burden of blame: A feminist study of mothers' experiences of mother blaming. *International Journal of Nursing Practice*, 10(4), 150–158.

Jambunathan, S., Burts, D. C., & Pierce, S. (2000). Comparisons of parenting attitudes among five ethnic groups in the United States. *Journal of Comparative Family Studies*, 31(4), 395–406.

Jean-Louis, E., Walker, J., Apollon, G., Piton, J., Antoine, M. B., Mombeleur, A., Thelismond, M., & César, N. (2001). Drug and alcohol use among Boston's Haitian community: A hidden problem unveiled by CCHER's Enhanced Innovative Case Management Program. *Drugs & Society*, 16(1–2), 107–122.

Jefferson, B. J. (2018). Policing, data, and power-geometry: Intersections of crime analytics and race during urban restructuring. *Urban Geography*, 39(8), 1247–1264. https://doi.org/10.1080/02723638.2018.1446587

Jensen, S. Q. (2011). Othering, identity formation and agency. *Qualitative Studies*, 2(2), 63–78.

Jensen, V., & DuBeck-Biondo, J. (2005). Mothers in jail: Gender, social control, and the construction of parenthood behind bars. In S. Lee Burns (Ed.), *Sociology of crime, law and deviance: Vol. 6. Ethnographies of law and social control* (pp. 121–142). Emerald Group Publishing.

Jordan-Zachery, J. S. (2008). A declaration of war: An analysis of how the invisibility of black women makes them targets of the war on drugs. *Journal of Women, Politics & Policy*, 29(2), 231–259.

Kaeble, D. (2018). Probation and parole in the United States, 2016. *Bureau of Justice Statistics Bulletin* (NCJ 251148). US Department of Justice.

Kelly, M. L., Herzog-Simmer, P. A., & Harris, M. A. (1994). Effects of military-induced separation on the parenting stress and family functioning of deploying mothers. *Military Psychology*, 6(2), 125–138.

Kent, M. M. (2007). Immigration and America's Black population. *Population Bulletin*, 62(4).

Kerrison, E. M. (2018). Exploring how prison-based drug rehabilitation programming shapes racial disparities in substance use disorder recovery. *Social Science & Medicine*, 199, 140–147.

Kim, M. E. (2020). Anti-carceral feminism: The contradictions of progress and the possibilities of counter-hegemonic struggle. *Affilia: Journal of Women and Social Work*, 35(3), 309–326.

King, L., Hinterland, K., Dragan, K. L., Driver, C. R., Harris, T. G., Gwynn, R. C., Linos, N., Barbot, O., & Bassett, M. T. (2015). Brooklyn Community District 16: Brownsville. *Community Health Profiles 2015*, 40(59), 1–16. https://www1.nyc.gov/assets/doh/downloads/pdf/data/2015chp-bk16.pdf

Kleinman, P. H., & Lukoff, I. F. (1978). Ethnic differences in factors related to drug use. *Journal of Health and Social Behavior*, 19(2), 190–199.

Kopak, A. M., & Hoffmann, N. G. (2014). The association between drug dependence and drug possession charges. *Drugs and Alcohol Today*, 14(2), 87–95.

Kreager, D. A., Matsueda, R. L., & Erosheva, E. A. (2010). Motherhood and criminal desistance in disadvantaged neighborhoods. *Criminology*, 48(1), 221–258.

Krieg, D. B. (2007). Does motherhood get easier the second-time around? Examining parenting stress and marital quality among mothers having their first or second child. *Parenting: Science and practice*, 7(2), 149–175.

Lal, S., Suto, M., & Ungar, M. (2012). Examining the potential of combining the methods of grounded theory and narrative inquiry: A comparative analysis. *The Qualitative Report*, 17(21), 1–22.

Larson, N. C. (2004). Parenting stress among adolescent mothers in the transition to adulthood. *Child and Adolescent Social Work Journal*, 21(5), 457–476.

LaVigne, N. G., Brooks, L. E., & Shollenberger, T. L. (2009). *Women on the outside: Understanding the experiences of female prisoners returning to Houston, TX*. Research Report. Urban Institute.

Leathers, S. J. (2005). Separation from siblings: Associations with placement adaptation and outcomes among adolescents in long-term foster care. *Children and Youth Services Review*, 27(7), 793–819.

Leverentz, A. M. (2014). *The ex-prisoner's dilemma: How women negotiate competing narratives of reentry and desistance*. Rutgers University Press.

Lipsitz, G. (2011). In an avalanche every snowflake pleads not guilty: The collateral consequences of mass incarceration and impediments to women's fair housing rights. *UCLA Law Review*, 59, 1746–1809.

López, V., & Chesney-Lind, M. (2014). Latina girls speak out: Stereotypes, gender and relationship dynamics. *Latino Studies*, 12(4), 527–549.

Lorde, A. (1984). *Sister outsider: Essays and speeches*. Crossing Press.

Lubiano, W. (1992). Black ladies, welfare queens, and state minstrels: Ideological war by narrative means. In T. Morrison (Ed.), *Race-ing justice, engendering power* (pp. 323–363). Pantheon Books.

Lynch, J. P., & Sabol, W. J. (2001). *Prisoner reentry in perspective*. The Urban Institute.

Maruna, S. (2001). *Making good: How ex-convicts reform and rebuild their lives*. American Psychological Association Press.

Massey, D. S., & Lundy, G. (2001). Use of black English and racial discrimination in urban housing markets: New methods and findings. *Urban Affairs Review*, 36(4), 452–469.

Mauer, M. (2009). *The changing racial dynamics of the war on drugs*. The Sentencing Project.

Mauer, M. (2013). *The changing racial dynamics of women's incarceration.* The Sentencing Project.

McAdams, D. P. (2008). Personal narratives and the life story. In O. P. John, R. W. Robins, & L. A. Pervin (Eds.), *The handbook of personality: Theory and research* (3rd ed., pp. 242–264). Guilford Press.

McCorkel, J. A. (2004). Criminally dependent? Gender, punishment, and the rhetoric of welfare reform. *Social Politics: International Studies in Gender, State & Society, 11*(3), 386–410.

McCorkel, J. A. (2013). *Breaking women: Gender, race, and the new politics of imprisonment.* New York University Press.

McGrath, A. (2017). Dealing with dissonance: A review of cognitive dissonance reduction. *Social Personal Psychological Compass, 11*(12), e12362.

McKim, A. (2017). *Addicted to rehab: Race, gender, and drugs in the era of mass incarceration.* Rutgers University Press.

McMahon, M. (1995). *Engendering motherhood: Identity and self-transformation in women's lives.* The Guilford Press.

Meier, A., Musick, K., Flood, S., & Dunifon, R. (2016). Mothering experiences: How single parenthood and employment structure the emotional valence of parenting. *Demography, 53*(3), 649–674.

Mendoza, A. N., Fruhauf, C. A., Bundy-Fazioli, K., & Weil, J. (2018). Understanding Latino grandparents raising grandchildren through a bioecological lens. *The International Journal of Aging and Human Development, 86*(3), 281–305.

Michalsen, V. (2011). Mothering as a life course transition: Do women go straight for their children? *Journal of Offender Rehabilitation, 50*(6), 349–366.

Middlemass, K. M. (2019). Black women excluded from protection and criminalized for their existence. In K. M. Middlemass & C. Smiley (Eds.), *Prisoner reentry in the 21st century: Critical perspectives of returning home* (pp. 83–95). Routledge.

Miller, J., Carbone-Lopez, K., & Gunderman, M. V. (2015). Gendered narratives of self, addiction, and recovery among women methamphetamine users. In L. Presser & S. Sandberg (Eds.), *Narrative criminology: Understanding stories of crime* (pp. 69–95). New York University Press.

Miller, R. J., & Stuart, F. (2017). Carceral citizenship: Race, rights and responsibility in the age of mass supervision. *Theoretical Criminology, 21*(4), 532–548.

Minaker, J., & Hogeveen, B. (2015). From criminalizing mothering to criminalized mothers: A introduction. In J. Minaker & B. Hogeveen (Eds.), *Criminalized mothers, criminalizing mothering* (pp. 1–24). Demeter Press.

Minton, T. D. (2013). Jail inmates at midyear 2012—statistical tables. *Bureau of Justice Statistical Tables* (NCJ 241264). US Department of Justice.

Mitchell, M., & Davis, J. (2019). Formerly incarcerated black mothers matter too: Resisting social constructions of motherhood. *The Prison Journal, 99*(4), 420–436.

Model, S. (1995). West Indian prosperity: Fact or fiction? *Social Problems, 42*(4), 535–553.

Model, S. (2001). Where New York's West Indians work. In N. Foner (Ed.), *Islands in the city: West Indian migration to New York* (pp. 52–80). University of California Press.

Morales, A., Yakushko, O. F., & Castro, A. J. (2012). Language brokering among Mexican-immigrant families in the Midwest: A multiple case study. *The Counseling Psychologist*, 40(4), 520–553.

Morrison, A. M., White, R. P., White, R. P., & Van Velsor, E. (1987). *Breaking the glass ceiling: Can women reach the top of America's largest corporations?* Pearson Education.

Mowatt, R. A., French, B. H., & Malebranche, D. A. (2013). Black/female/body hypervisibility and invisibility: A Black feminist augmentation of feminist leisure research. *Journal of Leisure Research*, 45(5), 644–660.

Moynihan, D. P. (1965). *The Moynihan report: The negro family, the case for national action*. US Department of Labor.

Mumola, C. (2000). Incarcerated parents and their children. *Bureau of Justice Statistics Special Report* (NCJ 182335). US Department of Justice.

Mumola, C., & Karberg, J. C. (2006). Drug use and dependence, state and federal prisoners, 2004. *Bureau of Justice Statistics Special Report* (NCJ 213530). US Department of Justice.

National Employment Law Project and In the Public Interest. (2016). *Reentry and employment for the formerly incarcerated and the role of American Trades Unions* [Policy brief]. http://www.nelp.org/publication/reentry-and-employment-for-the-formerly-incarcerated-and-the-role-of-american-trades-unions/

Nelson-Zlupko, L., Dore, M. M., Kauffman, E., & Kaltenbach, K. (1996). Women in recovery: Their perceptions of treatment effectiveness. *Journal of Substance Abuse Treatment*, 13(1), 51–59.

New York/New York III Supportive Housing Agreement. (2005). New York State Department of Health. https://www.health.ny.gov/diseases/aids/general/resources/docs/supportive_housing_agreement.pdf

New York City Bar (n.d.). *Do you have a criminal conviction history? A guide to your employment rights in New York*. http://www2.nycbar.org/pdf/report/Labor_reentry_pamphlet_employees09.pdf.

Newsome, Y. D. (2003). Border patrol: The U.S. Customs Service and the racial profiling of African American women. *Journal of African American Studies*, 7(3), 31–57.

Nieva, C. G., & Pulido, L. (2014). Beyond conflict and competition: How color-blind ideology affects African Americans' and Latinos' understanding of their relationships. *Kalfou*, 1(1), 87–116.

Novich, M., & Garcia-Hallett, J. (2018). Strategies for balance: Examining how parents of color navigate work and life in the academy. In *Contemporary Perspectives in Family Research: Vol.13, The work-family interface: Spillover, complications, and challenges* (pp. 157–184). Emerald Publishing Limited.

O'Reilly, A. (2019). Matricentric feminism: A feminism for mothers. *Journal of the Motherhood Initiative for Research and Community Involvement*, 10(1/2), 13–26.

Odum, T. C. (2017). *Our journey, our voice: Conceptualizing motherhood and reproductive agency in African American communities* [Doctoral dissertation]. University of Cincinnati.

Ortiz, S. Y., & Roscigno, V. J. (2009). Discrimination, women, and work: Processes and variations by race and class. *The Sociological Quarterly, 50,* 336–359.

Pager, D. (2003). The mark of a criminal record. *American Journal of Sociology, 108,* 937–975.

Palmer, P. (2010). *Domesticity and dirt: Housewives and domestic servants in the United States, 1920–1945.* Temple University Press.

Panettieri, G., & Hall, P. S. (2008). *The single mother's guide to raising remarkable boys.* Simon and Schuster.

Patel, R., & Philip, M. (2012). *Criminal justice debt: A toolkit for action.* Brennan Center for Justice.

Peter D. Hart Research Associates, Inc. (1998). *The road to recovery: A landmark study on public perceptions of alcoholism & barriers to treatment.* The Recovery Institute.

Phillips, S. D., Dettlaff, A. J., & Baldwin, M. J. (2010). An exploratory study of the range of implications of families' criminal justice system involvement in child welfare cases. *Children and Youth Services Review, 32,* 544–550.

Phinney, J. S., & Chavira, V. (1995). Parental ethnic socialization and adolescent coping with problems related to ethnicity. *Journal of Research on Adolescence, 5*(1), 31–53.

Potter, H. (2013). Intersectional criminology: Interrogating identity and power in criminological research and theory. *Critical Criminology, 21*(3), 305–318.

Premdas, R. R. (1995). Racism and anti-racism in the Caribbean. In B. P. Bowser, *Racism and anti-racism in world perspective* (pp. 241–260). Sage Publications.

Pruchno, R. (1999). Raising grandchildren: The experiences of Black and white grandmothers. *The Gerontologist, 39*(2), 209–221.

Purdie-Vaughns, V., & Eibach, R. P. (2008). Intersectional invisibility: The distinctive advantages and disadvantages of multiple subordinate-group identities. *Sex roles, 59*(5–6), 377–391.

Quets, G., Duggan, A., & Cooper, G. (2016). A gender lens on affordable housing. *Re: gender.* http://regender.org/Initiatives/GenderAndPrecarity/AffordableHousingPrimer

Raimon, M. L., Lee, A. F., & Genty, P. (2009). Sometimes good intentions yield bad results: ASFA's effects on incarcerated parents and their children. In S. Norton, K. Weber, O. Golden, & J. Macomber (Eds.), *Intentions and results: A look back at the Adoption and Safe Families Act* (pp. 121–129). Urban Institute.

Reddock, R. (2001). Conceptualizing "difference" in Caribbean feminist theory. In B. Meeks & F. Lindahl (Eds.), *New Caribbean thought: A reader* (pp. 196–209). The University of the West Indies Press.

Reece, S. M. (1995). Stress and maternal adaptation in first-time mothers more than 35 years old. *Applied Nursing Research, 8*(2), 61–66.

Reid, M., Kerr, B., & Miller, W. H. (2000). A study of the advancement of women in municipal government bureaucracies: Persistence of glass ceilings? *Women & Politics*, 21(1), 35–53.

Reilly, T. (2003). Transition from care: Status and outcomes of youth who age out of foster care. *Child Welfare*, 82(6), 727–746.

Reviere, R., Young, V. D., & Dawson, A. (2020). Mothers returning home: A critical intersectional approach to reentry. In K. M. Middlemass & C. Smiley (Eds.), *Prisoner reentry in the 21st century: Critical perspectives of returning home* (pp. 83–95). Routledge.

Rich, A. (1995). *Of woman born: Motherhood as experience and institution* (10th anniversary ed.). W. W. Norton.

Richie, B. E. (2001). Challenges incarcerated women face as they return to their communities: Findings from life history interviews. *Crime & Delinquency*, 47(3), 368–389.

Ritchie, A. J. (2017). *Invisible no more: Police violence against Black women and women of color*. Beacon Press.

Roberts, D. E. (1991). Punishing drug addicts who have babies: Women of color, equality, and the right of privacy. *Harvard Law Review*, 104(7), 1419–1482.

Roberts, D. E. (1993). Racism and patriarchy in the meaning of motherhood. *Journal of Gender & the Law*, 1(1), 1–38.

Roberts, D. E. (2012). Prison, foster care, and the systematic punishment of black mothers. *UCLA Law Review*, 59, 1474–1500.

Roberts, D. E. (2016). *Killing the Black body: Race, reproduction, and the meaning of liberty* (2nd ed.). Vintage Books.

Robison, K. J., & Miller, M. H. (2016). Decentering motherhood: Reentry strategies for women on parole and probation. *Women & Criminal Justice*, 26(5), 319–339.

Rogers, R. (2001). "Black like who?": Afro-Caribbean immigrants, African Americans, and the politics of group identity. In N. Foner (Ed.), *Islands in the city: West Indian migration to New York* (pp. 163–192). University of California Press.

Rogers, R. R. (2004). Race-based coalitions among minority groups: Afro-Caribbean immigrants and African-Americans in New York City. *Urban Affairs Review*, 39(3), 283–317.

Rogers, R. R. (2006). *Afro-Caribbean immigrants and the politics of incorporation*. Cambridge University Press.

Romero, M. (2008). Go after the women: Mothers against illegal aliens' campaign against Mexican immigrant women and their children. *Indiana Law Journal*, 83(4), 1355–1390.

Roscigno, V. J., & Bobbitt-Zeher, D. (2007). Sex discrimination in employment. In V. J. Roscigno (Ed.), *The face of discrimination* (pp. 57–72). Rowman & Littlefield Publishers.

Roscigno, V. J., Karafin, D. L., & Tester, G. (2009). The complexities and processes of racial housing discrimination. *Social Problems*, 56(1), 49–69.

Ryan, G. W., & Bernard, H. R. (2003). Techniques to identify themes. *Field Methods*, 15(1), 85–109.

Sabol, W. J., West, H. C., & Cooper, M. (2009). *Prisoners in 2008*. US Department of Justice, Bureau of Justice Statistics. http://www.bjs.gov/content/pub/pdf/p08.pdf

Sargent, C., & Harris, M. (1992). Gender ideology, childrearing, and child health in Jamaica. *American Ethnologist, 19*(3), 523–537.

Savarese, J. L. (2015). "Sadly . . . it appears the mother . . . saw more of the police . . . than [she] did [her] children": Theorizing soft criminalization in the child welfare system: An analysis of *Re S.F.* In J. Minaker & B. Hogeveen (Eds.), *Criminalized mothers, criminalizing mothering* (pp. 88–111). Demeter Press.

Scott, E. K., Edin, K., London, A. S., & Kissane, R. J. (2004). Unstable work, unstable income: Implications for family well-being in the era of time-limited welfare. *Journal of Poverty, 8*(1), 61–88.

Sered, S. S., & Norton-Hawk, M. (2014). *Can't catch a break: Gender, jail, drugs, and the limits of personal responsibility*. University of California Press.

Sharpe, G. (2015). Precarious identities: "Young" motherhood, desistance and stigma. *Criminology & Criminal Justice, 15*(4), 407–422.

Shaw-Taylor, Y., & Tuch, S. A. (2007). *The other African Americans: Contemporary African and Caribbean immigrants in the United States*. Rowman & Littlefield.

Shimizu, S. (2018). Beyond the box: Safeguarding employment for arrested employees. *The Yale Law Journal Forum, 128*, 226–243.

Siegel, J. A. (2011). *Disrupted childhoods: Children of women in prison*. Rutgers University Press.

Simkin, P., Whalley, J., Keppler, A., Durham, J., & Bolding, A. (2018). *Pregnancy, childbirth, and the newborn: The complete guide*. Hachette Books.

Smiley, C., & Middlemass, K. M. (2020). Thoughts, concerns, and the reality of incarcerated women. In K. M. Middlemass & C. Smiley (Eds.), *Prisoner reentry in the 21st century: Critical perspectives of returning home* (pp. 293–304). Routledge.

Smith, M. G. (1962). *West Indian family structure*. University of Washington Press.

Smith, S. S. (2010). A test of sincerity: How Black and Latino service workers make decisions about making referrals. *The ANNALS of the American Academy of Political and Social Science, 629*(1), 30–52.

Snell, T. L., & Morton, D. C. (1994). Survey of state prison inmates, 1991: Women in prison. *Bureau of Justice Statistics Special Report* (NCJ 145321). US Department of Justice.

Stack, C. B., & Burton, L. M. (1994). Kinscripts: Reflections on family, generation, and culture. In E. N. Glenn, G. Chang, & L. R. Forcey (Eds.), *Mothering: Ideology, experience, and agency* (pp. 33–44). Routledge.

Staley, E. M. (2008). *Female offenders: 2005–2006*. Research Highlight. New York State Department of Correctional Services.

Stanley, C. A. (2006). *Faculty of color: Teaching in predominantly white colleges and universities*. Anker Publishing.

Steffensmeier, D., Feldmeyer, B., Harris, C. T., & Ulmer, J. T. (2011). Reassessing trends in Black violent crime, 1980–2008: Sorting out the "Hispanic effect" in

Uniform Crime Reports arrests, National Crime Victimization Survey offender estimates, and U.S. prisoner counts. *Criminology*, 49(1), 197–251.

Steffensmeier, D., Ulmer, J. T., Feldmeyer, B., & Harris, C. T. (2010). Scope and conceptual issues in testing the race-crime invariance thesis: Black, white, and Hispanic comparisons. *Criminology*, 48(4), 1133–1169.

Stenius, V. M. K., Veysey, B. M., Hamilton, Z., & Andersen, R. (2005). Social roles in women's lives: Changing conceptions of self. *The Journal of Behavioral Health Sciences & Research*, 32(2), 182–198.

Stern, A. M. (2020). *Forced sterilization policies in the U.S. targeted minorities and those with disabilities—and lasted into the 21st century.* The Conversation. https://theconversation.com/forced-sterilization-policies-in -the-us-targeted-minorities-and-those-with-disabilities-and-lasted-into-the -21st-century-143144

Stevenson, B. E. (1993). "Rich tokens": The recruitment and retention of women-of-color historians. *Journal of Women's History*, 4(3) 152–157.

Strauss, S. M., & Falkin, G. P. (2001). Social support systems of women offenders who use drugs: A focus on the mother-daughter relationship. *American Journal of Drug and Alcohol Abuse*, 27(1), 65–89.

Sufrin, C. (2018). Making mothers in jail: Carceral reproduction of normative motherhood. *Reproductive BioMedicine and Society Online*, 7, 55–65.

Thacher, D. (2008). The rise of criminal background screening in rental housing. *Law & Social Inquiry*, 33(1), 5–30.

Thomas, J. L., & Bauer, L. (2019). As U.S. spends billions on foster care, families are pulled apart and forgotten. Retrieved January 13, 2020, from *The Kansas City Star*, https://amp.kansascity.com/news/special-reports/article23 8243099.html?__twitter_impression=true

Thornton, M. C. (1998). Indigenous resources and strategies of resistance: Informal caregiving and racial socialization in Black communities. In H. I. McCubbin, E. A. Thompson, A. I. Thompson, & J. A. Futrell (Eds.), *Resiliency in African-American families* (pp. 49–66). Sage.

Toussaint-Comeau, M. (2008). Do ethnic enclaves and networks promote immigrant self-employment? *Economic Perspectives*, 32(4), 30–50.

Travis, J. (2005). *But they all come back: Facing the challenges of prisoner reentry.* The Urban Institute Press.

Turner, C. S. V. (2002). Women of color in academe: Living with multiple marginality. *Journal of Higher Education*, 73(1), 74–93.

Turner, J. L. (2020). Black mothering in action: The racial-class socialization practices of low-income Black single mothers. *Sociology of Race and Ethnicity*, 6(2), 242–253.

Turney, K., & Wildeman, C. (2015). Detrimental for some? Heterogeneous effects of maternal incarceration on child wellbeing. *Criminology & Public Policy*, 14(1), 125–156.

US Census Bureau. (2013). *2011–2013 American Community Survey 3-year estimates* (S0201). Generated using American FactFinder, http://factfinder2 .census.gov

US Census Bureau (2019). *2018 population estimates by age, sex, race and Hispanic origin for the United States, states, and counties: April 1, 2010 to*

July 1, 2018. 2018 population estimates. https://www.census.gov/newsroom/press-kits/2019/detailed-estimates.html

Wakefield, S., & Garcia-Hallett, J. (2017). Incarceration effects on families. In *Oxford Research Encyclopedia of Criminology.* https://doi.org/10.1093/acrefore/9780190264079.013.232

Waldfogel, J. (1997). The effect of children on women's wages. *American Sociological Review, 62*(2), 209–217.

Wallace, D. (2015). Do neighborhood organizational resources impact recidivism? *Sociological Inquiry, 85*(2), 285–308.

Walsh, T. B., & Nieves, B. (2018) Military moms: Deployment and reintegration challenges to motherhood. In M. Muzik & K. L. Rosenblum (Eds.), *Motherhood in the face of trauma: Pathways towards healing and growth* (pp. 213–225). Springer.

Ward, K., & Wolf-Wendel, L. (2012). *Academic motherhood: How faculty manage work and family.* Rutgers University Press.

Ward, T., & Maruna, S. (2007). *Rehabilitation: Beyond the risk paradigm.* Routledge.

Waters, M. C. (1999). *Black identities: West Indian immigrant dreams and American realities.* Russell Sage Foundation.

Waters, M. C. (2000). Immigration, intermarriage, and the challenges of measuring racial/ethnic identities. *American Journal of Public Health, 90*(11), 1735–1737.

Waters, M. C., & Kasinitz, P. (2010). Discrimination, race relations, and second generation. *Social Research, 77*(1), 101–132.

Wells, K., & Guo, S. (1999). Reunification and reentry of foster children. *Children and Youth Services Review, 21*(4), 273–294.

Whalley, E. & Hackett, C. (2017): Carceral feminisms: The abolitionist project and undoing dominant feminisms. *Contemporary Justice Review, 20*(4), 456–473. https://doi.org/10.1080/10282580.2017.1383762

Wildeman, C., & Turney, K. (2014). Positive, negative, or null? The effects of maternal incarceration on children's behavioral problems. *Demography, 51*(3), 1041–1068.

Williams, J. C. (2001). *Unbending gender: Why work and family conflict and what to do about it.* Oxford University Press.

Williams, J. C. (2003). Beyond the glass ceiling: The maternal wall as a barrier to gender equality. *Thomas Jefferson Law Review, 26,* 1–14.

Williams, J. M., & Battle, N. T. (2017). African Americans and punishment for crime: A critique of mainstream and neoliberal discourses. *Journal of Offender Rehabilitation, 56,* 552–566.

Williams, J. M., Spencer, Z., & Wilson, S. K. (2021). I am not *your* felon: Decoding the trauma, resilience, and recovering mothering of formerly incarcerated Black women. *Crime & Delinquency, 67*(8), 1203–1136. https://doi.org/10.1177/0011128720974316

Zeng, Z. (2020). Jail inmates in 2018. *Bureau of Justice Statistics Bulletin* (NCJ 253044). US Department of Justice.

Index

addiction: stigmatized label as "addicts," 26, 156–58, 160, 166–67, 170, 177. *See also* alcohol use; recovery; substance use; treatment programs

Administration for Children's Services (ACS), 62, 75, 209n1, 213n6

adoption, 21, 39–41, 45, 71, 91, 153, 207n70

adult children, 189; financial problems and, 115–18, 127; housing and, 88–89

African American communities: cultural values, 100–103, 119, 154–56, 187–88; support and strains in, 124–25; use of term, 206n21; work ethic, stereotypes of, 100–103, 186–87. *See also* communities of color

African American mothers: caring for grandchildren, 56–57; community othermothers and, 67–68; employment, 99–104; family bonds, 65; finances and, 96, 119; post-incarceration motherwork, 17–18; protection of children, 36–37. *See also* mothers of color

African American women: controlling images of, 8–9, 100–103; incarceration rates, 13–14; in labor force, 211n16. *See also* women of color

Albion Correctional Facility, 73

Alcoholics Anonymous, 151

alcohol use, 130–31, 138, 145–46, 151, 153, 177. *See also* recovery; substance use

anger management, 43, 60, 73, 74, 76, 86

Appell, Annette, 73, 185–86

assault, 20, 28, 120–21

Astoria neighborhood, 125

Avila, Ernestine, 11

background checks, 93–95, 116

bail money, 14, 120, 128

Becton, Dajerria, 34

betrayal, 11, 54–55, 77

Black mothers. *See* African American mothers; Latina mothers; mothers of color; West Indian mothers

Black/white dichotomy, 7–8, 187

blame: for incarceration, 3, 37; of mothers for children's behavior, 51–52, 146; racialized oppression and, 7; social services and, 185–86; substance use and, 143, 160, 165–67; unemployment and, 184; welfare and, 11

Brownsville neighborhood, 33

bullying, 124–25

Bureau of Justice Statistics, 132

Burns, Stacy Lee, 160

carceral state: defined, 30; discipline and, 33; dissonance and, 174; resiliency of motherwork through dissonance within, 173–81; treatment programs as enforcers of state control, 159–64. *See also* criminalization; hypersurveillance; punishment

caregiving. *See* motherwork; shared mothering

child abuse, 54, 67

childcare, 71, 106–7, 128

child neglect: in foster care, 67; investigation of, 213n6; New York law on, 209n18; poverty conditions as, 63, 70–71, 175; reporting of, 63, 70; state surveillance and, 12–13; substance use and, 70

children: behavioral problems, 51–54, 146; care for (*see* motherwork; shared mothering); custody of (*see* custody); effects of maternal incarceration on, 3, 16–17, 47–56; emotional connections with mothers, 54–56, 60, 86, 136, 141–42, 178, 180 (*see also* mother-child communication); generational cycles and, 143–47; impact of maternal substance use and recovery on, 135–47; mental health of, 85, 209n18; participation in housing decisions, 78–81; perspectives of, 189–90

Children of Incarcerated Parents Program (CHIPP), 73–76

child support, 111, 113–14, 126, 140

child welfare system, 13, 39, 59, 209n1; barriers to mothers regaining custody, 62–64, 70–76; determining maternal fitness for custody, 70–76, 90–91, 175; distrust of, 67; housing requirements for maternal custody, 71–72, 88; mothers' substance use and, 134–35; poverty as sign of neglect, 63, 70–71, 175; prison visiting programs, 73–76; race and, 71–72, 90–91; supervised visits for mothers and children, 75–76. *See also* foster care

Christopher, K., 208n36

collective motherwork, 17. *See also* shared mothering

Collins, Patricia Hill, 12, 68

colorism, 207n1

communities of color: hypersurveillance in, 33–35, 58–59, 174, 212n45; support and strains within ethnic enclaves, 25, 122–25, 128–29. *See also* African American communities; Latinx communities; West Indian communities

community-based programs, 2, 14, 30, 68, 72, 104, 113, 123, 128, 160, 176, 183, 213n6

community-driven services, 26, 104, 183–84

Connections: A Guide for Formerly Incarcerated People in New York City, 83, 210n30

crime, 1–2; high-crime areas, 33–34, 123. *See also* drug crimes; money crimes; survival crimes

criminalization: ethnic enclaves and, 212n45; intersectionality and, 190; of substance use, 1–3, 14, 110, 132, 138, 176–77, 185

criminal legal system: fines and fees in, 106; justice, 75; men in, 2; mothers of color in, 3–4, 12–18, 176–77, 190; people of color in, 1–5; punitive policies, 14–15; "suspended moms" in, 213n11; women in, 3

criminal records: as barrier to employment, 17, 93–99, 105, 106–9, 118, 126, 184; fitness for child custody and, 72–73, 75; housing restrictions and, 82–83, 88; marginalization for, 176–77

cultural values, 25–26, 96; family bonds, 65; on money crimes, 25, 119–22, 127–28, 187–88; on substance use, 133, 154–56, 187–88

custody, 62–92; children's participation in housing decisions, 78–81; child welfare system and, 17, 24, 62–64, 70–76, 88, 90–91, 175; criminal records and, 72–73, 75; housing and, 64, 70, 76–78, 86–89; motherwork and, 21–22, 38–46; substance use and, 41, 43–44, 70, 144; temporary caregivers and, 76–78; types of arrangements, 21. *See also* nonresidential and noncustodial motherwork; shared mothering

day care. *See* childcare

de Blasio, Bill, 33, 214n25

defamation, 23, 25. *See also* stigmatized visibility of mothers of color

defensive othering, 165–69, 177, 182

Department of Homeless Services (DHS), 84–86

Department of Housing and Urban Development (HUD), 82–83

disability, 69, 112

discrimination. *See* employment, gender discrimination in; racial-ethnic discrimination

disempowerment, 5, 52, 74, 91, 157, 161, 163, 173–76, 180, 182, 184, 190
disengagement, maternal, trivializing of, 179–81
domestic servants, 10
Dominican Republic, 120
Drug Court, 160
drug crimes, 20, 106, 110, 119, 122, 124, 131, 134, 156, 185. See also substance use
drug policies, US, 14, 110, 138, 185; war on drugs, 1–3, 132, 176–77
drug testing, 44, 70, 74, 176–77
drug treatment. See treatment programs

Easterling, B. A., 213n11
East New York neighborhood, 38
education, 6, 15, 53–54, 97, 184
El Camino shelter, 39
emotional support, 128, 180, 188; recovery from substance use and, 148–50, 155–56
employment, 24–25, 93–109; child custody and, 71, 74; criminal records and, 17, 93–99, 105, 106–9, 118, 126, 184; ethnicity and, 99–104, 186–87, 211n16; family-friendly policies, 184–85; gender discrimination in, 24–25, 95–99, 210n7; glass ceiling in, 97, 104–5; human capital, 97; low-wage jobs, 98–99, 106–9, 112–13, 118–19, 126; marginalization of women of color, 95–104, 125–26, 211n16; maternal wall in, 104–11; motherwork and, 96, 104–9, 178, 184–85; racial-ethnic discrimination in, 103–4; single motherhood and, 104–5, 211n32; work-family conflict, 106, 108–9. See also unemployment; work ethic stereotypes; work schedules
empowerment, 92, 128, 147, 163–64, 175, 181–83
enablers, 147, 150–52
enslaved women, 9, 37, 97
ethnic enclaves: community support and strains in, 122–25, 128–29; criminalization and, 212n45
ethnic groups, 7–9; employment and, 25; interethnic stereotypes, 186–87; protecting children and, 36–37; in quantitative data sets, 19. See also African American communities; Latinx communities; West Indian communities
eugenics, 90

Fair Housing Act, 82
family bonds, 65. See also shared mothering

fathers: caregiving by, 66, 91; custody of children, 113–14
felony convictions, 93–95, 97–99, 106–9, 118, 126
feminism: Black, 7; matricentric, 5, 172, 190
finances: adult children and, 115–18, 127; carceral system fines and fees, 106, 111; childcare costs, 71, 106–7, 128; community support and, 122–23, 128; cultural beliefs and financial help, 25, 119–22, 127–28, 187–88; disconnected children and, 118–19; motherwork and, 96, 111–19, 126–27, 178; social pressures and, 123–25; underage children and, 112–14, 127. See also indebtedness; poverty; resources
Flatbush neighborhood, 122–23
Flavin, Jeanne, 14–15
Foner, Nancy, 206n21
foster care, 21, 41, 62, 64, 67, 69, 134. See also child welfare system
Foucault, Michel, 33
Fournier, Arthur, 121
Fried, Paula, 125
Fried, SuEllen, 125

gender: caregiving and, 5–6, 28–29, 104, 109, 112, 114; deviance from norms, 9, 14; discrimination in employment, 24–25, 95–99, 210n7; gendered consequences of incarceration, 28–30, 58–61 (see also motherwork); modeling for children, 43; race and, 5–6
generational cycles, 143–47
glass ceiling, in labor market, 97, 104–5
grand larceny, 20, 54
grandparents: caregiving by grandmothers, 66–67; children's behaviors and, 52–53; formerly incarcerated mothers caring for grandchildren, 56–58, 127, 180; "losing place" and, 48; negotiations over custody, 77–78; racial-ethnic interests and, 56–57
Gurusami, Susila, 35, 37

Haitian community, 36, 101–2, 120–21, 155, 170, 206n21
Harlem, 1–3, 40–41, 67–68, 124–25, 130
Harris, Angela P., 13
Herlihy, Daniel, 121
homelessness, 82, 168
homeless shelters, 38–39, 84–86, 214n25. See also shelter system
Hondagneu-Sotelo, Pierrette, 11

HourChildren program, 72, 80, 88
housing, 20–21; adult children and, 88–89; assistance programs, 72 (*see also* HourChildren program); child custody and, 64, 70, 76–78, 86–89; children's participation in decisions, 78–81; criminal records and, 82–83, 88; freedom and, 81, 92; loss of, 17; motherwork and, 81–92; post-incarceration barriers to, 81–91; public developments, 33, 38; reentry programs and, 83, 86–87, 92, 184; substance use and, 168; temporary, 24, 38; temporary caregivers and, 76–78; transitional, 79–80, 82, 111. *See also* nonresidential and noncustodial motherwork; shelter system
human capital, 97
hypersexuality, 10, 11
hypersurveillance: in communities of color, 33–35, 58–59, 174, 212n45; of parole, 30–32, 37, 58–59, 86, 123, 167, 174–76, 183; in reentry programs, 185; substance use recovery and, 138–39, 162–66

identity theft, 20, 113, 120–21, 126
incarceration: effects on children, 3, 16–17, 47–56; gendered consequences of, 28–30, 58–61 (*see also* motherwork); maternal identities and, 180; rates of, 3, 13–14; reincarceration for parole violations, 30–31; substance use during, 132, 135; treatment programs and, 160–61; visits with children during, 73–76
indebtedness, 106, 112–13, 120, 126–27, 140. *See also* finances
infants, 188–89
intensive mothering, 5–7, 9, 37–38, 43, 60–61, 63, 90, 137. *See also* motherhood, social constructions of
intersectionality, 6–7, 18, 170, 182
intimate partner abuse, 144

Jamaican community, 102, 122, 155
Jean-Louis, Eustache, 155, 170
Jezebel image, 9, 11

Kerrison, Erin, 161
kin networks: caregiving by, 65–67. *See also* grandparents; shared mothering

labor exploitation, 9–10
La Chingada (La Malinche), 11
La Llorona, 11

Latina mothers: caring for grandchildren, 56–57; employment, 99; family bonds, 65; finances and, 96, 119; post-incarceration motherwork, 17–18; protection of children, 36–37
Latina women: controlling images of, 8, 10–12; incarceration rates, 13–14; in labor force, 211n16
Latinx communities: cultural values, 154–56, 187–88; work ethic, stereotypes of, 128, 186–87. *See also* communities of color
La Virgen de Guadalupe, 11–12
Lorde, Audre, 1, 172
Lundy, Garvey, 82

Mammy image, 9–11
marginalization of women of color, 4, 90–91, 138–39, 161–63, 176–77, 183, 210n5; criminal records and, 176–77; employment and, 95–104, 125–26
Massey, Douglas, 82
maternal wall (in employment), 104; social policies and, 183–86
mental health, 73–76, 85–86, 113, 158
Middlemass, Keesha, 174
money crimes, 20, 117, 119–21, 126, 212n2; cultural values and, 25, 119–22, 127–28, 187–88
mother-child communication, 16, 21–22, 25, 31–32, 42–46, 49, 87, 145, 178, 180; with adult children, 189; restrictions on, 51, 59, 175; temporary caregivers and, 76–78
motherhood, social constructions of: reframing good mothering, 28–30, 37–46, 60–61, 87, 137, 147, 173–74, 178–81, 208n36; unbecoming a mother, 177; white middle-class norms of, 5–13, 16, 37, 72, 76, 89–90, 137, 172, 174, 178, 183 (*see also* intensive mothering)
mothers of color: in criminal legal system, 3–4, 12–18, 22–27, 176–77, 190; demographic characteristics, 19–20; ethnicities of, 7–8 (*see also* African American mothers; Latina mothers; West Indian mothers); invisibility as mothers, 3–5, 7, 45, 172, 174; power of, 190 (*see also* empowerment; resiliency). *See also* marginalization of women of color; stigmatized visibility of mothers of color
motherwork, 3–6, 23, 28–61; carceral state and, 28–30, 58–61; caring for grandchildren, 56–58, 127, 180; children's

behaviors and, 51–54, 146; custody of children and, 21–22, 38–46; defined, 5–6; disconnected children and, 42–46, 56, 118–19, 179–81, 208n22; employment and, 25; finances and, 96, 111–19, 126–27, 178; gaining positionality in children's lives, 47–49, 178; housing and, 81–92; during incarceration, 16–18; "losing place" with children, 47–49, 57; making up for lost time, 49–50, 57–58, 114, 116, 126, 178; nonresidential/noncustodial arrangements and, 31–32, 38–48, 90, 107–8, 113–14, 140, 152–53, 177–78; overcompensating, 50; parole and, 30–32, 37; police surveillance of communities and, 33–35; protection of children, 33–37; race and, 5–6, 29, 32–35, 45; reentry programs and, 4–5, 61, 170–71; resiliency through dissonance, 173–81; as role models, 43, 115–17, 127; substance use and, 43–44; treatment programs and, 170–71; troubled relationships and, 54–56; during unemployment, 109–11, 127; unseen post-incarceration obstacles, 46–61. *See also* mother-child communication; shared mothering
Muhammad, Bahiyyah, 3

Narcotics Anonymous, 149, 151, 159
New York City: Brownsville, 33; East New York, 38; employment laws, 95; ethnic groups in, 122–23, 187 (*see also* ethnic groups); Flatbush, 122–23; Harlem, 1–3, 40–41, 67–68, 124–25, 130; housing opportunities in, 83–84; South Bronx, 51, 130
New York Police Department (NYPD), 33, 62
nonresidential and noncustodial motherwork, 31–32, 38–48, 90, 107–8, 113–14, 140, 152–53, 177–78; shared mothering and, 39, 46, 60, 86–87, 91, 107

O'Reilly, Andrea, 5
organized crime, 54
othering, 4, 7, 10, 128, 164; defensive, 165–69, 177, 182. *See also* stigmatized visibility of mothers of color
othermothers. *See* shared mothering

parenting programs, 16, 24, 76
parole: child custody and, 70, 74–75, 86, 175; employment and, 108;

hypersurveillance of, 30–32, 37, 58–59, 86, 123, 167, 174–76, 183; maternal relationships and, 140; motherwork and, 30–32, 37; penal control through, 29–31, 58–59; substance use and, 166–67, 177; technical violations of, 30–31, 75, 86, 110, 135; treatment programs and, 158, 160
patriarchy, 3, 5, 7, 9–10, 12–13, 29, 64, 90, 183
penal control: of mothers of color, 3–4, 12–18, 29–30, 51–52, 173; through parole, 29–31, 58–59; social services and, 12–13, 185
personal responsibility rhetoric, 37, 51–52, 90, 160–61
Peyrot, Mark, 160
police surveillance, 33–35, 58–59, 174, 212n45
police violence, 6–7, 13, 34–35, 59
policy makers, 26, 183
poverty, 111, 123, 125; child custody and, 135; racialized, 2, 15–16; as sign of child neglect, 63, 70–71, 175. *See also* finances; resources; survival crimes
pregnancy, 6, 12, 14, 45, 84, 104, 106
prisoner reentry. *See* reentry programs
prostitution. *See* sex work
public housing developments, 33, 38
public safety rhetoric, 14. *See also* drug policies
punishment: invisible, 2; post-incarceration, 17, 22–27, 185; surveillance as, 33; treatment program policies as, 160

race: gender and, 5–6; motherwork and, 5–6, 29, 32–35, 45
racial dichotomy, Black/white, 7–8, 187
racial-ethnic discrimination, 6–7, 12–18; in employment, 103–4; housing and, 82–83; protecting children from, 35, 59
racial oppression, 1–9, 172; anti-Black racism, 90, 183; in carceral systems, 13–15; controlling images, 8–12, 100–103; institutional, 12–18; protection of children from, 36; substance use and, 161–62. *See also* marginalization of women of color
Reagan, Ronald, 11
recovering mothering, concept of, 180–81
recovery, 25–26, 130–71; acknowledgment and reinforcement in, 141–42; custodial rights and, 43; emotional support and, 148–50, 155–56; ethnic group views on,

recovery (*continued*)
154–56; family networks and, 151–56;
hypersurveillance and, 138–39, 162–66;
intimate partners and, 148–51; mother-
child relationships as motivation for,
132–37, 141, 169, 171, 176; motherwork and, 137–47; social support
networks, 147–71; stresses of reentry
and, 138–41. *See also* relapse; sobriety;
treatment programs
Reddock, Rhoda, 10
reentry narratives of mothers of color,
22–27. *See also* custody; employment;
finances; housing; motherwork; recovery
reentry programs, 2–3, 18–22, 26; anti-
oppressive efforts, 18, 173, 181, 185,
190; commonality in, 164, 182; *Connections* guide, 83, 210n30; hostility within,
166–70, 177; housing and, 83, 86–87,
92, 184; hypersurveillance in, 185;
internships at, 211n37; motherwork
and, 4–5, 61, 170–71; recommendations
for reform, 181–86; scare tactics and
warnings used in, 185; stigma and, 133;
substance use and, 158–59, 162, 166–71
relapse, 123, 136–37, 160; intimate partners
and, 150–51; life stresses and, 138–41,
169
research: future areas, 186–89; methods,
18–22
resiliency, 3, 15, 23, 42, 59, 111, 127,
173–81, 190
resistance, 59, 61
resources: access to, 2, 6–7, 11–12, 15–17,
29, 52, 59, 63, 147, 161, 172, 175; child
custody and, 75; guides to, 83, 210n30;
providing for children, 50; sharing
knowledge of, 122. *See also* finances;
welfare
Rich, Adrienne, 5, 189
Richie, Beth, 92
Rikers Island, 106, 120
Ritchie, Andrea, 8, 13
Roberts, Dorothy, 23, 138
Rockefeller Drug Laws, 110

Sapphire image, 9
Savarese, Josephine, 90
self-affirmations, 177, 179–81
sentencing decisions, 14
service work, low-wage, 98–99
sexism, 6
sexual harassment, 109–10
sexuality, 10–12

sex work, 20, 120–21, 131
shared mothering: biological family as
othermothers, 65–67, 152; child custody
and, 76–78; community members as
othermothers, 67–68; defined, 64–65;
nonresidential/noncustodial mothering and, 39, 46, 60, 86–87, 91, 107;
substance use and, 44, 68, 152–53;
temporary arrangements, 76–78, 91,
175, 189; validation of, 183
shelter system, 81–82, 84–86, 88, 89, 111,
130, 168. *See also* homeless shelters
Siegel, Jane, 189
single motherhood, 66, 69, 110; employment and, 104–5, 211n32
slavery. *See* enslaved women
sobriety, 25–26; motherhood as motivation
for, 132–37, 141, 169, 171, 176. *See
also* recovery
social capital, 123, 128
social inequalities, 6–8, 11, 15, 106, 113, 183
social support networks: cultural values
and, 187–88 (*see also* cultural values);
within ethnic enclaves, 25, 122–25,
128–29; validation in, 182. *See also*
emotional support
South Bronx neighborhood, 51, 130
Stanley, C. A., 210n5
stereotypes, 8–12, 100–103, 128, 186–87
sterilizations, forced, 90
Stevenson, B. E., 210n5
stigmatized visibility of mothers of color:
custody and housing, 63–64, 73, 90–92;
employment and finances, 96, 105,
121, 123, 127; within ethnic communities, 25; motherwork and, 37–46,
58–59, 173–81; paradox of visibility
and invisibility, 3–7, 172–75; reentry
programs and, 133; substance use and,
26, 132–33, 135, 137–38, 141, 154,
156–62, 165–70, 177, 178–79; use of
term "(m)others," 4. *See also* carceral
state; criminalization; penal control
substance use, 130–71; child custody
and, 41, 43–44, 70, 144; as coping
mechanism, 2, 26, 70, 133, 138–41,
144, 149–50, 154, 159, 176; as cultural
transgression, 154–56, 187–88; defensive
othering and, 165–69; disease narrative, 153; educating children to prevent
generational cycles, 143–47; enablers,
147, 150–52; housing and, 168; during
incarceration, 132, 135; motherwork
and, 43–44; racialized oppression and,

138; rates of, 132; shared mothering and, 44, 68, 152–53; stigmatizing ideologies of, 156–58, 160–61, 165–69, 174, 178–79. *See also* addiction; alcohol use; drug crimes; drug policies; recovery; relapse; treatment programs

Sufrin, Carolyn, 16

Supplemental Security Income (SSI), 69, 112, 117

support groups, 51–52

surveillance. *See* hypersurveillance

survival crimes, 15, 113, 131, 161

Tapia, Ruby, 30

temporary housing, 24, 38

toddlers, 188–89

transitional housing, 79–80, 82, 111

transnational mothers, 43, 60, 137, 208n36

Travis, Jeremy, 2

treatment programs, 26, 74, 82, 131, 144, 147–48, 150; commonality in, 164, 182; as enforcers of state control, 159–64; hostility within, 165–66, 170, 177; motherwork and, 170–71; recommendations for reform, 181–86; in reentry programs, 158–59. *See also* recovery

Trinidad and Tobago, 10

Turner, C. S. V., 210n5

unemployment, 96, 117, 178, 184, 211n37; financial challenges of, 112; motherwork during, 109–11, 127. *See also* employment

validation, 182

war on drugs. *See* drug policies

Waters, Mary, 100

weapons possession, 20

welfare, 106; ethnicity and, 101–3; substance use and, 157; Welfare Queen image, 10–11, 37

West Indian communities: cultural values, 119–23, 154–56, 169–70, 187–88; family bonds in, 65; support and strains in, 122–23, 128–29; use of term, 206n21; work ethic, stereotypes of, 100–103, 128, 186–87. *See also* communities of color

West Indian mothers: caring for grandchildren, 56–57; employment, 99–104; finances and, 96, 119–21; post-incarceration motherwork, 17–18; protection of children, 36–37

West Indian women: controlling images of, 8, 9–10, 100–103; in labor force, 211n6

white mothers: in criminal legal system, 15; substance use, 138, 162. *See also* intensive mothering; motherhood, social constructions of

white privilege, 5–7, 13–15, 82, 162

Williams, Joan, 104

women: invisibility of, 3–4; social norms of womanhood, 9–12. *See also* gender

women of color: ethnicities of, 8, 12 (*see also* African American women; Latina women; West Indian women); housing discrimination and, 82–83. *See also* marginalization of women of color; mothers of color

Women's Prison Association, 113

work ethic stereotypes, 100–103, 128, 186–87

work schedules, 107–8, 126. *See also* employment

Founded in 1893,
UNIVERSITY OF CALIFORNIA PRESS
publishes bold, progressive books and journals
on topics in the arts, humanities, social sciences,
and natural sciences—with a focus on social
justice issues—that inspire thought and action
among readers worldwide.

The UC PRESS FOUNDATION
raises funds to uphold the press's vital role
as an independent, nonprofit publisher, and
receives philanthropic support from a wide
range of individuals and institutions—and from
committed readers like you. To learn more, visit
ucpress.edu/supportus.

www.ingramcontent.com/pod-product-compliance
Lightning Source LLC
Chambersburg PA
CBHW030403270326
41926CB00009B/1246